All Canada in the Hands of the British

of the British

CAMPAIGNS & COMMANDERS

GREGORY J. W. URWIN, SERIES EDITOR

CAMPAIGNS AND COMMANDERS

ALL CANADA IN THE HANDS OF THE BRITISH

General Jeffery Amherst and the 1760 Campaign to Conquer New France

Douglas R. Cubbison

UNIVERSITY OF OKLAHOMA PRESS | NORMAN

Also by Douglas R. Cubbison

"The artillery never gained more honour": The British Artillery in the 1776 Valcour Island and 1777 Saratoga Campaigns (Fleischmanns, N.Y., 2007)
The American Northern Theater Army in 1776: The Ruin and Reconstruction of the Continental Force (Jefferson, N.C., 2010)
The British Defeat of the French in Pennsylvania, 1758: A Military History of the Forbes Campaign against Fort Duquesne (Jefferson, N.C., 2010)
Burgoyne and the Saratoga Campaign: His Papers (Norman, Okla., 2012)

Library of Congress Cataloging-in-Publication Data

Cubbison, Douglas.
  All Canada in the hands of the British : General Jeffery Amherst and the 1760 campaign to conquer New France / Douglas R. Cubbison.
      pages cm. — (Campaigns and commanders ; volume 43)
  Includes bibliographical references and index.
  ISBN 978-0-8061-4427-6 (hardcover : alk. paper) 1. Amherst, Jeffery Amherst, Baron, 1717–1797—Military leadership. 2. Québec (Québec)—History—French and Indian War, 1754–1763—Campaigns. 3. United States—History—French and Indian War, 1754–1763—Campaigns. 4. Montréal (Québec)—History, Military—18th century. 5. Canada—History—1755–1763. I. Title. II. Title: General Jeffery Amherst and the 1760 campaign to conquer New France.
  E199.C956 2014
  355.00971409′033—dc23
                          2013033142

All Canada in the Hands of the British: General Jeffery Amherst and the 1760 Campaign to Conquer New France is Volume 43 in the Campaigns and Commanders series.

The paper in this book meets the guidelines for permanence and durability of the Committee on Production Guidelines for Book Longevity of the Council on Library Resources, Inc. ∞

1 2 3 4 5 6 7 8 9 10

Interior layout and composition: Alcorn Publication Design

"*Montreal is now . . . the Sole Object to Compleat the Glory of His Majesty's Arms in these Parts, the Reduction of all Canada depending entirely on the Fall of that Place; I therefore Intend to Advance on them by their three Avenues; Namely, from Quebec up the River St Lawrence; from Lake Ontario down the River St Lawrence; and from Crown Point by the Isle au Noix.*"

GENERAL JEFFERY AMHERST, JUNE 12, 1760

"*I [have] come to take Canada and I did not intend to take anything less.*"

GENERAL JEFFERY AMHERST TO GOVERNOR MONSIEUR DE VAUDREUIL, OUTSIDE THE CITY OF MONTREAL, SEPTEMBER 6, 1760

Contents

Illustrations

Figures

Tables

Preface

I transferred from the U.S. Military Academy at West Point to serve as the command historian with the 10th Light Infantry Division (Mountain), Fort Drum, New York, in May 2006. Shortly thereafter I was asked to join the board of the Fort La Presentation Association, a nonprofit community organization that owns the archaeological site of Fort de la Présentation, the French outpost that figured prominently in the 1760 campaign. The board requested that I assist them with securing National Register of Historic Places recognition for the archaeological site. While performing background research on the fort's role in the Seven Years' War, I was surprised to uncover a void in scholarship on Jeffery Amherst's campaign of 1760, which completed the defeat of Canada and, in large measure, New France. Accordingly, as professional responsibilities and the exigencies of a two-month deployment to Afghanistan and other historical projects allowed, I slowly began to accumulate research on the campaign. This book is the result of this effort, which has consumed five years' research, study, and analysis.

One observation from General Amherst specifically caught my attention. Writing in his private journal, he recorded: "I believe never three Armys setting out from different & very distant Parts from each other, Joyned in the Center, as was intended, better than we did and it could not fail of having the effect of which I have just now seen the consequences."[1] As a lifelong student of military history, and as a former U.S. Army officer, I realized that Amherst was entirely correct, and just what a remarkable achievement his 1760 campaign had been. Three substantial armies, traveling by different routes separated by hundreds of miles across wilderness, wild rivers, and an ocean, had arrived at the objective nearly simultaneously. And I pondered three questions. First, was this Amherst's intent, or was it simply good fortune? Second, if it was a deliberate component of Amherst's plan, how did he utilize the British army's command and control system of the mid-eighteenth century (Command and Control, Communications, and Intelligence, or C3I, in modern parlance) to implement his plan? The third question, of course, was how these three separate columns individually fulfilled their assigned missions. This treatise attempts to investigate these discussion points.

A primary purpose of this study is to examine the operations of the three principal columns that constituted Amherst's 1760 campaign, from the perspective of the British forces that set the tempo and initiative of that year's campaign, and thus to explore how General Jeffery Amherst conquered Canada using three detachments. Amherst could exercise direct command and control over only one of these columns, separated one from another by a strong French army that occupied interior lines of maneuver. The second objective of this book is to assess how Amherst employed command and control, and thus this campaign serves as a case study of how the British army practiced command and control at mid-century, during the two conflicts that did so much to influence the formation of the four nations of Britain, Canada, France, and the United States.

During this campaign, three sieges were undertaken. One of them was a counterattack directed against Quebec by the French, and the other two were performed by the British invaders attempting to force a path into the interior of Canada. Both of the British sieges stand out in that the French defenders were installed on islands in the midst of rivers, considerably complicating the British operations. These intriguing sieges have never received adequate research and analysis, particularly when viewed within the context of mid-eighteenth century siegecraft, military engineering, and artillery employment.

During his penultimate movement up the St. Lawrence River from Quebec to Montreal, Brigadier General James Murray fought a military campaign distinctive for the mid-eighteenth century in that it employed the extensive use of maneuver and what would today be recognized by the U.S. Army as population-centric counterinsurgency. The campaign stripped the support of the Canadian militia and Native American allies from the cause of New France, resulting in the collapse of French resolve and determination and the capitulation of Montreal, now badly outnumbered and abandoned, without a fight. Murray's tactics and techniques were innovative and creative, and well deserve study by military professionals and historians.

In undertaking that study, I strive to demonstrate that the 1760 campaign was among the most significant and most instructive campaigns of the Seven Years' War as it was conducted in North America.

Acknowledgements

I wish to acknowledge the assistance of Ms. Wendy Newell and other members of the Fort Drum Library, Fort Drum, New York, and Ms. Heather Turner and other members of the Reference Department of the Combined Arms Research Library, Fort Leavenworth, Kansas, who located numerous references and sources for me that would have otherwise been unobtainable. This book could not have been prepared without their generous and always uncomplaining assistance.

Assistance was also provided by the following archivists/librarians at the following institutions: Mr. Bill Copeley of the New Hampshire Historical Society; Ms. Norma Kein of the Old Berwick Historical Society, South Berwick, Maine; My friend, Dr. Tim Abel, formerly of the Jefferson (New York) County Historical Society assisted me with research on numerous occasions; Mr. Simon Blackett of the Invercauld Estate, who generously provided me copies of the letters of Lieutenant Alexander Farqharson; and the Connecticut Historical Society assisted me with a copy of the Asa Waterman Diary.

My good friend of more years than either of us is willing to admit, Dr. Walter L. Powell of Gettysburg, Pennsylvania, assisted me with research on Jean-Daniel Dumas of the French Marines. A mutual friend of ours, Mr. Bob Messner, provided me with a transcribed copy of Dumas' manuscript, the original of which currently resides with the Braddock's Battlefield Association, Braddock, Pennsylvania. Another friend of mine, Mr. William Tatum, Sol Feinstone Scholar at the David Library of the American Revolution, Washington Crossing, Pennsylvania, performed a helpful review of an earlier draft of this manuscript.

MAPS

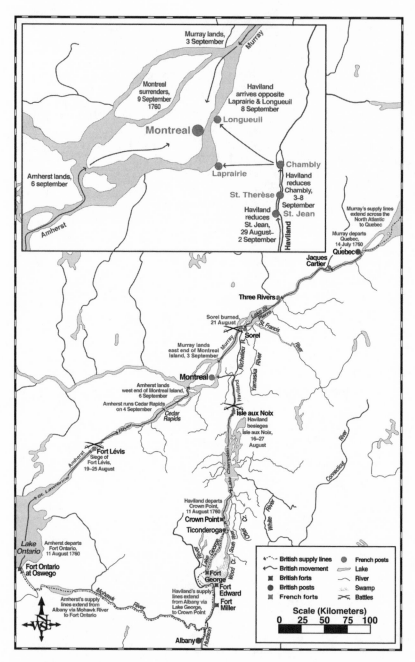

Amherst's 1760 Campaign. Map prepared by Michael F. Beard, SunSyne Graphics, Johnson City, Tennessee. Copyright © 2013 The University of Oklahoma Press.

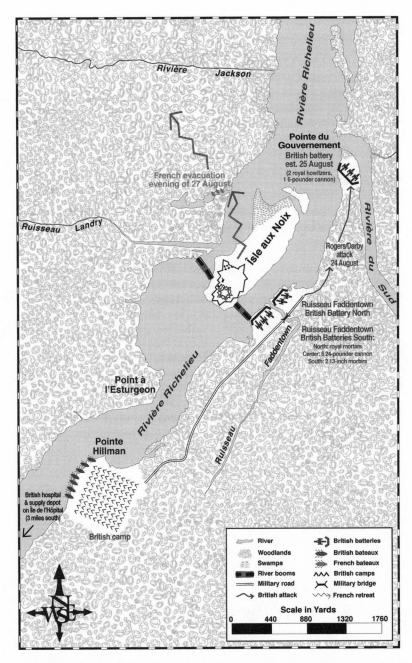

Rivière Jackson

Rivière Richelieu

Pointe du Gouvernement
British battery est. 25 August
(2 royal howitzers, 1 6-pounder cannon)

French evacuation evening of 27 August

Ruisseau Landry

Île aux Noix

Rogers/Darby attack 24 August

Rivière du Sud

Ruisseau Faddentown British Battery North

Ruisseau Faddentown British Batteries South:
North: royal mortars
Center: 6 24-pounder cannon
South: 2 13-inch mortars

Point à l'Esturgeon

Rivière Richelieu

Faddentown

Ruisseau

Pointe Hillman

British hospital & supply depot on Île de l'Hôpital (3 miles south)

British camp

River		British batteries	
Woodlands		British bateaux	
Swamps		French bateaux	
River booms		British camps	
Military road		Military bridge	
British attack		French retreat	

Scale in Yards

0   440   880   1320   1760

N S E W

Siege of Fort Île aux Noix, 16–28 August 1760. Map prepared by Michael
F. Beard, SunSyne Graphics, Johnson City, Tennessee. Copyright © 2013
The University of Oklahoma Press.

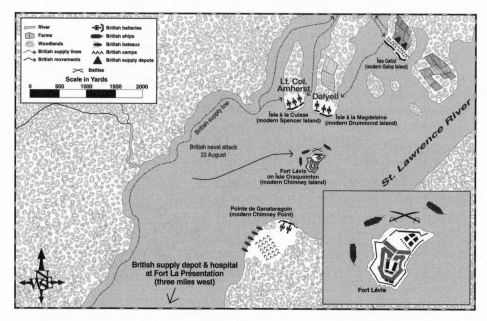

Siege of Fort Lévis, 18–25 August 1760. Map prepared by Michael F. Beard, SunSyne Graphics, Johnson City, Tennessee. Copyright © 2013 The University of Oklahoma Press.

ALL CANADA IN THE HANDS OF THE BRITISH

"THE ENTIRE REDUCTION OF CANADA"

War on the Saint Lawrence to 1760

On January 7, 1760, William Pitt, First Earl of Chatham, secretary of state for the Southern Department, and the political leader of the British government who directed and coordinated Britain's war efforts, wrote to General Jeffrey Amherst, the Commander in Chief of the British Army in North America. This letter contained Pitt's instructions to Amherst for his execution of the 1760 campaign:

> The reduction of Montreal was evidently the great and essential object, which remained, to compleat the glory of His Majesty's Arms in North America. . . . To this great end, it is His Majesty's pleasure, that you do attempt the invasion of Canada, with the Forces under your command, either in one body, or by different operations, at one and the same time, by a Division of the said forces, into separate and distinct bodies, according as you shall, from your knowledge of the Countries, thro' which the War is to be carried, and from emergent circumstances not be known here, judge the same to be most expedient; and that you do proceed to the vigorous attack of Montreal, and exert your utmost efforts to reduce that place, as well as all other posts belonging to the French in those parts.[1]

Amherst received Pitt's letter relatively expeditiously, as he wrote to Colonel John Bradstreet from his winter quarters in New York City on February 16, 1760: "I am now to Inform You, that the Packett has brought me Letters from Mr. Secretary Pitt, directing me to make all necessary preparations for pushing the War with the utmost Vigour as early in the Year as the Season will permit, and thereby Compleat the great work so Successfully begun of rendering His Majesty entire Master of Canada."[2] As the senior British general officer in North America, General Jeffery Amherst was to play the lead role in the campaign that Pitt had just called for.

Amherst was born in 1717, and had entered military service as a cornet with Major General John Ligonier's Regiment of Horse in 1735.[3] His most significant military service had been as an aide-de-camp to General Ligonier in Flanders during the War of the Austrian Succession. Serving under this highly skilled, aggressive, and efficient commander throughout the European continent, Amherst had the opportunity to observe a true master at work. He had been present at the engagements at Dettingen in 1743 and Fontenoy in 1745. Amherst clearly impressed General Ligonier throughout this war. In the Campaign of 1747, Amherst became aide to William, Duke of Cumberland, the son of King George II, who had saved his father's monarchy at Culloden in April 1746.[4] He had the opportunity both to observe the duke closely and to impress him.

Early in the Seven Years' War in Europe, Amherst briefly served under the well-regarded Prussian general Prince Ferdinand, Duke of Brunswick, who commanded a Hanoverian "Army of Observation" cooperating with the British in Flanders. Amherst and the Duke of Brunswick doubtless had discussions regarding military leadership, administration, and logistics while serving together in what was then regarded as "the cockpit of Europe."

When Pitt determined to replace the British military leadership in North America with younger, more active commanders, General Ligonier (by now the overall British Commander in Chief) recommended Amherst for the position. Amherst was at this time a relatively junior colonel, and although King George II "took a lot of persuading" he eventually approved the appointment of Amherst as a major general responsible for commanding the British combined naval and land operation in 1758 against Louisburg, the strongest and most prominent French fortress in New France. The fort on Cape Breton Island was generally considered to be the guardian of the North Atlantic gate to Canada. Amherst crossed the North Atlantic barely in time to join the army already en route to Louisburg. He had immediately taken charge and promptly directed the capture of Louisbourg.[5] Late in 1758 Amherst was appointed commander in chief in North America, and he personally commanded one of the three major British columns, directed against French Fort Carillon, in the 1759 campaign. Under his leadership, the British won three great victories in North America, with the captures of Quebec, Fort

Joshua Reynolds, Sir Jeffery Amherst (1765). Passage of Cedar Rapids of St. Lawrence River, September 4, 1760, in background. Courtesy of Mead Art Museum, Amherst College, Amherst, Massachusetts.

Carillon, and Fort Niagara. Amherst proved himself to be a highly capable and competent senior general.[6]

The situation in February 1760 reflected the major accomplishments of the British Army and Royal Navy in North America during the previous campaign season. In the eastern Saint Lawrence River Valley, Major General James Wolfe had won a great victory at Quebec in September 1759. In the process, both Wolfe and the French commander, the Marquis de Montcalm, were killed. Wolfe's army had occupied the premier city of Canada, Quebec, which had been badly battered by the summer's siege. To secure their prize, the British had installed a substantial winter garrison in Quebec under the command of one of Wolfe's Brigade commanders, Brigadier General James Murray. To the south, Amherst himself had led a British army up the Hudson River–Lake George–Lake Champlain corridor in 1759 and had engaged Fort Carillon at Ticonderoga in a formal siege. The French had left behind a minor caretaking garrison to delay Amherst. Before this garrison retreated, they detonated the powder magazine in the southeast bastion, and in the resulting maelstrom the stone and timber French fort was partially burned. Shortly thereafter, the small French garrison of Fort Saint Frederick at Crown Point similarly detonated their magazine and withdrew down Lake Champlain. Once at Crown Point, Amherst's advance was stymied by the need to construct a naval flotilla. There were no roads at the time around Lake Champlain, and the French operated a small but effective naval force that dominated the lake. Amherst had to first construct and then operate a fleet on Lake Champlain. He would engage and defeat the French flotilla in the fall of 1759, but this came too late in the campaign season for him to exploit his victory. While Amherst was waiting for his vessels to be built, he occupied his time by performing minimal repairs to Fort Ticonderoga. He also constructed Fort Crown Point, an enormous new fortification, to guard against any future French counterattack up Lake Champlain from Canada. He dispatched a strong ranger corps commanded by New Hampshire major Robert Rogers against the Indian village of Saint Francis, which for decades had been a source of trouble for New England. Rogers succeeded in his mission and destroyed the village, but his rangers took serious casualties during their withdrawal through the wilderness. The British armies also gained a major success when a strong column captured Fort Niagara, effectively sundering all posts on the Great Lakes from the remainder of Canada. Although this siege had been successfully concluded by July 1759, one of Amherst's key subordinates, Brigadier General Thomas Gage, had failed to exploit that accomplishment. He squandered the remainder of the summer in idleness at Fort Ontario at Oswego on Lake Ontario.

Thus, the 1759 campaign had ended with three large British armies encamped on the periphery of Canada: to the east down the Saint Lawrence River at Quebec, to the south up Lake Champlain at Fort Crown Point, and to the west up the Saint Lawrence River and Lake Ontario at Fort Ontario (also known as Fort Oswego). The French defenses were concentrated at Montreal, with three fortified positions to defend against any potential British attacks. A small force at Jacques Cartier was intended more to keep an eye on the British force at Quebec than to defend against any serious attack by that garrison. A strong fortified position at the island of Île aux Noix was to safeguard the Richelieu River from any invasion down Lake Champlain. Another strong fortified position in the middle of the Saint Lawrence River, near the Catholic mission Fort de La Présentation, was to obstruct any British line of advance up the river.

To prepare for the campaign of 1760, Amherst opened negotiations with the numerous Indian nations that inhabited the interior of the continent. Amherst regularly corresponded with Sir William Johnson, Superintendent of Indian Affairs for the Northern Department, regarding diplomacy and relationships with the various First Nations.

William Johnson, born in Ireland in 1715, had moved to the Mohawk Valley in New York colony in 1738 to manage the large estates of his uncle, British admiral Peter Warren. Over the next ten years, Johnson established himself as one of the most prominent residents of the Mohawk Valley, and purchased thousands of acres for his own. Johnson was physically powerful, personable, intelligent, hard working, and ambitious. He established profitable trading relationships with the Indians of the region. Johnson was adopted into the Mohawk Tribe of the Iroquois Confederation, and eventually became regarded as a Chief of the Nation. Active in the New York militia, during King George's War he had been effective at raising and dispatching Mohawk raiding parties against Canada. By 1755 he was a senior officer in the militia, and agent to the Iroquois Confederation. Accordingly, he commanded the provincial column operating against Fort Saint Frederick on Lake Champlain. His victory at Lake George in September 1755 was one of only two British successes that year, and King George II rewarded him with a baronetcy and the appointment as the Northern Superintendent of Indian Affairs in North America. Johnson had raised New York provincial militia in an attempt to relieve Fort William Henry in 1757, and led a large force of Iroquois warriors in the 1758 expedition against Fort Carillon. In 1759 he had marched at the head of a similar large contingent of Iroquois warriors against Fort Niagara, had assumed command when General Prideaux was killed, and had received the French surrender to considerable acclaim.[7] During the preparation for the campaign, Johnson and Amherst worked closely together to plan and prepare for the coming operations.

In late April, Amherst traveled up the Hudson to Fort George. Although it was spring, the river was frosty and speckled with ice. Here he met with Johnson and representatives of a number of Indian nations and presented a formal speech at the small fort on April 27, 1760. Amherst promised the friendship of the British, and laid the foundation for the participation of various Indian tribes in the forthcoming campaign. He also promised, "I mean not to take any of your Lands." He then proposed arrangements for leasing land for military posts and their necessary gardens, noting that "they shall remain your absolute Property." He assured the Indians that he would "promise you some Presents as a Consideration for the Land where such Forts & trading Houses are or may be built upon." These commitments by Amherst as an official representative of "the King my Master" would eventually be formalized by Sir William Johnson later that summer and fall into the treaties of Oswegatchie and Caughanawaga.[8]

Although the French army in Canada was rather the worse for wear as a result of the heavy engagements and defeats of 1759, it remained a potent striking force. With the highly capable and experienced François de Gaston, Chevalier de Lévis in command, it retained the ability to launch at least one formidable counterattack. De Lévis would carefully and craftily weigh the odds and, when he adjudged the moment to be right, aggressively carry the fight to the British.

Thus, Amherst faced a complicated tactical challenge. His three armies at Fort Ontario at Oswego, Fort Crown Point on Lake Champlain, and Quebec formed the rim of a wheel, while a smaller but still formidable French army held the hub at Montreal. Amherst determined to proceed along three axes of advance: west from Quebec on the Saint Lawrence River, north on Lake Champlain, and east from Oswego on Lake Ontario and the Saint Lawrence River. His intent was "that I may force them to divide their Troops, which will Weaken them in every Part, and that I may press on them as nearly as may be, by those Routes at the same time."[9] This book will examine how Jeffery Amherst overcame this challenge and exercised successful command and control, as it was practiced by the British army in the middle part of the eighteenth century, to defeat and conquer Canada.[10]

Under his orders from Pitt, Amherst's mission was straight-forward enough: seize Canada to contribute to the collapse of New France. The specifics were left entirely up to Amherst, who decided to launch columns from each of the three bases that had been established in the successful campaigns of 1759. The capital of Montreal would be the objective of the 1760 campaign. Amherst himself would lead the largest army down the Saint Lawrence River from the logistical base at Fort Oswego. Colonel William Haviland commanded another major column that would continue Amherst's campaign of the previous fall north down Lake Champlain. Finally, Brigadier General James Murray led a column principally employing Royal Navy vessels operating from Quebec to Montreal on the Saint Lawrence River. If Amherst could successfully concentrate these three armies in front of Montreal, he would possess more than adequate combat power to subdue the considerably smaller French army. As British army commander in North America, Amherst would guide the British regiments, artillery, and naval vessels toward this end.

One modern combat veteran has famously stated that "The business of the military in war is killing people and breaking things." Although often quoted, this adage is entirely inaccurate. Any military leader, of any rank, has to possess a range of certain characteristics. An effective military leader has to be self-confident (sometimes to the point of arrogance or egotism), self-reliant, proud, and resolute. He has to be courageous, brave, determined, focused, and dynamic. Most effective military leaders also have to be ambitious. As one example, Civil War brigadier general John White Geary would write to a U.S. senator in 1862, "He that is without ambition is unworthy to wear a sword."[11] In short, leaders have to be strong and committed men. In battle, the actual contest is between two military leaders rather than between two military forces. A victorious leader utilizes his military might, which sometimes in fact does entail killing people and breaking things, to shatter the will of his opponent, to destroy his resolution and confidence, and to eliminate his focus and determination. An effective military leader breaks the will, morale, confidence, and resolve of his opponent. Military defeat is something that happens inside the mind of a leader.

It must be noted that this result is often achieved by separating the leader from his subordinates. The effective application of violence serves this purpose quite well, but there are other techniques. During this campaign, Brigadier General James Murray, who commanded Amherst's column on the Saint Lawrence River, effectively employed maneuvers and measures directed against the Canadian population to outflank the French military opposition, and to divide the militia and Indians from the cause of Canada.

The core of General Jeffery Amherst's strategy was to defeat not the armies of Canada, but a single man, Pierre François de Rigaud, Marquis de Vaudreuil-Cavagnal, the governor of Canada. The Marquis de Vaudreuil was born in Quebec in 1698, when his father was governor of Canada. He had briefly served in in the Troupes de la Marine—companies raised and controlled by the French Ministry of Marine—and had subsequently proven himself to be a skilled, courageous, efficient, and ambitious leader and administrator. When he was appointed as governor in 1755, he was the first Canadian-born governor of the colony. The Marquis de Vaudreuil was absolutely committed to the cause of France, and until Amherst could crush his resolve to defend that colony, Canada would remain undefeated.

As the New Year of 1760 was ushered in with a round of social events in the capital city of Montreal, Governor de Vaudreuil's Canada found itself in desperate straits. In 1755 and 1756 Canada had been reinforced by over three thousand French regulars, who had put a serious strain on the agricultural resources of the settlement. Canada was barely self-sufficient at the onset of hostilities. Exacerbating the situation, the harvests of 1756, 1757, and 1758 had been meager. An aggressively prosecuted British blockade had become progressively more efficient every year and had limited supplies arriving from the home country. The operations of General Wolfe around Quebec in the summer of 1759 had devastated the agricultural production of that region, the longest occupied and most well established of New France. Continuous militia service had seriously reduced the availability of labor and doubtless played a role in the three successive years of poor harvests. By 1759 the island of Montreal "was so depopulated that the crop had to be gathered by a common effort, and even though women and girls, old men and boys all turned out, the work went slowly." Eventually, de Lévis was forced to detach militia from his already depleted army to bring in the harvest. By 1760, agriculture in Canada had for all practical purposes collapsed. Because of the large militia drafts over several years, numerous farms had gone out of cultivation. Many holdings had been abandoned when militiamen failed to return from campaign, and the supply of livestock had been seriously depleted as animals had been taken from the farm fields for military purposes. The dire shortage of provisions severely constrained French military operations.[12]

Furthermore, the economy of Canada had been plagued for years with shortages of coins of precious metals. As was typical of any fledgling colony, Canada imported more goods than it exported, such that silver and gold coin tended to flow back to France to pay commercial debts, rather than remaining in circulation in Canada. Shipments of hard money from France were few and far between. As a result, in 1685 paper money was officially issued for the first time, and was used intermittently thereafter. On several occasions, stamped and countersigned playing cards were actually pressed into service because the colony suffered from a shortage of paper. This paper money was not officially sanctioned and generated inflation. The paper currency was generally viewed without trust or confidence, further eroding its value. Thus, Canada's economy had been forced to operate with an improvised monetary system, which had collapsed under the rigors of the war by 1760.[13]

Canada had another problem. The Marquis de Vaudreuil was a competent political governor, and he had seen previous service as a commissioned officer with the Ministry of Marine, but he generally lacked military skills. Louis Antoine de Bougainville, a French soldier and senior officer who would earn great fame, was completely unimpressed with him. Although not always an impartial observer, Bougainville found de Vaudreuil to be "a man, limited, without talent, perhaps free from vice, but having all the faults of a petty spirit." Bougainville further noted that though the governor was fascinated by military strategy and tactics, he had served on only one active campaign, a minor Indian raid launched from Canada. Upon receipt of a message from de Vaudreuil on July 31, 1758, Bougainville scorn-fully recorded in his journal, "Letters from the Marquis de V as usual, that is to say, vague, ridiculous, or captious, not answering at all to reason, to facts, to proof."[14]

Although Canada under de Vaudreuil's leadership had experi-enced military successes between 1755 and 1757, the tide had turned against the colony in 1758. British arms had gained major victories in the 1759 campaign that had reduced Canada to Montreal, a por-tion of the Saint Lawrence River valley, and the Richelieu River val-ley. Still, Canada remained in the fight and maintained formidable defenses, with large contingents of the French Army stationed at Montreal, Îsle aux Noix, and astride the Saint Lawrence River, near the confluence of the Oswegatchie River.

General de Lévis commanded a small, but highly trained, well-seasoned, and extremely competent regular army, supplemented at least on paper by a large force of Canadian militia and Indians. The core of the French army had crossed the North Atlantic in 1755 and fought under Baron Dieskau at Lake George in September of that year, with massive reinforcements following in 1756. The heart of de Lévis's army consisted of the eight regular battalions of La Reine, La Sarre, Languedoc, Royal Rousillon, Guyenne, Berry (two battal-ions), and Béarn. These regiments had known victory at Oswego in 1756, Fort William Henry in 1757, Fort Carillon in 1758, and they had fought with stubborn valor as they had gained glory and honor at Fort Niagara and Quebec in 1759.

Lévis could depend on approximately 3,500 regulars, 3,000 mili-tia of the districts of Montreal and Three Rivers, and approximately 400 Indian warriors. Counted among the regulars were a number of companies and other small detachments of French Troupes de la Marine, who garrisoned the majority of the small posts throughout Canada and New France. These numerous independent companies of French marines were raised and under the control of the French Ministry of Marine, which was in turn responsible for the supervi-sion of all colonies. These soldiers were thus not actual "marines" serving onboard naval vessels but infantrymen who safeguarded the various posts of the French colonies. These independent com-panies were under a separate chain of command and played a dif-ferent role from the regulars of the French Army. By 1760, many of these marines were highly capable and experienced warriors.[15] Although it was a relatively small army, it was very familiar with the military conditions of Canada, and provided de Lévis with a powerful striking force.

To the west, up the Saint Lawrence River valley, the French had constructed Fort Lévis, a strong fortification on an island in the middle of the river. It was just downstream from the confluence of the Saint Lawrence and the Oswegatchie River, at the site of present-day Ogdensburg, New York. Here in 1749 the Abbé Piquet had established a religious mission for a mixed Indian community, and Fort de La Présentation had been constructed to secure this mission.[16]

By the late 1740s, French growth had reached the upper Saint Lawrence River valley. French colonial leaders recognized the need to establish settlements at the western extremity of the Saint Lawrence River, upstream beyond the final set of rapids, but before the deep waters of Lake Ontario were reached. An early French post was established at Fort Frontenac on the Cataraqui River (modern Kingston, Ontario), but another post closer to the terminus of the Saint Lawrence River was desirable. Additionally, "a great number of Iroquois Indians having expressed their willingness to embrace Christianity, it has been proposed to establish a mission in the direction of Fort Frontenac. Abbé Piquet, a zealous Missionary in whom these nations have evinced much confidence, has been put in care of it." Abbé Piquet arrived on May 30, 1749 to establish a storehouse and chapel at a site that he found to be "advantageously situated . . . on the bank of the River la Présentation, at the head of all the rapids, on the west side of a beautiful basin formed by that river, capable of easily containing forty or fifty sloops . . . A handsome town could be hereafter built there."[17] Piquet called the fort "La Présentation," a name chosen for the fact that the date of his arrival coincided with the Catholic Feast of the Presentation of the Blessed Virgin Mary. Piquet celebrated the first mass at the fort on June 1, 1749.

The initial post was destroyed by a Mohawk raid on October 26, 1749, "the stockades of the fort . . . being burnt. Abbé Piquet's house alone was saved. The loss by this fire is considerable. It would have been greater were it not for four Abenakis, who on this occasion gave a proof of their fidelity. The man named Perdreaux had half of his hand carried away. His arm had to be cut off. One of the Abenakis received a gun shot; the ball remained in his blanket."[18]

Subsequently, the French engineer Etienne Robert, Sieur de la Morandière, was dispatched to "draw a plan of barracks for this detachment, and a store for the provisions."[19] Regarding armament, it was noted that "they have caused five guns, of two pound caliber, to be sent to Abbé Piquet for his little fort, so as to inspire the Indians with confidence, and to convince them that they will be safe there."[20] A "Return of Artillery in Canada" for 1749 recorded "5 iron guns of the caliber of 2 pounders" at "Fort Souegatsi."[21] By 1749 cannon of this small size would have been of no value against a European army, but they certainly would have created an extremely loud report that would have impressed the Natives.

French Army Captain Pierre Pouchot described this post as "a square fort there, the buildings of which formed the bastions. The curtains were of large upright stakes 15 to 16 feet high. The missionaries, the commandant, his little garrison & the storekeeper for the trade of the missionaries appointed by the King all occupied the four main parts of this facility. . . . There is a reef in the river almost at the end of the Indian village where the Abbé Piquet had set up saw mills."[22] By 1756 Fort de La Présentation was a thriving settlement. Piquet's religious influence on the community was apparent, as allegedly La Présentation was one settlement where brandy was not given to the Indians.[23] Bougainville observed in July 1756 that "there is in the fort a captain of colonial troops as commander, but all real control is ecclesiastical."[24]

A conference with the Iroquois Indians settled at La Présentation was held at Quebec on September 20, 1751. At the conclusion of these discussions, the Natives specifically noted, "If we were in more comfortable circumstances, our village would increase perceptibly. We want 37 kettles; it is the women who ask them." Their request was granted by the French.[25] Assuming that one cooking kettle was provided for each fire maintained by an extended family unit in a longhouse, this suggests that 37 such families resided at Fort de La Présentation, which would thus have supported approximately six to eight longhouses, and a community of 500 to 600 Natives. This would be a typical sized village, and for the settlement to be this well established after only two years suggests that the community was prospering under Piquet's tutelage.

Throughout the Seven Years' War, several French military observers recorded accounts of the post. Adjutant Anne-Joseph-Hippolyte de Maurès de Malartic of the Regiment Béarn passed through La Présentation with his regiment on July 28, 1756: "This fort consists of four buildings, in the form of a bastion, the curtains whereof are palisades. It is good against Indians, but would be quite untenable against Regulars that might wish to attack it, as it is commanded on all sides."[26] A German soldier serving with the French marines and subsequently captured by the English reported in August 1759 regarding La Présentation: "The Garrison consisted of 50 Men, who were generally employed Cutting Timber for 2 Store Houses which were built within the Fort and were almost finished when he left it, the one was for the Commandant, the other for the Priests. Of whom they have three." He also recalled "drawing Stones from near Swegatchy for building."[27] An English captive who subsequently escaped from Canada reported of La Présentation: "From Cadaraqui he went down the river St. Laurence to Montreal & in the way called at Sweegatchie which is a small stockaded fort & a great many Indian houses & Indians there."[28]

Beginning with the French military advance down the Ohio Valley in 1753, Fort de La Présentation served as a storehouse for supplies intended for the "upper country forts" west of Lake Ontario. These included Forts Niagara, Detroit, Michilimackinac, and the Ohio Country posts.[29] Each of these stores was under the supervision of a French royal storekeeper, who was stationed at the fort and also responsible for the maintenance of the Indian trade. In the summer of 1756, Bougainville further observed that "the Abbé Piquet, able missionary . . . built a fort of squared posts, flanked by four strong bastions, palisaded without and with a water-filled ditch. Beside the fort is the village of a hundred fires, each that of an Iroquois chief, all warriors. . . . Abbé Piquet teaches them and drills them in the French military exercises."[30]

At various times throughout the war, the French officers dispatched raiding parties from La Présentation, or supported major operations against English posts, principally at Oswego or along the Mohawk River.[31] In the winter of 1756 the French launched a large, aggressive raid from Fort de La Présentation against Fort Bull, a small English post guarding the critical supply line running from the Mohawk River to Fort Ontario. Under the command of French engineer Lieutenant Gaspard Joseph Chassegros de Léry, this French raiding party consisted of approximately one hundred Native warriors and 250 French regulars and Canadian militiamen. It was organized and equipped at La Présentation, and headed south on March 12, 1756.[32] This raid destroyed Fort Bull and considerable English stores and effectively isolated Fort Ontario, setting the conditions for its capture by the French that summer. De Léry's Expedition returned to La Présentation early in April.

During the French campaign to capture the English fort at Oswego the next summer, the French army under the Marquis de Montcalm passed through Fort de La Présentation, and spent the evening of July 21, 1756, encamped there. That night, Montcalm held a council with the Fort de La Présentation Iroquois Indians, and recruited them for the ensuing attack. Following his successful capture of Oswego, the French army and Montcalm again passed through Présentation on their way back to Montreal.

In November 1757, another French raid was launched from Fort de La Présentation on the settlement of German Flats in the Mohawk Valley, resulting in its destruction on November 12.[33] Following the reduction of the French Fort Frontenac by the English colonel John Bradstreet in August 1758, Captain Francois Lefebvre Duplessis Faber and 1,800 soldiers were ordered on August 30 to take up position at Fort de La Présentation to block any further English incursion up the Saint Lawrence River. This marked the first deliberate French defense of the upper Saint Lawrence River valley. For the next eighteen months, Fort de La Présentation would be the center of this French defensive position.

The Marquis de Vaudreuil noted in a letter dated September 2, 1758: "A camp is about to be formed at La Présentation to protect the Colony at that side; annoy the English at Chouaguen [Oswego] . . . have parties out from whom I shall obtain information respecting the movements of the English and their force."[34] In the summer of 1759 the French marine captain the Chevalier de la Corne Saint-Luc was assigned a similar position and role, although he only had four to five hundred Canadian militia and a few French marines assigned to him. From here in early July, reinforced by the Indians from La Présentation led by Abbé Piquet, he launched an unsuccessful spoiling attack on the English garrison guarding supplies at Oswego.[35]

Following the fall of Fort Niagara in early August 1759, Montcalm's principal subordinate de Lévis was sent to Fort de La Présentation with an additional five to six hundred men. At this time Lévis determined to construct a new fortification on Île Oraquointon (modern Chimney Island), which then became the principal French defensive post guarding the western entrance to the Saint Lawrence River.[36] This post, carefully positioned to block both the north and south channels of the Saint Lawrence River, entirely obstructed the river and safeguarded Montreal from any British advance from Lake Ontario. British brigadier general Gage had been instructed to seize Fort de La Présentation and the new fort in the late summer of 1759 following the capture of Fort Niagara. He had failed entirely, incurring the great displeasure of Amherst through his lack of action.

Fort de La Présentation was too flimsy and poorly positioned to withstand a deliberate siege. During the winter of 1759–1760, once the new Fort Lévis was defensible, the French abandoned Fort de La Présentation and shifted their operations to their new post. Many of the Indians departed. On July 13, 1760 a French detachment was sent to the older fort to begin its demolition, although it appears that they only removed the roofs.[37] Still, Indian raiding parties were regularly dispatched from La Présentation in the summer of 1760, suggesting that the Iroquois Indian village and at least some French presence remained at the post. The Marquis de Vaudreuil noted on June 24, 1760 that: "He has constantly parties of Indians of La Présentation" performing scouting duties.[38]

To the south, the Richelieu River was similarly obstructed by another set of strong entrenchments constructed at the low-lying Île aux Noix (literally, the Island of Nuts), located in the middle of the river. Heavy log booms had been constructed to interdict the east and west channels of the river. The remnants of the small French Lake Champlain fleet were based out of the island fortress.

Île aux Noix was a formidable position. Although the island was a miserable location for habitation, its placement in the midst of the river rendered it nearly impregnable against a direct assault, and any formal siege would be very difficult. A fortification here entirely obstructed the Richelieu River, and swamps extending to the east and west of the river prevented any large force from out-flanking it. Until the French fortifications at Île aux Noix could be captured, any further British advance from the south would be impossible.

Although the situation of the French in Canada in the winter of 1759 and spring of 1760 was grim, it was by no means untenable. During the long winter, the French leadership in Montreal was well aware that the British garrison of Quebec was suffering severely from illness, and would be continuously weakened until fresh provisions, medicine, and reinforcements reached them in the spring. Although similar intelligence was lacking for Oswego and Crown

Point, it was not unreasonable to assume that those garrisons, isolated by the harsh winter in remote wilderness posts at the ends of long and tenuous supply lines, would be in similar circumstances.

In 1759 the French had constructed strong citadels at Îsle aux Noix and Fort Lévis. These defenses were by no means impregnable, but they could not be bypassed by any British advance. They would have to be reduced by a formal siege that would require preparation time and absorb considerable resources before any advance into the interior of Canada was feasible. Although the fortifications on the eastern Saint Lawrence River at Jacques Cartier were nowhere near as strong, there were French Canadian militia and Indian warriors in the area. The post constituted a powerful rallying spot from which a defense of the river against any incursion from Quebec could be centrally conducted. It was also reasonable to assume that any British advance would be delayed until provincial troops could be raised from the various colonies. This was always a slow process, and likely to be even slower in 1760, after over five years of campaigns and the victories of 1759 that for many signaled the end of the war. Such a delay might be more than sufficient to enable a relief column with reinforcements, ordnance, munitions, and supplies to arrive from France.

By necessity, any British advance in 1760 would have to be segmented and traverse scores of miles of wilderness, constituting a logistical nightmare for the British commanders and officers. Lévis's small but highly effective French army could maneuver along interior lines of communications along the rivers and lakes of Canada. With the strong military fortifications constructed in 1759 and the natural defenses imposed by distance and terrain, the French leadership in Montreal knew that they faced a formidable challenge in 1760, but they were by no means entirely vulnerable. A resolute resistance had every prospect of permitting Canada to survive for another campaign season.

CHAPTER 2

"WORTHY ANTAGONISTS!"

Winter of 1759–1760 in Quebec

Quebec surrendered to the British army on September 18, 1759. Throughout the summer the city had been pounded, in some cases literally to dust, by the British artillery. A large French army had occupied the city throughout the year, consuming prodigious quantities of provisions and firewood. During the blockade of Quebec, British major general James Wolfe had launched numerous light infantry and ranger raids on the surrounding countryside, focused on destroying crops and French magazines of rations and fodder. The adjacent farms, which provided the majority of the fresh food for the city, had been absolutely devastated.

Buildings in the city had been burned, shattered, and rendered uninhabitable. Sergeant James Thompson of the grenadier company of Colonel Simon Fraser's 78th Highlanders recalled: "We found the Buildings in general in a most ruinous condition, and infinitely worse than we could have imagined; for, besides those burnt, there was hardly a house in the Town that was not injured by either shot or shells; nor were they habitable without some repairs."[1] When Thompson and his Highland soldiers were assigned quarters in a house, they discovered that it "was scarcely habitable from the number of shells that had fallen through it."[2] Nearly all available firewood had been consumed by the French. The British army had been fully engaged in military operations against the city and was far too busy to make any preparations for the winter. Thus, the British garrison began its occupation of the city facing considerable challenges.

The defense of Quebec was entrusted for the winter to Brigadier General James Murray, Wolfe's oldest brigade commander, though junior in seniority. He had been born in Ballencrief, Scotland, on January 21, 1712, to a minor member of the Scottish peerage.[3] Murray had entered the British army in 1740 as a nineteen-year-old second lieutenant in the newly raised 4th Regiment of Marines. Almost immediately, he served in the expedition to Cartagena, Colombia, in 1740. Because of gallantry in the assault on Cartagena, and since he had survived the decimation of that force by disease, Murray was rewarded with a commission as captain in Colonel John Wynard's 15th Regiment of Foot on November 20, 1741.[4] Murray's two brothers had been active Jacobites in the 1745 rebellion, though Murray himself remained loyal to King George II and served with honor and distinction with his regiment in Flanders throughout the Scottish uprising. He was severely wounded at the Siege of Ostlund, Belgium, in the summer of 1745. Yet Murray had apparently (and entirely unfairly) been judged guilty by association of the nefarious activities of his brothers, and his advancement in the British army had clearly been retarded as a result.[5] Murray had participated in an aborted amphibious raid on Rochefort, France, in 1757; had distinguished himself at the siege of Louisbourg in 1758; and had proved to be a reliable and dependable brigade commander under Wolfe at Quebec. By the fall of 1759, General Murray was a highly accomplished officer. He had seen nearly two decades of commissioned service in the British army, including considerable combat experience in Flanders during the War of the Austrian Succession and in North America.

The Chevalier Johnstone had fought with the Jacobites throughout the 1745 rebellion, been present at Culloden, and then fled to France to avoid punishment. He had subsequently served as an officer with the French Army. Although he might have been favorably biased toward a fellow Highander, Johnstone would write of his opponent: "General Murray, who does the greatest honor to his country by his great knowledge of the art of war, good sense and ability."[6]

Murray's garrison was entirely isolated once the ice settled in Saint Lawrence Bay, an event that usually occurred in early December and typically continued through early May. Making the situation even worse, a large British army had to be maintained in the city. In October 1759, Murray designated 7,300 rank and file as the winter garrison. In hindsight, this force was far too large to be sustained for the winter in Quebec, but it was adjudged necessary due to the proximity of the French camp of observation at Jacques Cartier, and the presence of the main French force comparatively close at Montreal.

A relatively robust and capable advance guard of French regulars, marines of the French Colonial Service, Canadian militia, and Indian warriors was stationed at Jacques Cartier under the command of Captain Jean-Daniel Dumas, an experienced and capable marine officer. Born in 1721, Dumas had served with the French Army on the European continent throughout the War of the Austrian Succession. Transferred to Canada in 1750, Dumas was best known for leading the French and Indian forces that had crushed the British column under Major General Edward Braddock near Fort Duquesne in early July 1755. In recognition of his leadership, he had been made a knight of the Order of Saint Louis, quite rare for an officer under thirty-five years of age. Early in 1759 he had been commissioned major general inspector for the troops in Canada. Dumas had extensive service at Fort Duquesne in the Ohio Country. He had gained considerable knowledge coordinating with the various Indians supporting the French fort there, and he possessed substantial experience with what was then referred to as *petite guerre,* or Small War. Dumas fully intended to put his skills and knowledge to use to harass Quebec throughout the winter. Murray noted that "as it was not impossible that by the intrigues of the enemy . . . our principal magazine might be burned or destroyed," he took precautions to disperse his valuable stores of provisions on November 11. The next day, Murray also wrote of Dumas's first efforts against his garrison, in which "the enemy [had] the impudence to come and carry off cattle from the neighborhood of the town."[7] Following the winter's travails, Murray would write to Amherst, mentioning "the designs which were formed and partly attempted against me in the winter."[8]

Murray's garrison took possession of Quebec on September 29, 1759. Quartermaster Sergeant John Johnson of Lieutenant General Robert Anstruther's 58th Regiment of Foot recorded Murray's actions to secure the approaches to the city:

> We . . . Secured ourselves in it, in the best manner we were able: by posting a large number of detachments, round about, in the Skirts of the Woods, which surrounded the town on all Sides. . . . The detachments were to watch the motions of the Enemy's Army, who for some time Lay hovering round about the Garrison; as also to be a check upon their Skulking Parties of Indians and Canadiens; who during the Winter Season were a great disturbance to the Garrison, as well as to the Inhabitants, within the Country towns and

Plantations, who had taken the Oath of Allegiance to the English Government. Although, a vast number of the Canadians, as well as the French inhabitants who had settled in Canada . . . brought in their Arms daily, and took the Oath of Allegiance to Brigadier General Murray the Governor; as also a great number within the said circuit laid down their Arms, and took the oath of Neutrality tendered to them.[9]

Throughout the long winter, Murray remained concerned that Dumas's advanced detachment would launch a surprise attack against the city, and he issued stringent orders that his garrison maintain its alertness. Quartermaster Sergeant Johnson recalled that "our Orders were . . . to lye on our Arms: No Officer, or Soldier, unless he was Sick, was allowed to undress, or go to Bed; Nor were we on any pretence, allowed to put off our Accoutrements during the night . . . by which precaution we were always in readiness to turn out at a Moment's warning, without the least hurry or confusion, in case of a Surprize."[10]

Whenever Murray dispatched parties to gather firewood, they encountered harassing fires from the Canadian militia and Indians. Accordingly, the general determined to secure an outer perimeter around the city. He established advanced posts at Saint Foy on November 11 and at Lorette the next day. These detachments occupied and fortified churches and were equipped with artillery.[11] Later in the winter Murray also constructed blockhouses around the city, particularly at Point Lévis.

To support the establishment of his intelligence network and to reduce the harassment that his garrison faced, Murray also implemented measures to achieve neutrality in the Canadian countryside around Quebec. He initiated a concentrated effort to gain the goodwill of the French Canadian population; today such a campaign would be considered counterinsurgency. It is conceivable that Murray, whose Scottish homeland had been devastated following the Jacobite Rebellion, and who had seen firsthand the brutal treatment that his superior General James Wolfe had inflicted on Quebec in the previous campaign, was hesitant to implement such a scorched-earth policy himself.

As early as November 12, Murray published a manifesto warning the Canadian citizens of the "misfortunes" they would bring on themselves if they failed to keep quiet, while representing the French as "a beaten, dispirited army, which had already abandoned them." This manifesto presented regulations for the inhabitants, established a civil jurisdiction for them, and "appointed Colonel Young chief judge, taking into the other offices some of the men of the best character that I could find in the place."[12] Murray simultaneously wrote to Amherst:

> Untill I have the honor to receive your orders I shall follow the natural disposition of my heart, which dictates Clemency. This conduct can do no hurt . . . it may have a permanent advantage; the Canadians have been taught to look upon us as Barbarians, whose only view was their destruction; hence the obstinate resistance they have made and the eagerness they shew'd to take up arms against us; They begin now to be astonish'd with our conduct, will soon be convinced that there is no deceit in it, and hardly here after [be] so easily be persuaded to take up arms against a nation they must admire & who will always have in in their power to burn and destroy. Sufficient examples they have had this summer of the horrors of war; they were not treated tenderly before we had the good fortune to take Quebec; they will remember that no doubt and it may be supposed they will not forget any instances of Clemency & generosity that may be shewn them, since they have been entirely in our power.[13]

Thus, Murray assured the inhabitants that if they did not cause trouble for him, he would not cause trouble for them, while simultaneously reestablishing a rudimentary civil government with a system of justice. This went far in returning the immediate vicinity of Quebec to some semblance of normality.

Murray continued his efforts, using the proverbial carrot and stick. On November 20 he "ordered Major Hussey, commanding the detachment at Lorette, to summon the inhabitants of that parish, to make them deliver their arms, swear them, and burn the houses of those who might be still with the army."[14] These were neither idle threats nor idle promises.

In early February a French marine captain, one Saint Martin, launched a raid in force against Point Lévis, opposite Quebec. Murray neatly parried Captain Saint Martin's thrust but was not amused to discover that his force had contained a considerable party of Canadian militia. He was "informed the French detachment had concealed itself for two nights in houses at Point Lévis, within about six miles of our post, without any of the inhabitants giving the least notice." He acted promptly. On February 26 Major Eliot of Colonel James Shaw Kennedy's 43rd Regiment, with three hundred infantrymen and sailors, was dispatched to burn a number of houses of inhabitants on the south shore of the river who could not account for themselves. Their hapless families were driven into the Canadian winter. Murray issued a proclamation, strongly expressing regret at having to take such a terrible step, and again warning the inhabitants of what they must expect if they violated their oaths of neutrality.[15]

Quartermaster Johnson remembered another of Murray's initiatives:

> As the Canadian Inhabitants had suffered exceedingly during the late Campaign, and had lost all they had; either by their Own people plundering them, [or by] destroying their Substance on the other hand: and We, who were their Enemies, destroying all we came near on the other hand . . . they were now in the deepest distress, even for common nourishment. General Murray therefore, out of humane and tender regard to their calamities, ordered One day's provisions to be Stopped weekly from each Officer and Soldier, and to be distributed amongst the inhabitants . . . the Soldiers out of a tender and compassionate regard for their fellow Creatures, willingly acquiesced with the above order, and parted freely from their Subsistence for them.[16]

That this policy had a positive effect on the Canadians cannot be doubted. Murray had already begun to demonstrate charity on behalf of King George and to dilute the Canadians' support for King Louis. By the end of December, Murray could report: "Quebec had only capitulated for itself, but now the Province, from the Cape Rouge on the northern, and from the Chaudiere [River] on the southern shore, had submitted; the inhabitants had taken an oath of fidelity, and surrendered their arms; my orders were obeyed everywhere within this extent, and the parishes within reach of the garrison assisted us to carry in our wood; they furnished bullocks for our use, and hay, straw, and oats for the draft cattle; it is true that for these they were paid."[17] Murray's efforts quickly began to foster reconciliation between the Canadian citizens and the British army, and more important, he had discovered a successful formula that he would employ with considerable effect that spring.

Murray supplemented his intelligence network and treatment of the French Canadian citizens with aggressive patrolling and scouting performed by his rangers and light infantrymen on snowshoes. Murray employed the information that he garnered to launch recurring raids using these rangers and light infantry, augmented by grenadiers, on the various French posts. Generally successful, these raids secured Quebec and kept Dumas's irregulars at arm's length. Murray achieved the upper hand during this winter's series of small wars. This proved to be fortuitous, for Murray and his army were much less fortunate in their struggle against what proved to be their greatest enemy, the brutal Canadian winter. Although the garrison was secure, and Murray's actions had ensured that the inhabitants were neutral, if not friendly (at least in exchange for British hard specie), temperatures were frigid, the fall of snow both consistent and heavy, and the garrison had not been provided with adequate winter clothing. By mid-December, conditions were already becoming nearly unbearable. The winter became "insupportably cold," as recorded by Lieutenant Malcolm Fraser of the Highlanders.

In particular, the poor men of Fraser's 78th Highlanders assigned to the garrison, clad in the Scottish kilt, suffered terribly. A more inappropriate dress for the frigid Canadian temperatures and biting wind could scarcely be imagined. Adequate firewood had not been stockpiled for the winter in the garrison, and the men had to march daily no less than four miles to Sainte-Foy to cut wood, and then haul it back to the city on sledges. Fraser recorded in his journal on December 20: "This is a very severe duty; the poor fellows do it however with great spirit, tho' several of them have already lost the use of their fingers and toes by the incredible severity of the front, and the country people tell us it is not yet at the worst. Some men on sentry have been deprived of speech and sensation in a few minutes, but hitherto, no person has lost his life, as care is taken to relieve them every half hour or oftener when the weather is very severe."[18] Sergeant Thompson with the same regiment recalled that, although his quarters miraculously possessed a stove, "some days [the men] were almost frozen to death or suffocated by the smoke and to mend the matter they had nothing better than green wood."[19] Often the garrison awoke in the morning to find their blankets covered in snow and ice.

The garrison had also not been provided with sufficient medical care. A June 24, 1760, report by James Napier, the British Director of Hospitals, reported that a single surgeon, Francis Russell, accompanied by one apothecary's mate, David Ord (or Orde), were present at Quebec. Apothecary Alexander Vere arrived at Quebec on April 30, too late to provide any assistance during the long winter.[20] For a garrison as large as Murray commanded in Quebec, over 7,000 men at peak strength, this was a woefully insufficient medical staff. Although the Canadian population generously provided care and lodging for the sick, the small number of British medical practitioners certainly did nothing to prevent or arrest the spread of disease.

The Quebec garrison was without adequate firewood, clothing, doctors or quarters, yet the greatest shortfall was in rations. Because the British established the garrison so late in the year, no opportunity to stockpile fresh food or vegetables had existed, and in any event the year's campaign had exhausted all local sources of supply. Thus, the army had to rely on salt pork, salt beef and bread as the core constituents of their diet. The inevitable result was scurvy.

Scurvy is a disease caused by a deficiency in vitamin C, an essential nutrient normally obtained from fresh vegetables and fruits and readily obtained in a simple vitamin pill today. Soldiers in isolated eighteenth-century winter garrisons, surviving on the standard army ration, and sailors serving on extended cruises at sea were particularly susceptible to this disease. This was largely caused by inadequacies in the contemporary preservation of foodstuffs. The only foods that could readily survive for extended periods without refrigeration had to be smoked, salted, or pickled in brine, destroying much of their nutritional value. Most fruits and vegetables could simply not be preserved in such a manner. Accordingly, the core army and navy ration consisted of salted meat and bread. So long as this ration could be supplemented with fresh fruit and vegetables, scurvy would not break out. But when such items were not available, as was the case in the hastily established Quebec garrison in the fall of 1759, scurvy was nearly inevitable. The timing of the onset of scurvy is somewhat variable depending on how much vitamin C is in a particular soldier's body, and individual physical and dietary differences. However, once scurvy erupted it was devastating to an army. Soldiers initially were fatigued and lethargic, as the disease progressed they increasingly became too weak to handle their weapons, easily exhausted, and incapable of performing extended military service. Eventually, they collapsed. In protracted cases, scurvy inevitably resulted in death. Only an infusion of acceptable nutrients would reverse the condition. By 1760, the British Royal Navy was at the forefront of investigating this disease and had already detected its root cause, but had not yet identified effective and viable preventative measures, much less a cure.[21] Over a century later, scurvy still bedeviled the United States Army during the 1864 Atlanta campaign and in remote garrisons on the western plains frontier during the Indian Wars.

Murray noted on February 29: "The men growing sickly; to ease the duty, took off some of the guards, and ordering a quantity of ginger to be delivered out to the several regiments, to be mixed with the men's water, to correct it." By March 9 Murray further noted: "The sickness still on the increase, notwithstanding every measure was taken to prevent it spreading; and the cause being manifestly the scurvy, gave orders this day about the method of boiling and preparing the salt pork, it being impossible to procure fresh provisions or vegetables." Although Murray was desperately attempting to arrest the spread of scurvy, variations in cooking the salt provisions would do nothing to alleviate its severity. By the end of the winter the disease had become an epidemic. Murray recorded on April 25: "Two hundred men having fallen ill this last week."[22] By this point, the garrison had recorded over six hundred deaths due to illness (a 9% mortality rate), and had nearly 3,000 men (38%) on the sick rolls.[23] Murray would write in May 1760 that "the Excessive coldness of the Climate, and constant living upon salt provisions, without any vegetables, introduced the scurvy among the Troops, which, getting the better of every precaution of the Officer, and every remedy of the Surgeon, became as universal as it was inveterate, in so much, that before the end of April one thousand were dead, and above two thousand of what remained, totally unfit for any service."[24] A young soldier, James Miller, remembered the horrors of the winter:

A severe winter now commenced, while we were totally unprepared for such a climate, neither fuel, forage or indeed anything to make life tolerable. The troops were crowded into vacant houses, as well as possible, number fell sick, and the scurvy made a dreadful havock among us. The duty became extremely hard, for after being up all night on guard, the men were obliged to go near six miles through the snow, to cut wood, and then to bring it home on sledges. From the severe frost, the wood was as hard as marble, and Europeans who had never been accustomed to cut wood, made but small progress, a constant and daily supply was however necessary, and required the greatest perseverance. In short, the fatigues of the winter were so great, that the living almost envied the dead.

Liquors were extremely scarce, and when the men could procure them, they generally drank to excess, it was no uncommon thing, in the morning to find several men frozen to death from the above cause . . . Many men lost the use of their hands and feet during the winter.[25]

Quartermaster Sergeant John Johnson of Ansthruser's 58th Regiment of Foot remembered of the grim appearance of the scurvy: "We had amongst us also during the Winter Season an inveterate Scurvey, and which proved Mortal to Numbers, especially to the Wounded men."[26] Quartermaster Johnson recorded that by April, the members of Quebec's garrison: "Through the hardness of their Duty; the Severity of the Weather, and the Want of provisions and nourishment, we were reduced to mere Skeltons."[27]

As the army suffered and struggled, in the midst of the winter Murray was faced with the necessity of coordinating with the British authorities in Boston, and with General Amherst in New York City. Naval communication was impossible so long as the Saint Lawrence River was choked with the ice of winter from early December. Heavy snowfall, frigid temperatures and the presence of the Îsle aux Noix garrison rendered communications by way of Lake Champlain unfeasible. In late December 1759, Murray handed a packet of dispatches to Lieutenant Butler of the Rangers, accompanied by an escort of four of his enlisted soldiers, to carry on snowshoes to Amherst in New York City. Butler, discovering that he was in imminent danger of being intercepted by Indians friendly to the French, had been forced to return to Quebec.[28] Accordingly, Murray dispatched engineer Lieutenant John Montresor on an arduous and difficult cross-country trek, using a little known route far to the southeast to swing around the hostile Indians and the French garrisons on the Richelieu River, following the Chaudière River south then southeast from Quebec to New England. Montresor succinctly described his journey:

I left Quebec the 26th day of January, crossed the river St Lawrence in Canoes through & over the ice to Point les Peres, from thence marched into the woods & cut through the village and concessions of St Charles, from thence struck S and by West upon the river Chaudiere--a few miles above the village of Nouvelle Basse, from thence to the Forks of Chaudiere, continuing on the southern Branch till we arrived at the Notch of the Allegany Mountains, till I arrived at the Great Chaudiere Pond, still keeping the same course, passed the height of land down to the little Chaudiere pond, passed the carrying place and struck on a stream or Branch of Ammerascagen [the modern Kennebec] River which I followed till I arrived at the settlement of the Township of Topsham [on the Kennebec River, close to Casco Bay].[29]

Montresor's dry, technical report in no way conveys the arduousness of this midwinter cross-country journey on snowshoes through scores of miles of wilderness once the French settlements on the Chaudière River were left behind. Montresor's trip from Quebec to Boston required a full month, and his arrival was by no matter certain. His party ran desperately low on food, but they still managed to push through in a desperate race against starvation. Lieutenant Montresor was eventually able to deliver Murray's letters in Boston. Such difficult, dangerous cross-country treks could scarcely be considered to be a reliable or dependable conduit of communications and coordination. In fact, Montresor's successful delivery of his dispatches had been a closely run event, as the men nearly starved to death in the deep Maine snows. This was the only communication between Murray and Amherst until the ice departed the river in late April.

Throughout the winter, while Murray was frozen in Quebec, de Lévis and the Marquis de Vaudreuil had planned a counterattack against the city. They believed that its capture would be critical to permit the small, battered French army to effectively employ its interior lines of communication in order to defeat in detail the two other likely British columns moving against them by way of Lake Champlain and Lake Ontario.[30] General de Lévis was determined to retain the initiative by going on the offensive in the spring, before the British could act. The experienced Jean-Daniel Dumas, a friend of de Lévis's who shared his military views, would later write: "The Canadian war was of the defensive kind; however the French generals acted always offensively, and obtained unbelievable successes while maintaining that character to its limit" and further that "The defense of the colonies must be more active, one must march toward the enemy."[31] Dumas and Lévis were clearly in agreement, as was Governor de Vaudreuil.

The French intentions were not unknown to Murray, and as early as November he received intimations through his rapidly expanding intelligence sources that such a French incursion was to be expected. He had written to Amherst on January 25, 1760, that "we wish for nothing more than the Visit Monsr de Lévis has threatened to pay us; If he really intends it, I suppose he will think proper to put it off till the Spring; I am told he may then bring all the force they have in Canada against us."[32] Lieutenant Fraser of the Highlanders recalled in early March that "They have threatened to attack us all winter, and the General seems now to think them in earnest."[33] Fraser echoed in mid-April: "A few days ago, the General despatched a small schooner down the river to meet the Fleet and hurry them up, as he expects to be attacked as soon as the river is clear of Ice above the Town."[34] Murray wrote in his journal on April 17 that "the best intelligence was now procured that the French had armed six ships, which had remained in the river last autumn, with two gallies which they had built; that they designed to bring down this squadron, with a number of boats, to transport the troops to the Cap Rouge."[35] Murray later confirmed to Pitt that: "In this Situation I received certain Intelligence that the Chevalier Gaston de Lévis was assembling his Army, which had been cantoned in the Neighborhood of Montreal, that he had completed his eight Battalions . . . and was determined to besiege us, the moment the St. Lawrence was open."[36]

As Murray's intelligence suggested, de Lévis intended to land at the Cape Rouge River, ten miles west of Quebec, close enough for the possibility of a *coup de main*, or surprise attack, directly on Quebec from the landing boats and march column. Murray had established advanced posts at Ancienne Lorette, Sainte-Foy, Point Levy and Sillery to prevent just such a French assault. Murray dispatched a detachment of Light Infantry at Cap Rouge, and reinforced the post at Sainte-Foy. On April 22, Murray noted in his journal that he had sent two 18-pounder cannon to this post, "drawn with infinite labor and trouble."[37] As Murray had anticipated, these posts forced De Lévis to transfer his landing to Saint Augustin, approximately two miles (three kilometers) upstream of Cap Rouge. A landing at Saint Augustin would have to cross the Cap Rouge River before it could move against Quebec, and was thus distant enough to render any possibility of a French surprise against Quebec unfeasible. On March 2, Lieutenant Fraser of Fraser's Highlanders specified: "Captain Cameron of our regiment was pitched upon by the General as a proper person to command at Lorette, as he spoke French, and by that means may the more readily procure intelligence of the enemy's motions."[38]

By establishing these advanced positions, Murray conducted what George Washington would later christen a "war of posts" in miniature. This does not mean that he intended to permanently defend this string of posts, nor in any of his letters to his superiors did he ever commit to such a course of action. Rather, by establishing these advanced posts he extended his control of the countryside west of Quebec, forced de Lévis to land on the far side of the Cap Rouge River, denied de Lévis close intelligence of the situation of the Quebec garrison, and at the same time expanded the ground over which he could push his light infantry and ranger patrols out to the west. Thus, Murray used this string of reinforced advanced posts to ensure that he had established viable security for Quebec.

In New France, the predominant lines of transportation and commerce followed the waterways. Roads were relatively few and served primarily to connect adjacent communities. Although they possessed some limited local value for military operations, they were generally devoid of military application to support major movements or campaigns. Accordingly, de Lévis could not maneuver his army from its winter quarters in Montreal and along the Saint Lawrence River until the ice melted from that river. Lieutenant Fraser observed the river from the city of Quebec: "About the 23rd or 24th of this month [April], the Ice on the River St. Lawrence broke, and began to come down the river in great sheets extending from one side to the other of the river . . . the Ice below, has been broken some time ago."[39] The Highlander lieutenant was correct, for as early as April 10 the ice had sufficiently melted at Montreal to permit the French to initiate their long-anticipated movement forward, although not without difficulty. Many of the boats still had to be dragged a distance across the ice. By April 20 they were well on their way downstream on the ice-choked river.[40] Although the transit down the river was both difficult and dangerous, de Lévis was determined to steal a march on Murray and attack him at the earliest conceivable opportunity. In addition to bringing with him nearly the full strength of Canada, it is significant that de Lévis would be supported by no less than 270 Indian warriors. These were principally from Caughnawaga and Saint Francis and were often (although imprecisely) referred to as the Canadian Iroquois.[41]

Murray received confirmation that the French had initiated their movement through a set of bizarre circumstances at 3:00 A.M. on the morning of April 27. As Captain Knox related, about 2:00 A.M., following a horrific early spring storm the evening before: "The watch on board the Racehorse sloop of war in the dock [at Quebec] hearing a distressful noise on the river, acquainted Captain McCartny therewith, who instantly ordered out his boat, which shortly after returned with a man whom they found almost famished on a float of ice." The British sailors warmed the man up until he was able to speak, and were astounded at the tale that he related: "That he is a Serjeant of the French artillery, who, with six other men, were put into a floating battery of one eighteen pounder; that his batteau overset in the great storm above mentioned, and his companions he supposes are drowned, that he swam and scrambled, alternately, through numberless floats of ice, until he fortunately met with a large one, on which, through with great difficulty, he fixed himself." It was from this block of ice that he had been rescued, nearly perished from the effects of his immersion and the cold. The thankful sergeant, who must have been ecstatic that he was still alive, reported "that the French squadron, consisting of several frigates, armed sloops, and other craft . . . laden with ammunition, artillery, provisions, entrenching tools and stores of all kind, were coming down to the Foulon at Silery; where they were to meet the army under M. de Lévis and M. Bourlamacque." Doubtless still shivering, the French sergeant further stated, "They are made to believe that they will be reinforced by a powerful fleet and army from France, before an English ship can enter the river; and they are in daily expectation of a frigate laden with ammunition and stores." Immediately upon hearing this rendition, Captain McCartney had the man swaddled in navy wool blankets and carried in a sailor's hammock to General Murray, whom McCartney did not hesitate to awaken for an interview with the French sergeant.[42] Although the information was scarcely unexpected, Murray now had precise intelligence of the French approach, and he wasted little time in responding.

Murray's advanced posts served him well, as they forced de Lévis to divert to the north to cross the Cap Rouge River on the evening of April 26. The same terrible storm that had cast the beleaguered French artillery sergeant adrift had also bedeviled de Lévis's soldiers. He would record in his journal: "It was a most awful night, with terrible storm and cold, which caused the army great suffering, as it was not able to finish crossing till far into the night. The bridges having broken down, the soldiers crossed in the water. The workmen had much difficulty in effecting repairs in the dark, and, but for the lightning, we should have been forced to halt."[43]

April 27 proved to be a miserable day, "with a thick and cold misting rain" reported by Captain Knox.[44] Murray realized that the moment had arrived to evacuate his advanced posts, none of which were sufficiently robust to have any real hope of holding out against the full strength of the French army. Accordingly, he marched from Quebec with the grenadier battalion and Amherst's 15th Regiment of Foot and two field pieces to cover the withdrawal of the small garrison at Sainte-Foy. Colonel Charles Otway's 35th Regiment of Foot and the 2nd Battalion of Royal Americans were dispatched to Sillery on a similar mission. Murray prudently safeguarded his movements with a strong reserve consisting of Colonel Philip Bragg's 28th, General Peregrine Lascelles's 47th, and Ansthruser's 58th Regiments of Foot, along with Fraser's Highlanders.[45] Murray found the French "in possession of all the woods from Lorette to St. Foy, and just entering the plain: however they declined attacking me in the advantageous position I had taken."[46]

Throughout his operations west of Quebec, Murray employed his elite flanking companies in ad hoc battalions. In the British army in North America during the Seven Years' War, each regiment consisted of eight companies of line or battalion infantry, one company of grenadiers, and one of light infantrymen. Grenadiers were larger, stronger and more imposing men whose height was exaggerated by specialized hats, often made of bearskin. They had originally been organized to throw hand grenades in defensive or offensive siege operations, a measure that required considerable strength to fling them into the enemy's works. The light infantrymen were typically more active and agile soldiers, selected for their innovation and intelligence, trained and equipped to operate independently. It was common practice to join these specialized companies together into a battalion during active field operations, thus creating an elite grenadier or light infantry unit for special services.

Murray was in a tactically superior position, and it was in his best interest to fight de Lévis as far outside of the city as possible, so as to delay his advance until the Royal Navy relief fleet made its appearance at Quebec.[47] However, he realized that remaining in the field overnight, with his men soaked and cold, in vestiges of uniforms that had not been replaced in over a year and had seen months of hard service during the winter, and suffering from the effects of scurvy and various ailments, would simply destroy his army. Murray noted "the weather very bad," and he had to abandon a transient field advantage in the interests of preserving his command. To his credit Murray did not hesitate to evacuate "all my posts" and withdraw his command into the city for the night, even if it meant abandoning the two 18-pounder cannon at Sainte-Foy, after their trunnions had been knocked off to render them permanently useless.[48]

Murray's drenched, chilled, and nearly drowned army returned to the city through the Saint Louis and Saint John's gates. Knox reported "the army being extremely harrassed, and wet with a constant soaking rain, were allowed an extraordinary jill [gill] of rum per man; and some old houses at St. Rocque were pulled down to provide them with fire-wood, in order to dry their clothes."[49] Quartermaster Sergeant Johnson echoed: "It rained very hard all that Afternoon, and we marched back to the Garrison, wet to the Skin."[50]

The next morning, Murray's organized his army into three divisions: a right column that marched out Saint John's Gate under Colonel Burton with Amherst's 15th, Anstruther's 58th, the 2nd Battalion Royal Americans and General Daniel Webb's (late Colonel Dunbar's) 48th Foot. A left column departed from Saint Louis Gate under Colonel Fraser with his own Highlanders, Kennedy's 43rd, Lascelles's 47th, Bragg's 28th Foot and Fraser's Highlanders. A reserve corps commanded by Lieutenant Colonel Young included Otway's 35th Regiment of Foot and Young's own 3rd Battalion of the Royal Americans. The Light Infantry Battalion covered the right (north) of the army; with a company of volunteers under Captain McDonald of Fraser's Highlanders and Captain Moses Hazen's Company of Rangers on the left (south) flank.[51] Captain Knox reported that the army was accompanied by a substantial force of artillery: "consisting of eighteen pieces of cannon, two twelve-pounders, with sixteen six-pounders and two howitzers."[52] The best estimate of Murray's strength is that he carried 3,364 infantrymen forward. He faced a considerably stronger French force that deployed no less than 6,661 muskets, although de Lévis's army was only accompanied by three 6-pounder cannon.[53]

Murray's columns marched to occupy the high ground of the Buttes à Neveu, the farthest east topographical ridge of the Plains of Abraham, and the closest to the ramparts of Quebec. It was Murray's intention to construct fortifications along this ridgeline, creating an additional set of outerworks in front of the city that de Lévis would have to seize before he could initiate a formal siege of Quebec. Murray had been contemplating such an effort for months, he had stockpiled materials such as fascines and pickets, but the severe winter weather and onset of scurvy had prevented him from doing so.[54] Murray provided his soldiers with spades, shovels, and picks, and accompanied his infantry columns with large numbers of artillery pieces to outfit the new fortifications. The low ground to the west of the Buttes à Neveu was choked with snow, melting ice, slush and mud and constituted a significant obstacle to any French approach to the ridgeline. It afforded Murray with a strong position. From the ridgeline, Murray watched the French army begin to emerge from the woodline and begin to deploy.

At this moment, James Murray committed his sole error of the winter's garrison, an error of huge magnitude that almost lost for him the entire campaign and his life's reputation. Even Murray's biographer cannot defend this decision, noting: "It seems impossible to contend that Murray was justified in quitting the high ground and advancing to meet the enemy."[55] Believing that he had a great opportunity of striking the French army while they were segmented and vulnerable on the march, he abandoned his commanding ground on the Buttes à Neveu and attacked the French. In doing so, he left behind a tactically and operationally sound position, and rendered himself vulnerable.

While he remained on the Buttes à Neveu, Murray left de Lévis with few good alternatives. General de Lévis could, of course, abandon his plans for an attack on Quebec and return the French army to Montreal; he could establish a tight blockade around Quebec, rather than establishing a true siege, and wait for reinforcement from France; he could initiate his siege of Quebec from the second ridge west on the Plains of Abraham (where the battle would in fact be fought this morning) to reduce the British earthworks on the Buttes à Neveu before he could continue the siege against Quebec proper. As a last resort, de Lévis could simply launch a frontal attack on the British position on the Buttes à Neveu. The first two alternatives were unthinkable, for de Lévis had to not only win big, but win fast, at Quebec. Abandoning the effort to capture Quebec would, for all practical purposes, constitute a surrender of Canada. Likewise, initiating a siege against the Buttes à Neveu would consume considerable time and resources, two commodities that were already in painfully short supply for the French military and Canada. And so long as Murray remained on the Buttes à Neveu, a French attack would have to be pressed against a British army on easily defensible high ground, fighting behind earthworks, liberally supplied with artillery. Both flanks rested on open ground and were protected by musketry and artillery fire from the walls of the city proper. The low ground to the British front had been inundated by the heavy rains and was still choked with partially melted snow and thick mud, which created a wet ditch to obstruct any French infantry maneuvers. None of these alternatives would have been particularly palatable to de Lévis.

Subsequently, Murray came under considerable criticism by his subordinate officers and soldiers for his decision. Malcolm Fraser commented: "It seems he observed the enemy some formed at the edge of the wood, some forming, and the rest marching from St. Foy. The bait was too tempting, and his passion for glory getting the better of his reason, he ordered the Army to march and attack the enemy. . . . His conduct on this occasion is universally condemned by all."[56] Quartermaster Sergeant Johnson was absolutely scathing in his condemnation of Murray's leadership on this day: "Let it be further considered and we shall find no honour could have arisen to General Murray, for such mad, enthusiastic Zeal . . . it must be confessed that it is the duty of a General commanding an Army, to form every Scheme, and draw every plan, and to exert every faculty for the service of his Country; but it may be as readily believed that no State ever yet gave his General Orders to throw away the lives of his men without some seeming probability of success . . . it was therefore General Murray's duty to use all possible means to preserve it, and to defend it to the last extremity, and not lavishly to throw away such brave men, on a vain dulusion, of gaining to himself great honour."[57]

Murray strongly defended his decision, consistently arguing that he had a great opportunity to crush the French in detail, while they were still extended on the march and in the process of forming a cohesive line of battle. On April 30 Murray wrote to Amherst in this vein: "While the Line was forming I reconnoitred the Enemy . . . the greatest part of their Army was on the March—I thought this was the lucky moment, and marched with the utmost Order, to

Attack them before they had formed."[58] However, it is impossible to disagree with the assessments by the British soldiers who paid the price in blood for Murray's audacious gamble: that it was reckless and ill conceived, and that it abandoned a sound defensive position and advantageous tactical situation.

Without hesitation Murray's battalions followed their General's commands to close with and destroy the enemy. Captain Knox recalled that "we descried the enemy's van on the eminences of the woods of Sillery, and the bulk of their army to the right marching along the road of St. Foy. . . . Upon this discovery . . . the troops were ordered to throw down their intrenching-tools and march forward, this being deemed the decisive moment to attack them."[59]

The low ground to the British front (west) that should have served as an effective barrier to any French advance, rather became a trap for Murray's army. Knox complained "In the course of the action we were insensibly drawn from our advantageous situation into low swampy ground, where our troops fought almost knee-deep in dissolving wreaths of snow and water."[60] Quartermaster Sergeant Johnson, who accompanied the supply trains in the rear of the regiments and experienced the debacle at first hand, was bitter about the result: "The Ammunition waggons were hardly no sooner out of the Gates, but they were bogged in deep pits of Snow, and therefore intirely unable to come up to us, to our assistance."[61] The British thus found themselves, upon their advance, to be deprived of their formidable advantage of artillery at the critical moment in the engagement.

Even worse, the British movement forward had placed both of their flanks on precarious ground. To the north, the Highlanders found themselves fighting French grenadiers for the possession of the Dumont Mill in a vicious, hand-to-hand struggle. The Chevalier Johnstone, a hardened Scottish Highlander and veteran of Culloden who witnessed the contest from the French lines to the rear, was simultaneously appalled at the carnage and astounded at the feats of martial valor: "Worthy antagonists! The Grenadiers with their bayonets in their hands, forced the Highlanders to get out of it by the windows; and the Highlanders getting into it again by the door, immediately obliged the Grenadiers to evacuate it by the same road, with their daggers. Both of them lost and re-took the house several times, and the contest would have continued whilst there remained a Highlander and a Grenadier, if both generals had not made them retire."[62]

To the south, a knoll partially covered by a copse of dense trees and brush called the attention of the British to secure their left (southern) flank, for this ground was the key to this portion of the field. The detachment of volunteers commanded by Captain Donald McDonald of Fraser's Highlanders, a "brave and experienced officer" according to Murray, seized a couple of partially constructed redoubts, and then vanished into the woods, never to be seen again. McDonald's Company of Volunteers was destroyed to the last man. Sergeant James Thompson recalled that McDonald's "Volunteers rush'd forward to the attack of a small Redoubt, which he entered, and from which he drove away the French, many of whom were cut to pieces, but there came upon him a stronger body of French that overpower'd and completely butcher'd his whole party, and he himself was found cut and hack'd to pieces in the most shocking manner! There was an end of him!"[63] When Hazen's Ranger Company followed in their rear, they were driven in disarray and panic from the forest in short order and played no further role in the engagement. With this flank endangered, Murray transferred Kennedy's 43rd Foot, a fine regiment but one that was extremely understrength, from his rear to reinforce it. This was a well-considered tactical move that bought his left flank time, but failed to permanently stabilize it.

Although the British center was but slightly engaged, both flanks were involved in intensive fighting. A heavy band of woods to the north allowed the Canadians and Natives to pour a deadly accurate sniping fire upon the British right (northern) flank that claimed a horrific toll of the English officers. Miller, with Amherst's 15th Foot, remembered: "we unfortunately advanced, which gave them an opportunity of cutting us up, they being drawn up under cover, and taking aim at leisure, while we could only see them through the intervals of the trees. In short, in half an hour Ten Officers from Twenty were dropped, twelve Serjeants from twenty four, and near two hundred Rank and file from less than four hundred in the field!"[64] The superior French numbers permitted them to outflank both ends of the British line, and the terrain afforded the French a considerable advantage. Captain Mackellar observed with his engineer's eye: "The action which lasted full three hours was chiefly upon the Flanks, there the Enemy made all their Efforts without making scarce any attempt towards the centre."[65]

At a critical moment in the fighting, Captain Jean-Guillaume Plantavit de Lapause de Margon, adjutant of the Guyenne Regiment, misunderstood or misinterpreted orders from de Lévis and ordered a general withdrawal, rather than the intended tactical adjustment of the French flank to better ground slightly to their rear. The French lines were thrown into confusion and the British in turn pressed forward in anticipation of the decisive moment of the battle. As related by the Chevalier Johnstone, "M. Dalquier [Lieutenant Colonel Jean d'Alqier de Sarrian, Commander of the French Left Brigade and 2nd Battalion, Béarn Regiment] a bold, intrepid old officer, turned about to his soldiers when La Pause gave him M. de Lévis' order to retire, and told them, 'It is not time now, my boys, to retire when at twenty paces from the enemy, with your bayonets upon your muskets, let us throw ourselves headlong amongst them, that is better.' In an instant they fell upon the English impetuously, with thrusts of bayonets hand to hand, got possession, like lightning of their guns; and a ball which went through Dalquier's body, which was already quite covered with scars of old wounds, did not hinder him from continuing giving his orders."[66] The fighting was at close range and absolutely brutal. When Sergeant Thompson's company commander was grievously wounded, he had to step forward to assume leadership of the grenadiers. Thompson found that so many casualties covered the ground that he had to place his foot on his wounded captain in order to maintain an effective place within the ranks.[67]

With both of Murray's flanks enfiladed and withering under intense fire, the British found themselves compelled to retire from the field. During the retreat, James Miller recalled: "The Commanding officer, of the Corps, did all that man could do to keep it in a body, in order to cover the retreat, ordering them to turn round frequently, and fire by platoons, or volleys, in the hurry, he had like to have lost his wig, he however put it under his arm, with great san froid, and said 'damn the old wig' a name by which he is known to this day by the old soldiers."[68] Although retreats are rarely orderly by their very nature, the withdrawal of the British army seems to have been performed in the best possible order given the circumstances. The redoubt constructed on the Buttes à Neveu served to provide some element of protective fire to the retreat, before it too had to be abandoned. The low ground now to their rear caused particular difficulties to Murray's columns. Lieutenant Fraser remembered, "Most of the Regiments attempted to carry off their artillery, but the ground was so bad with wreaths of snow in their hollows, that they were obliged to abandon them, after nailing them up [spiking them], as well as [abandoning] the intrenching tools."[69] Captain Knox similarly remembered, "It was utterly impracticable to draw off our artillery under those unhappy circumstances."[70]

The evening of April 28 found the British army, badly battered, temporarily disorganized, but still full of fight and confidence, safely ensconced behind the fortified walls and bastions of Quebec. Its commander was not in the least defeated or demoralized. The fortifications could have certainly been stronger, but they were more than sufficient to defeat any infantry assault or *coup de main* that the French could contemplate. The French were in no condition to launch any sort of attack.

General de Lévis recorded in his journal: "Our loss has been considerable, especially in officers. The battalions of La Sarre and Béarn, who were on the left [north], as well as those of Berri and of the Marine, have suffered considerably. The grenadiers have been reduced to a very small number."[71] He would record, by rank, name and organization, no less than 105 officer casualties, including 23 dead. Among the key leadership losses were de Lévis's deputy commander, Brigadier General François-Charles de Bourlamaque, who suffered a serious wound with "part of the calf of the leg cut by a cannon ball." Lieutenant Colonel Marie-Joseph Toussaint de Carnay, the commander of the Guyenne Battalion was mortally wounded. He would die outside of Quebec on May 9. Lieutenant Colonel Trivio, of the 2nd Battalion of De Berri, was slightly wounded. Lieutenant Colonel Jean d'Alquier de Servian, of the Béarn Battalion, was critically wounded with a "gunshot wound in the side." Two of the marine company commanders were also slightly wounded; the native Canadian Chaptes de La Corne Saint-Luc, Commandant of the Indians, was slightly wounded, while the commander of the Montreal Battalion of the Canadian Militia was killed.[72] Lévis would report 630 of his irreplaceable 3,610 French regulars killed or wounded; along with 203 of the Canadian Militia, for total losses of 938 officers and enlisted men, or no less than over fourteen percent of his total force.[73] Among the most valuable of his soldiers, the eight battalions of French regulars, the casualty rates exceeded twenty percent. The wounded Bourlamaque would write his friend Bougainville, in command at Isle aux Noix, "We have lost the elite of the officers of La Sarre, Berry, Béarn and La Marine, all wiped out, so too our Grenadiers, 1000 men are killed or wounded I believe."[74] Making the situation even worse was that the French army contained a mere sixteen surgeons, who must have been absolutely overwhelmed with the casualties, thus throwing the care of their grievously wounded comrades on the army itself.[75] The devastating losses temporarily crippled the French army until it could be reorganized. Captain Knox would record: "The enemy did not pursue with that spirit which the vast importance of their victory required; the truth was, they were very roughly handled; and from their losses, which fell mostly upon the flower of their army, they were heartily sick of it."[76]

The British army had also absorbed heavy losses, with 130 officers killed or wounded, as well as 979 rank and file. Fully a third of the men that Murray had carried through Saint Louis and Saint John's Gates that morning became casualties. The highest ranking casualty had been Lieutenant Colonel John Young, the commander of the 3rd Battalion, Royal Americans, who had been killed. Perhaps the most significant loss was that of Murray's chief engineer, the highly experienced and talented Major Patrick Mackellar, who was so seriously wounded that he could contribute no further to the defense of Quebec. From a matériel standpoint, the British lost the twenty-two field pieces that they had brought onto the field. Most were spiked and abandoned as they lay trapped in the mud and deep snow in the low ground west of the Buttes à Neveu.

General de Lévis failed to perform any effective pursuit of the British army. In large part, this failure was the result of not only the severe casualties that his army had absorbed but also the same terrain conditions that had plagued Murray, specifically the difficulty of travel over the low ground west of the Buttes à Neveu, which any French pursuit would have to traverse. By the end of the day, the British were locked behind Quebec's sturdy gates and curtain walls, and de Lévis had no viable plan to drive them out or force their capitulation. He could only hope that a large French relief fleet would arrive from Europe.

Much has been made of the battle of Sainte-Foy. This is entirely reasonable and to be expected, as it appeared (in 1760 and in retrospect today) to have been a romantic revenge for the debacle between Wolfe and Montcalm in September 1759, which forever lost for France the city of Quebec. In reality, the battle had no influence whatsoever on the Campaign of 1760 or the fate of Canada. Dawn had broken on April 28 behind a dense cloud bank, with the French army outside of Quebec, and the British army inside of Quebec.

The sun set on April 28 with the French army still outside of Quebec, and the British army still inside of Quebec. The French army was now in possession of the Buttes à Neveu, with a few damaged British artillery pieces and several score British entrenching tools as their only real gains of the day. Both were valuable acquisitions, but whether or not de Lévis could make effective use of them remained to be seen.

The British army was disorganized but unbroken, fully capable of further resistance as it would shortly demonstrate. It remained behind the city walls, which were perhaps vulnerable to artillery, but were insurmountable until heavy guns could be brought to bear on them. The French army was incapable of exploiting their tactical victory at Sainte-Foy. The victory had no effect at all on the situation of the British garrison in Quebec, on the French army outside of the walls, or on the overall military situation along the Saint Lawrence River. The French would still have to lay siege to the city, they were still dreadfully short of artillery and munitions with which to do so, and they were still reliant on the arrival of a healthy supply fleet from France. Nothing had changed, except for the loss of many a brave man from both nations.

But little of this was apparent late on the day of April 28. From the British perspective, the day's affairs had been an utter fiasco. Few of the redcoats would have disagreed with the words of James Miller: "The Corps was broken, and retreated to their former ground, happy would it have been, had they never left it."[77]

CHAPTER 3

"THE WHOLE GARRISON WERE ALERT, THE GENERAL WAS INDEFATIGABLE"

The Siege of Quebec

The fortifications of Quebec that Murray defended had initially been constructed by the French between 1672 and 1682, but they were not effectively designed, or even finished. In 1757, de Bougainville noted: "The fortifications are so ridiculous and so bad that they can be taken as soon as they are besieged."[1] They had scarcely been strengthened since.

In 1760, it was the land defenses facing the Plains of Abraham to the west that would predominantly concern Murray and de Lévis.[2] These fortifications consisted of a lineal curtain wall, with four bastions pierced by two gates. The left (south) flank was anchored on a promontory overlooking Cap Diamant (in English, Cape Diamond). This flank was built as a large redoubt, constructed of fascines to safeguard the powder magazine. In later years, the considerably stronger Quebec Citadel would be constructed here.[3] Northward from the Saint Lawrence River were the Glacière Bastion; the Saint Louis Bastion; the Saint Louis Gate, opening to the Sillery Road; the Saint Ursula Bastion; the Saint John's Gate, opening to the Sainte-Foy Road; and the Saint John Bastion. From this last bastion, the works turned to the east, paralleling the Saint Charles River, and essentially refused the right flank of the city. These works were protected by a poor ditch to the west, according to de Lévis "the depth of which in some places is only 5 or 6 feet."[4] Sergeant James Thompson of the Highlanders, an alert and attentive soldier with experience in carpentry and construction, adroitly noted: "The Fortifications, which consisted only of the fronts-towards the Land, were little more than half-finished, and could have held out but a very few days after the opening of our batteries; for, there being neither ditch, cover'd-way, nor out-works, the Scarp-wall was exposed to view in many places from the top of the parapet to the foundation. The inside was equally imperfect, and its defense in many places impracticable, even for small arms."[5] Compounding its deficiencies of construction, the curtain wall contained numerous cannon that had been relatively poorly maintained. They were sited from the flanks of the bastions, where they could provide effective enfilading fire on any infantry assault, but would be incapable of controlling the ground to the west. The cannon could not resist a formal European siege from the landward side. This was a critical flaw, and rendered the city extremely vulnerable. Furthermore, Quebec lacked a well-defined glacis, a standard feature of a fortress that consisted of a level and open field in front of a fortification's walls, which extended to the maximum range of its cannon. This precluded the besiegers from approaching the fortress without being both exposed and vulnerable.

Murray had recognized that these works were defective. However, throughout the brief time available to him from late September to the onset of winter in November, his efforts had to be focused on preparing the badly battered city for the winter garrison. Although Murray planned substantial improvements to the city, these could not be implemented until the ground had thawed in early May.[6] Throughout the winter, Murray had working parties under the direction of Sergeant Thompson continuously manufacturing fascines and pickets so that construction could be initiated immediately as the weather permitted. Thompson and his Highlanders produced no fewer than 45,500 fascines over the winter months.[7] In the event, when Murray attempted to construct earthworks on the Plain of Abraham as late as April 25, he discovered that "it was hardly possible to drive the first Piquets [pickets], the Thaw having reached no farther than Nine Inches from the Surface."[8]

Murray completed seven blockhouses to sweep the ground to the front of the works, and one redoubt located northwest of the Saint Louis Gate intended to cover sorties from Quebec proper. He had constructed another redoubt on the Buttes à Neveu that had been abandoned following the fight on April 28. These seven blockhouses were formed of heavy logs and timber, and thus could be constructed above ground level. They were installed from fifty to

250 yards outside the city.[9] The redoubt was constructed predominantly of fascines, and thus could also be built above the frozen ground.[10] Murray noted in a letter to Amherst on May 19, 1760: "[Engineer Lieutenant John] Montresor tells me you seemed surprised at the precautions I had taken in building block-houses in the winter."[11] Murray had earlier noted that "the place is not Fortified, and Commanded every where towards the Land."[12] Thus, Murray had constructed these seven blockhouses and single fascine redoubt to provide the main land defenses of Quebec with at least rudimentary outworks that enabled him to control the ground in front of his bastions.

The fortification of a house or similar strong structure, or the construction of such defensive works, was a well-established principle of field or urban fortification.[13] Fortifications became progressively stronger during this period, as increasingly more extensive and formidable outworks were designed and constructed so that they could withstand the main brunt of an assault. While in earlier years these advanced works had been solely occupied by infantry, by the middle of the eighteenth century they were being equipped with formidable batteries of ordnance. In doing so, the defenders gradually converted a lineal defense into a defense in depth. Military engineers designed increasingly more complex outworks that became sprawling defensive belts that were often considerably larger and more extensive than the original fortress that they were intended to cover. These powerful extended works became a dominant feature of the eighteenth century landscape.[14]

Time and weather constraints precluded Murray from implementing such expansive outworks as were common in Europe and as he intended. By the spring of 1760, the blockhouses and redoubts were little more than rudimentary outposts. Still, any French siege would have to reduce these defenses before the French could extend formal siege lines and install breaching batteries against Quebec's curtain walls proper, or launch an infantry assault on any breach in the old French fortification. These blockhouses and redoubts were clearly of limited value, but they afforded Quebec a legitimate and supplemental defense. General de Lévis would have to overcome them before he could entertain any hope of seizing the city of Quebec itself.

On the evening of April 28, Murray could do little except "to give his soldiers time to rest and endeavour to keep the enemy out of the town."[15] Late in the evening, Murray published General Orders that set the tone and tempo for the remainder of the defense of Quebec:

> The 28th of April has been unfortunate to the British arms, but affairs are not so desperate as to be irretrievable; the General often experienced the bravery of the troops he now commands, and is very sensible they will endeavour to regain what they have lost; the fleet may be hourly expected, reinforcements are at hand; and shall we lose, in one moment, the fruits of so much blood and treasure? Both Officers and men are exhorted patiently to undergo the fatigues they must suffer, and to expose themselves cheerfully to some dangers; a duty they owe to their King, their Country, and Themselves.[16]

Murray wasted little time putting his rousing orders into effect: "I ordered Capt. Holland to visit the works, and all the officers and men to parade for work at five next morning."[17] Since Major Mackellar had been seriously wounded, Captain Samuel Johannnes Holland, a Dutchman who had joined the Royal American Regiment of the British Army and had already been acting as an assistant engineer at Quebec, was designated his temporary replacement.

There was clearly some disorder within the British army, entirely to be expected within an army that had sustained a defeat and been driven in retreat. The day following the defeat Murray "observed a good deal of drunkenness among the men, ordered all the spirits in the lower town not belonging to the King to be spilled. As many of them were breaking into the houses . . . ordered one to be hung for an example to the rest."[18] Captain Knox confirmed: "Immense irregularities are hourly committed by the soldiery, in break-open store and dwelling houses to get at liquor: this is seemingly the result of panic and despair, heightened by drunkenness; one man was hanged this evening *in terrorem*, without any trial, which it is hoped will effectually prevent farther disorders, and influence the soldiers to a lively sense of their duty."[19] These efforts were succesful, for by May 1 the army had returned to good order and discipline. Captain Knox documented: "If the enemy have, or do still entertain, thoughts of storming the place, it seems too late, and they have let slip a golden opportunity; had they followed their blow on the 28th, 29th or 30th, before the soldiers recollected themselves . . . Quebec would have reverted to its old masters." By this date, Knox stated proudly, "We no longer harbour a thought of visiting France or England, or of falling a sacrifice to a merciless scalping knife. We are roused from our lethargy; we have recovered our good humour, our sentiments for glory, and we seem, one and all, determined to defend our dearly purchased garrison to the last extremity."[20]

Private James Miller recalled: "No sooner had we got within the walls, than every one began labouring on the fortifications."[21] Beginning early on the morning of April 29, Murray's soldiers started cutting embrasures through the curtain walls.[22] As previously noted, most of the guns already emplaced in Quebec's works were oriented for enfilading fire, perfectly sited to repulse an infantry assault but of limited utility in resisting any formal French siege. Apparently the French intent had been to erect batteries *en barbette*, to fire over the ramparts, but Murray did not approve of employing his valuable cannon and gunners in such an exposed manner. Accordingly, chisels, hammers, and crowbars had to be used to remove the masonry in order to cut the embrasures. Engineers had to carefully supervise the work to ensure that the parapet was not unnecessarily weakened. In the meantime, cannon, ammunition, and gunpowder had to be moved up to the ramparts under the supervision of the Royal Artillery.

The French artillery struck the first blow on this date. Murray reported: "At eleven this morning the enemy brought up a twelve-pounder, and fired several shot through the great block-house. The powder magazine [of the blockhouse] catched [fire], blew up the roof, and burned it to the ground. A captain and about twenty-five men were disabled. This was unlucky, as it was our most advanced work, roomy, strong, and hors d'insulte, having three pieces of cannon in it.[23] Murray could not have been pleased to have lost one of his outerworks, quite literally at the very first shot. However, de Lévis must also have been alarmed, for his 12-pounder cannon had been dismounted "by some accident in firing" suggesting that either the skills of his artillerymen or the construction of his artillery carriages were deficient.

That night, Murray launched a small sortie of one officer and twenty men, a standard tactic when besieged. The fact that he launched such a raid on the initial evening of the siege indicates that, notwithstanding his defeat two days earlier, Murray remained aggressive and determined to carry the fight to the French. He may also have suspected that de Lévis had supply problems, and he would have been well aware that the French army was encamped in tentage in the raw, wet Canada spring weather, which would render the French vulnerable to sickness and declining morale. He certainly desired to expedite this deterioration within de Lévis' ranks. Murray reported one prisoner being taken in his first sortie. On April 30, Murray ordered his men to encamp "in their respective alarm posts." He positioned his entire infantry command along the works, so that they could immediately man the entirety of the walls against a French incursion, considerably improving the security of the city.[24] The same day, Murray began mounting cannon to fire against the French siege lines, placing six 24-pounders on the wall. Seven more cannon were mounted on May 1, apparently as rapidly as embrasures could be cut, for Murray experienced "great difficulty" in this process. Beginning the next day Murray ordered "a small party . . . to lie out every night along the high bank of Cape Diamond, to watch the enemy's motions and prevent any surprise on that side."[25] Captain Knox recorded one particularly successful raid on May 6: "Our rangers sallied out last night, went up to the enemy's trenches unperceived, poured in a smart volley, and returned immediately, without having a single shot fired at them; they are advanced every evening about half-way between the town and our chain of blockhouses, where they remain on their arms until day-break."[26] Thus, Murray continuously maintained security to the front of his defenses.

The renowned British military engineer and artillery expert John Muller wrote, "The intent of Sallies is to fall upon and destroy a part of the Approaches not quite finished, or not well supported, to nail up the Guns upon the Batteries, or to surprize a part of the guard in the Trenches." Muller amplified: "Sallies, when made with due precuation and judgement, are one of the principal means to lengthen a Siege" and "Sallies are also proper to be made when the Fortification is bad . . . it is best, in [this] case, to keep the enemy at a distance as long as possible" and this was certainly the case at Quebec.[27] Muller strongly advised that when defending a position, "Another precaution the Governor should take, is to send every night, from the time the Place is invested, several small parties, of ten or twelve men, commanded by a serjeant, with orders to lay on their faces, all round the skirt of the glacis, to keep strict silence, and listen with great attention to whatever passes"[28] Murray, who depended upon the arrival of a fleet from England for his relief, had every interest in extending the duration of de Lévis's siege through every means possible. His vigorous actions outside of the city's walls were fully in accord with established siege protocols and military engineering treatises of the time.

Holding a picquet in front of the city's fortifications or launching a probe against the French works were extremely dangerous propositions. Although such tactics proved highly beneficial to the defense of Quebec, these activities were not without risk and loss. Captain Knox documented the demise of one such party: "Ensign Maw, of the forty-third regiment, with two non-commissioned and twenty volunteers, sallied out last night, hoping to get a prisoner for intelligence, but unfortunately, his sight not being equal in goodness to his spirit and ability, he fell into the enemy's hands, and six of his men were killed and wounded."[29]

In the meantime, de Lévis struggled to initiate his formal siege. The French marshal de Vauban was still considered to be the foremost expert on siege operations, which he had established and formalized during the previous century. Vauban had developed a standardized sequence all sieges were expected to follow, which artillerymen and engineers of the time observed scrupulously. The first step, familiarizing the army and its leaders and engineering officers with the terrain, was scarcely necessary in this case. Simultaneously, the necessary supplies, ordnance for a siege train, and munitions were to be prepared. General de Lévis chose to disembark his military train at the Anse au Foulon, the same cove where Wolfe had landed his army and ascended to the Plains of Abraham and victory in September 1759 (now known as Wolfe's Cove). The second step was to secure the besieging army against attack, either from outside of the besieged city, or from a sortie launched from the besieged army. This was intended to be done by constructing two rings of fortification: "lines of countervallation" were entrenchments "made to secure the army against any attempt from the garrison"; and "lines of circumvallation" that were defenses "made to secure the army against any attempt that the enemy may make from the field."[30] In the case of Quebec, there was no British field army that could possibly relieve the garrison. Thus, lines of circumvallation were entirely superfluous and were never constructed.

The only direction from which a relief force could come was up the Saint Lawrence River. Accordingly, de Lévis had intended to dispatch two small frigates to pass down the river to attack any British vessels as they arrived, thus serving as the nautical equivalent of a line of circumvallation. These were the *Atalante*, commanded by the highly capable and well seasoned French naval captain Jean Vauquelain; and the *Pomone*, commanded by one Monsieur Sauvage. However, these vessels proved incapable of passing by the guns of Quebec, so they instead remained near the Anse au Foulon to cover the landings of the French supplies.[31]

General de Lévis chose to establish no lines of countervallation, although the British propensity for sorties was revealed quite early in the siege. He later noted that: "the ground is solid rock, which becomes almost bare" on the Plains of Abraham, implying that available men and materials had to be focused on constructing the approaches, parallels and batteries of the siege, rather than being expended on a line of countervallation.[32] However, redoubts could certainly have been constructed of timber and dry-laid stone (as they would be by the American Continental Army at West Point eighteen years later) or fascines (precisely as Murray had done at Quebec that same winter), and their absence strongly suggests a lack of engineering acumen and ingenuity on the part of the French army.

Once these actions were completed—or in the case of de Lévis *not* completed—the siege proper could be initiated. First, a series of trenches called approaches had to be excavated. These ditches zigzagged toward the enemy citadel, following a convoluted but carefully selected path to avoid being outflanked. Thus, a single cannon ball could not bounce its way down a trench, destroying everything and dismembering everyone in its path. These approaches offered a means for both men and material to be moved forward in safety to press the siege. The French engineers working under de Lévis constructed a single approach beginning in the dead ground west of the Buttes à Neveu, under the cover of a large patch of woods that extended between the Sainte-Foy and Sillery Roads.

The approaches, or in front of Quebec the single approach, led to a series of fortified lines that ran parallel to the defender's fortifications. As their alignment suggests, these lines were designated as "parallels." These parallels were essentially the protected lines from which a siege could be carried forward. Muller noted that "they serve as places of Arms for the guards of the Trenches, who by that means are under cover, and at hand to support the workmen upon all occasions." Most commonly, there were three parallels constructed. A first parallel, at the greatest distance from the defending fortification, supported the preliminary cannon and mortar batteries used at the opening of the bombardment. A second and more advanced parallel moved the artillery batteries into a position from which the defenders' fire could be silenced and a breach in the enemy defensive works opened. A third parallel would be far forward, at the edge of the covered way or initial defenses of a fortress, from which the actual infantry assault could be launched through the breaches in the defensive walls into the opposing town. In a few extraordinary cases, an even farther forward fourth parallel might be required. Muller recommended: "The first Parallel is always made within 300 fathoms [a fathom is approximately six feet, or two yards] of the covert-way [covered way], whether the Trenches are opened nearer or farther from the place; if it can be made nearer, it would be so much the better. The second 140 fathoms from the first; or if the garrison is weak, it is often made close to the glacis. The third Parallel is always made near, or upon the glacis . . . this Parallel is on that account made wider and deeper, as also with more care than the rest of the works, especially as the troops designed for the Attacks of the covert-way, and other out-works, are to be placed there; for which reason, its parapet is made with steps, so that the troops may march out in order of battle without confusion."[33] For a variety of reasons, as will subsequently be discussed, the French in front of Quebec constructed only the first parallel, and failed to construct even a second set of approach trenches forward of this first parallel.

General de Lévis, in consultation with Nicolas Sarrebource de Pontleroy, the French engineer in chief of Canada, and Captain Fiacre-François Potot de Montbeillard of the French Royal Artillery, commanding that branch in Canada, determined to align their firing batteries against the bastions of Saint Louis, Glacière, and Cape Diamond, as "the revêtment was badly constructed at that point."[34] However, this entry in his journal is misleading, as de Montbeillard lacked adequate artillery to mass effective fire against three bastions simultaneously. Accordingly, he actually concentrated his efforts against the Glacière Bastion alone.

The parallels were intended, as Muller specified (and as Vauban decades before had mandated), to support batteries of artillery that would wreak the devastation necessary to subdue the defensive fire of the enemy fortification, to smash the outer works into rubble, and to begin a breach through the walls so that an infantry assault could be ultimately launched. To accomplish this, two types of firing batteries were constructed. The first consisted of cannon, firing solid iron balls at a low, nearly flat, trajectory directly against the enemy works to shatter them. A variation of this was known as "richocet fire," which employed slightly reduced gunpowder charges so that the cannon balls would bounce across the ground. Given the rocky nature of the ground in front of Québec, ricochet fire proved effective here. The second type of batteries consisted of mortars or howitzers, firing explosive shells at high angle over the enemy defenses to explode with havoc in the rear areas among the defensive infantry, artillery crews, and logistical infrastructure of the citadel. The cannon fired through embrasures or openings cut through a protective earth, wood, and sod parapet; while the mortars could fire over their own defenses and were protected by a heavy epaulment or earthen bank dense enough to repulse artillery balls fired in response by the defensive guns.

The French engineers made very slow progress in their advancement of the siege lines. In fact, it would take de Pontleroy and de Montbeillard nearly two weeks, to May 11, until the first parallel was completed and its batteries could open fire. This was an extraordinarily long period of time to open a single approach and parallel. Muller (and Vauban) specified that: "The work is thus continued day and night with all possible speed, advancing as far by night as possible, and finishing by day what was begun by night; and if the same number of workmen is not sufficient, more are ordered for that purpose, that nothing may be wanting to carry the works with all expedition as far as the second Parallel."[35] The French in front of Quebec failed to maintain anything approaching this schedule. General de Lévis complained: "The parallels and batteries could not be finished except after incredible difficulties: the work was all rock. The earth had to be brought a very great distance in sacks." Captain Knox, observing the accurate fire from the walls of the citadel city sweeping the ground to the front of the walls, noted: "The troops are indefatigable in forwarding their work; and our batteries fire vigorously on the enemy, who remain very quiet in their camp and trenches; this inclines us to think that no measures will be taken on their part, until the arrival of a fleet."[36]

General de Lévis was a victim of the dire logistical situation in Canada in the spring of 1760. New France had always suffered from inadequate resources. As previously discussed, the colony consistently lacked enough precious metal coinage to carry on commerce, and had to resort to various paper currencies with decidedly mixed results, and this financial system had effectively collapsed by the spring of 1760. Because of a combination of heavy calls on the Canadian militia and poor weather, the harvests of 1756, 1757 and 1758 had all been poor. In any event, with the arrival of the large army of French regulars in Canada in 1755, the colony could no longer feed itself.[37] Canada had almost no capacity for the production of military supplies, with the exception of a single iron foundry at Three Rivers that was capable of casting limited quantities of artillery shot and shell. With the fall of Fortress Louisbourg in 1758 and the presence of a blockading British Royal Navy fleet in the Saint Lawrence supporting operations against Quebec throughout 1759, the French ability to resupply from the home country had been seriously curtailed. By the spring of 1760 Canada's supply condition had reached a critical stage, bordering on catastrophic collapse.[38] General de Lévis recalled: "'Twas never expected, when leaving Montreal, that we could take Quebec with the mere resources the country was able to furnish."[39] Rather, de Lévis relied exclusively on the hope for fortuitous arrival of a relief fleet from the home country.

Still, both the Marquis de Vaudrieul and de Lévis had done much to exacerbate this situation. The French had limited resources, but enjoyed the substantial advantage afforded by interior lines of communication. It appears that a maximum effort against one of the English columns should have been attempted, with a bare minimum economy-of-force mission against the other two English columns. Ostensibly, the operation against Quebec that de Lévis launched in April 1760 was intended to be just such a maximum effort. However, the Marquis de Vaudrieul and de Lévis had syphoned off major assets of manpower, artillery, munitions and provisions for the construction of substantial fortifications at Îsle aux Noix and Fort Lévis. As a result, de Lévis's thrust against Quebec, although the primary effort of Canada in 1760, suffered from inadequate resources. In fact, resources were so lacking that his siege operations were severely constrained to the point of ineffectiveness.

One significant disadvantage that hindered de Lévis was inadequate forces. Vauban had suggested the ratio of besiegers to defenders should be five to one. Following the Battle of Sainte-Foy, approximately 5,700 soldiers (including Natives, who were of limited utility for sieges) were available to de Lévis. Murray's garrison contained approximately 2,500 soldiers. Thus the French siege was conducted with only a two to one advantage, scarcely sufficient for effective offensive operations.

Further complicating the French progress was that Murray swiftly opened numerous embrasures to place a heavy volume of artillery fire on the French works. General de Lévis recorded with consternation: "The enemy soon had 60 cannon unmasked on the attacked fronts. This artillery, served with the greatest activity, not only retarded the construction of the batteries, but also prevented the workmen transporting material; the balls plunging behind the heights, left no spot protected. The troops were even obliged several times to encamp." Murray reported as early as May 3 that the garrison had expended no less than 1,623 shots and shells, from guns as large as 24-pounder cannon and thirteen-inch mortars, and he reported that: "Our fire retards the enemy, who seems to advance slowly."[40] Clearly, the British fire was absolutely devastating. Murray's garrison consistently maintained this level of firepower, and Murray carefully monitored how much ammunition he was expending on a daily basis, to ensure "that we should not by too early a profusion disable ourselves from giving them a warmer fire when they should approach closer."[41] Murray recorded firing 690 shot and shells on May 4, but only 201 the next day. Murray continued his sorties, and "the Rangers were ordered out to fire upon the enemy's workmen two or three times, in order to retard them." On May 6, Murray's Royal Artillery gunners smothered a French battery under construction, demolishing it before it could be completed. That day Murray's batteries discharged a thundering barrage of no less than 834 shots and shells.[42] Captain Knox recalled on May 8: "Some [French] deserters who came in to us this morning say that it is incredible the execution made among them by our shot and shells; that their Officers are lavish in their encomiums [tributes] on our Gunners, and the admirable service of our artillery."[43]

Observing that high ground to the south overlooked the Cape Diamond Bastion, and that the French first parallel was being extended in that direction, on May 6 Murray ordered two cavaliers to be constructed within that bastion "to mount heavy cannon upon them." According to an earlier work by Muller, that expanded on previous military engineering treatises prepared by Vauban and the distinguished military engineer Baron Menno van Coehorn, "a Cavalier is a work raised generally within the body of the place, ten or twelve feet higher than the rest of the works.

Their most common situation is within the bastion, and made much in the same form . . . The use of cavaliers is to command all the adjacent works and country about it; they are seldom or never made but when there is a hill or rising ground which overlooks some of the works."[44] Thus, the construction of cavaliers by Murray was perfectly in accordance with established siege principles, and demonstrated his mastery and knowledge of the art and science of siegeworks.

On May 7, Murray had four monstrous 32-pounder cannon dragged up from the lower town of Quebec, guns that dwarfed anything that the French could employ. Both days saw continuous heavy firing by the British, on May 8 no less than another 1,159 shots and shell. This extraordinary volume of fire paid dividends, for on the morning of May 9 Murray "observed that the last night's fire had prevented the enemy's working, and had almost ruined their batteries." Murray maintained his heavy rate of fire this day, pounding away with another 1,193 rounds of artillery.

Although the overwhelming rate of fire was having a significant detrimental effect on the French ability to move their siegeworks forward, it was not without hazard. The majority of the British guns were of cast iron, which were prone to shatter under heavy use. In fact, three years earlier, at the siege of Fort William Henry, the British defense had collapsed when every one of their heavy iron cannon had failed under just such conditions.[45] Murray was similarly plagued by such damage. He lost his first gun when one 24-pounder cannon split as early as May 4. One week later, May 10 was a particularly expensive day as another 24-pounder failed, as did three garrison carriages supporting the heavy cannon barrels. Later on this same date another 24-pounder burst as it was being fired, killing two gunners and wounding two others. Still, the indomitable Captain Knox recalled "we have not a mortar or gun mounted that was not employed, and without the smallest intermission."[46]

Murray continued his adroit preparations to resist any possible French assault, which he recognized was increasingly likely as the French might be made desperate by the arrival of a Royal Navy vessel. Accordingly Murray "had the coehorns [small four-and-two-fifths-inch mortars] laid in readiness in case the enemy should attempt to advance under favour of the batteries they had opened."[47] Murray also had one half of his garrison standing to arms, at their alarm posts on the walls and within the bastions, at any given time throughout the night, in the event that the French determined to launch a surprise infantry assault under cover of darkness.[48]

On May 9, a momentous event occurred: the first ship of the spring arrived at Quebec. General de Lévis desperately hoped that the ship would be the vanguard of a French supply fleet transporting ammunition and heavy artillery from France, which would enable him to press his siege more aggressively. The British defenders were resolute, but exhausted and in ill health, and they desperately sought relief. At about 9:00 in the morning the Royal Navy 28-gun frigate HMS *Lowestaff* sailed up the center of the channel of the Saint Lawrence River and anchored off Quebec. The British had won the naval race to Quebec.

Murray's garrison was ecstatic. Quartermaster Sergeant Johnson recalled: "But who can express the joy which we felt on this occasion; none but we who needed the benefit arising from it."[49] James Miller similarly recalled "our great joy" on this occasion, as the British garrison ringed the ramparts and cheered in enthusiasm.[50] HMS *Lowestaff* subsequently landed a number of her trained gunners to reinforce the garrison's tired artillerymen. Its cargo included a quantity of cannon shot and shell, and gunpowder to augment the stocks of Québec's garrison. The presence of these comparatively fresh seamen and additional ordnance stores was a welcome addition for Murray.

The French finally opened their batteries in the first parallel on May 11, but in short order they proved to be woefully insufficient. The French directing engineer and artilleryman de Pontleroy and de Montbeillard initially installed two richochet batteries, consisting of six cannon at the left (north) of the parallel; and four cannon generally in the center of the parallel. They also installed a small battery of two nine-inch mortars to the north of the six-gun battery.[51] These guns were undersized for the job at hand, as noted by de Lévis: "Twas composed of 6 iron 18 and 12 pounders, only one 24, and although the best in the Colony had been selected, the most of the guns were, on the second day, unfit for service, and the remainder soon threatened to be in the same state." On May 12, de Lévis uncovered another battery of an additional three cannon, two 24-pounder cannon and one 12-pounder cannon, to the right (south) of the parallel.[52]

It should be noted, in defense of the French engineers and artillerymen, that these batteries were perfectly positioned to allow enfilading fire on the Glacière Bastion. Muller specified that the richochet batteries should be "perpendicular to that work" and the French batteries were so positioned.[53] And de Lévis's instincts were proven correct—the construction of the Glacière Bastion was faulty, and this bastion was vulnerable to being breached. On May 12 Murray wrote in his journal: "The chief acting engineer reported to me, at four this afteroon, that having observed the enemy direct their fire very briskly to the [Glacière Bastion] he had been out to observe the effect, and was surprised to find it so great, owing, as he suppposed to the rotteness and badness of the wall. I went myself to examine it, and found it in the condition reported. This was a matter of astonishment, the enemy having fired but a short time, and at such a distance as rendered the effect very surprising."[54]

Although their approach had merit, the French failed to mass their fire against the vulnerable point in the British walls. Lieutenant Forbes noted: "On the 11th May the French opened two Batteries mounting thirteen guns, and one of two mortars. Their heavy metal consisted of one twenty-four and two eighteen-pounders, the rest were all light. They did not seem to confine their fire entirely to any particular part of the walls, otherwise I believe they might in time have made a breach, and their fire was not very smart. We were masters of a much superior fire, and annoyed the besiegers at their Batteries very much. Their fire became every day more faint, and it was generally believed they intended to raise the siege."[55]

In response to the opening of the French batteries, on May 11 the English gunners discharged a staggering 2,023 shots, including twelve from the massive 32-pounders. A similar rate of fire was maintained on May 12, as Murray documented the expenditure of another 1,542 rounds, although this was not without a price as he lost one more 18-pounder cannon and another 12-pounder cannon to fractures. Still, Murray doubtless considered such a cost to be acceptable, for the overwhelming rates of fire on both days simply proved devastating to the French. Murray observed that "we silenced four of the enemy's cannon and hurt their batteries much."[56]

In addition to being outgunned by the British, de Lévis was woefully short of gunpowder, and had no choice but to limit "the fire of the batteries to 20 shots in each 24 hours." Absent supplies from France, most of his shot and shells had been produced that winter at the iron foundry at Three Rivers. Murray, always aggressive at gaining intelligence regarding the French army, instructed soldiers to retrieve the French cannon balls so that he could ascertain the precise size of guns that he was facing. He adroitly noted that "both shot and shells appear new."[57]

At the same time, the British resistance was stout and unwavering, and the British soldiers had full confidence in Murray's leadership. Lieutenant Fraser recorded in his journal: "Our works were carried on briskly. The General seemed resolved from the first to defend the place to the last. This, nobody doubted, and every one seemed to forget their late misfortune, and to place entire confidence in the General's conduct, which all must acknowledge very resolute."[58] Quartermaster Johnson remembered the high morale in the garrison:

> Notwithstanding all the forementioned impediments, through the alacrity of the Officers and Soldiers, who were all equally inured to hardships, and hard duty with the Common Soldiers, the work was finished in an astonishing manner before the enemy opened their Batteries against the town. None but those who were present on the Spot, can imagine the grief of heart the Soldiers felt, to See their Officers doing the common labour of the Soldier, equal with themselves; to see them yoked in the harness dragging up Cannon from the Lower town, the same as themselves—to see Gentlemen . . . to be at Work at the Batteries with the Barrow, Pickax and Spade, with the same Ardour as themselves. These were noble examples . . . it shows a true Spirit of Patriotism, and is highly praise worth; but indeed at this time the men had no need of Commanders, being Actuated by a Spririt of Zeal for the Service, and the example of their Officers, every one was striving who should out do his fellow.[59]

Viewing the heavy labor that his men were performing, Murray doubled their provisions, and of greatest import, their rum allowance. Captain Knox recorded that "the General and Lieutenant Governor visit the guards and working parties frequently, to encourage the men, and influence them to diligence and alertness."[60] Such efforts were clearly successful, as James Miller recorded that "The whole garrison were alert, the General was indefatigable."[61]

The French did have some success, for Murray reported the morning of May 12 that the scarp wall of the La Glacière Bastion had been "knocked down" and that "last night 200 men were employed to repair the embrasures and clear the rubbish in the ditch below the face and counterguard of the La Glasiere bastion."[62] Murray was ensuring that the debris from the damaged wall did not fill the ditch in front of the bastion, which would greatly simplify any French infantry assault. Murray was, once again, fully acting in accordance with well-established engineering principles of the time. That the French were aware of the damage that they caused is unlikely, for they failed to subsequently concentrate their artillery against the weak spot. In any event, the French shortage of gunpowder and shot and shells meant that they could not exploit the small advantage that they had gained, even if they had been aware of it.

By May 13, the British had clearly demonstrated their dominance of the battlefield, and they actually reduced their volume of fire to a comparatively modest 1,012 shot and shell, still far more than the volume of fire that the French were able to maintain. Murray observed of his gunnery this day "The French had made no visible progress during these last twenty-four hours." Material casualties among the British guns continued, as one thirteen-inch mortar failed this day. The next day the British again reduced their rate of fire to a mere 419 shot and shell. Still, these proved more than adequate, as Murray reported: "At the break of day the enemy played ten guns from their different batteries, which were partly silenced by us at noon. From this time their fire has been very slack the whole day, and little or no damage has been done to the wall."[63]

In addition to mounting his artillery, Murray was extremely aggressive at implementing improvements to his fortifications, and continued his efforts at intelligence gathering. On May 10 Murray noted in his journal that he was installing a line of pickets in the ditch of the Cape Diamond Bastion; and on May 11 he constructed traverses (earthen ramparts intended to prevent flanking fire by artillery) on the La Glacière Bastion, and continued to emplace pickets in both that bastion and the Cape Diamond Bastion. He noted that by May 15 that damage caused to the surviving blockhouses by French artillery fire had been "quite repaired." Captain Knox, as early as May 6, surveyed the defenses of the city and observed: "The parapet wall, surrounding the countryside of the town, is now strengthened considerably, being reveted with fascines, and a quantity of earth rammed down between the [fascine] lining and masonry work; this has been executed with astonishing diligence and perseverance, by day and night."[64]

On May 5 Murray "sent two faithful Canadians down the river to gain intelligence of the enemy, and know if there was any shipping in the river."[65] On May 16 Murray received his answer when additional Royal Navy vessels arrived at Quebec, the seventy-gun HMS *Vanguard*, the thirty-two-gun HMS *Diana*, and the armed provincial schooner *Lawrence*. With the arrival of the British fleet, Murray no longer felt constrained by his ammunition supplies, and he unleashed an overwhelming barrage of artillery fire against the French, as he intended to launch a powerful attack on the French the next morning. In anticipation of the assault, Murray pounded the French works this day with an amazing 2,913 shots and shell, the largest single day's expenditure of ammunition during the siege. Captain Knox, a veteran of major sieges in Europe, recorded: "I believe I may venture to advance, that there never was such tremendous firing heard as our artillery displayed this evening for near two hours."[66] The French guns were absolutely smothered by this barrage, for Murray reported that "The enemy fired only four shells and a few shot."[67]

With the arrival of the Royal Navy fleet in full strength, on the night of May 16 de Lévis did not hesitate to retreat. Under cover of darkness, he abandoned his camps, heavy baggage and artillery and withdrew for Jacques Cartier. May 17 proved to be a memorable day in front of Quebec, on both land and sea. On the Saint Lawrence River, Murray launched his three Royal Navy ships against the French fleet supporting de Lévis's operations from the river. He had previously positioned his two small frigates, the *Atalante* and *Pomone*, to safeguard his river logistical line, as a nautical line of circumvallation. However, de Lévis recognized that these two small vessels "were not in a condition to resist the enemy's vessels and protect our transports." At daybreak the British vessels moved upstream, and while maneuvering to escape them the *Pomone* ran aground near Sillery, and was abandoned by her crew. Only the *Atalante*, commanded by the indomitable Vauquelin, stood to fight against all odds at the Point-aux-Trembles. Heavily outgunned, the courageous French frigate was shattered and driven ashore. When the French vessel exhausted its ammunition, the Captain ordered the mizzenmast chopped down, and the crew used it as a raft to escape ashore. Vauquelin then nailed the French colors to the mainmast, and with a few of his officers continued to fight his vessel. The British were astounded at the selfless service to country, dedication to duty, and incredible courage displayed by Captain Vauquelin (although it did not prevent them from seizing the frigate and cutting the French flag down). So impressed were they by Vauquelin that the Royal Navy provided him with unconstrained passage to France.[68] Captain Vauquelin's sacrifice of his ship was intended to provide time for some of the smaller French vessels to flee, but the British pursuit was relentless. Only the small *La Marie* escaped, the others were driven ashore and either captured or burned. Lévis also reported the loss of "a great number of batteaux."[69]

Murray, meanwhile, had intended to sortie that morning with the majority of his garrison, determined to strike a hammer blow against the French army: "I instantly pushed out with these corps, in hopes to come up with their rear; but they were too expeditious, their rear crossed the Cape Rouge [River] before we could reach them." Murray seized a handful of prisoners (doubtless stragglers who had stayed behind to loot), considerable baggage, large quantities of military supplies including entrenching tools and scaling ladders, and no less than 36 pieces of artillery, including six that had been captured from the British just a few weeks earlier.[70] Sergeant Thompson of the Highlanders had more important interests in the French camp than artillery and tools: "They thought that we had received a powerful reinforcement, and they scamper'd away . . . . Our men soon were sent out and then regal'd themselves upon their soup and pork which they had left cooking on the fire."[71] The French siege of Quebec was raised by noon of May 17.

On May 23, Murray reported to Amherst: "I have the honour to acquaint you that the Enemy raised the siege of Quebec the 18th Instant having lost one thousand men, all their magazines & 36 pieces of cannon, tents, scaling ladders, four petards and one thousand stand of small arms, in short every thing that is necessary for the defense of their Colony & ensuing Campaign in so much that [I am] almost Confident they will make very little further resistance. The poor men under my Command have behaved to admiration, their labours and exploits are so romantic that had I time, I would not recite them."[72] The French had suffered severely during the siege. Captain Knox claimed, although he did not record his source of information, that "the regiment Guyenne lost . . . three hundred by our shot and shells."[73] De Lévis would report no less than eleven officers as casualties, with five of these men being killed.[74] Of the rank and file, he reported 68 men killed and 127 wounded, proportionally extremely heavy losses.[75] Captain Knox recorded that the British casualties "did not exceed thirty, killed and wounded."[76] Exacerbating the grim situation caused by de Lévis's withdrawal from the front of Quebec, the Canadian Indians that had fought at Sainte-Foy lost confidence in the ability of Canada to achieve victory, and abandoned the colony's cause. This marked the last occasion that a French army would be supported in Canada by appreciable numbers of Native warriors.

Throughout the siege, Murray had consistently demonstrated highly developed military engineering skills and knowledge. Immediately following the retreat from the battlefield of Sainte-Foy, the British army had experienced inevitable disorganization, but Murray had swifly restored order. His draconian hanging of a soldier taken in the act of plundering on April 30 went far in returning his army to good order and discipline. From this point forward, Quebec was never in any real danger of falling to the French. Murray's winter establishment of the blockhouses and redoubt as outerworks, although a bare minimum of such fortifications, proved to be effective. When combined with his frequent sorties and positioning of strong, alert parties in front of the city's walls throughout the nights, Murray entirely dominated the ground between Quebec's ramparts and the French parallel. Murray aggressively mounted his artillery and cut scores of embrasures through the parapet, and once his guns had been installed Murray's gunners swept the ground to the west with devastating gunfire that severely inhibited the French ability to carry forward their siegeworks. Murray continuously strengthened his works, reinforcing the parapets with fascines and earth, installing pickets in the ditch, repairing the outer blockhouses as they were damaged, and constructing two cavaliers in the Cape Diamond Bastion. The British defense of Quebec had been superlative.

The actions of de Lévis, in contrast, failed to demonstrate a resolution to conquer Quebec. A few hours of vulnerability existed following his victory in open battle at Sainte-Foy, but the heavy French casualties and abysmal ground in front of Quebec prevented him from contemplating any sudden assault, and the opportunity swiftly passed. The French construction of siegeworks was, at best, dilatory. The works were not aggressively pushed forward, and never progressed beyond the opening of the first parallel. It should be noted in defense of the French efforts that the condition of the ground in the spring of 1760—variously rocky or frozen solid or boggy—significantly hindered their progress. The French failed to construct any lines of countervallation to safeguard against a sortie by the British garrison. When they finally did get their batteries into action on May 11 and 12, they failed to concentrate their fire against the vulnerable La Glacière Bastion. This bastion was clearly poorly constructed, a fact that the French engineers were well aware of, and by only the second day of the French bombardment it was crumbling and falling into the ditch. Had French gunfire been concentrated on the weak La Glacière Bastion, and a second parallel been pushed forward against the point of this bastion, conditions that favored a succesful French infantry assault on Quebec could have been achieved. General de Lévis failed to mass his fire to exploit this advantage.

Clearly the French were constrained by lack of ammunition, and by the relatively small size of their artillery, but an attack on Quebec had been contemplated for months, and was unquestionably the French major military effort of the 1760 campaign. As the critical French line of effort, it should have received priority for supplies and reinforcements, rather than permitting critical artillery, ordnance stores, and manpower to be diverted to Fort Lévis and Isle aux Noix.

General de Lévis's primary planning principle throughout the conduct of the siege of Quebec was, as he himself admitted, "hoping that the Court would, before long, send by the [Saint Lawrence] river some succors in artillery and provisions, which would enable him to terminate the siege of Quebec in a few days."[77] However, this seems unreasonably optimistic. His engineers and artillerymen had made no provisions to construct approach trenches forward of his first parallel, much less a second or third parallel, or to create additional firing batteries to emplace this additional artillery should it materialize. Thus, considerably more than "a few days" would have been necessary to carry the siege of Quebec forward to a successful conclusion for French arms.

Furthermore, de Lévis clearly understood that a naval race to gain the St. Lawrence was underway, and that even if the French supply fleet won the race to Quebec, it would likely only precede the British Royal Navy by a few days. And, once arrived, the French ships would have been fully engaged in unloading their artillery and munitions at the Anse au Foulon; and thus been rendered extremely vulnerable on the arrival of the British fighting vessels. Although de Lévis believed that the French ships could have disembarked their armament in safety, this was more delusion than sound military logic, and it was much more likely that the French ships would have been decisively engaged and destroyed on the arrival of the Royal Navy. In the event, when the French escort frigate *Machault* and the French supply vessels belatedly arrived in New France in June, they would be trapped in Chaleur Bay and utterly destroyed by the Royal Navy.[78] General de Lévis's leadership in front of Quebec in May 1760 was insipid, uninspired, and was entirely devoid of a determination to conquer.

Both French contemporary observers and historians have been highly complimentary of de Lévis, who would later become a Marshal of France. The Marquis de Montcalm, under whom de Lévis served from 1756 to 1759, assessed him to be "practical, sensible and alert, with an admirable capacity to think for himself when thrown on his own resources."[79] The Chevalier Johnstone believed that "There needed only the arrival of a ship from France with artillery and ammunition to crown M. de Lévis with glory. The English in Quebec confessed that the first flag that would appear in the St. Lawrence would decide the question, if Canada should remain in possession of the English or return to the French."[80] Murray's biographer, Major General Mahon, a highly accomplished soldier in his own right who was a Knight of the Bath and Companion of the Star of India, believed that de Lévis's plans were "bold and skilfully executed."[81] A modern Canadian historian has referred to him as a "born soldier," a favorite of the Marquis de Vaudreuil, and complimented his daring plan against Quebec.[82]

Yet for all this acclaim, de Lévis demonstrated little real strategic or tactical skills in front of Quebec in April and May 1760. The French army under his leadership had won a limited tactical success at Sainte-Foy on April 28, but this accomplishment had been obtained only at a crippling cost in his irreplaceable French regulars and officers, and this victory had been achieved more by Murray's flawed tactics and the vagaries of terrain than any real talent on de Lévis's part. He had failed to effectively press a siege against the relatively weak and fragile defenses of Quebec, and he had then retreated precipitously upon the appearance of the English fleet, absorbing devastating losses in matériel and morale that Canada could ill afford.

General de Lévis would claim that "a single [French] frigate would have involved the surrender of Quebec and assured us the possession of Canada for another year."[83] However, there is no real support for this assertion. Rather, all surviving British accounts indicate that the Quebec garrison was more than adequately equipped with artillery, ammunition and provisions; was well fortified; was alert and active; and most importantly possessed high morale and was superbly led by a resolute Brigadier Murray. Certainly the garrison was physically exhausted, but as an old noncommissioned officer with many years of service in the U.S. Army and several tours of duty in Vietnam once intimated (in gratuitously profane verbiage) to the author, a good night's sleep and service in the infantry and artillery are mutually exclusive! And Captain Knox, in particular, observed in early May that "our gallant soldiers actually say, they [the French] had better desist, lest they catch a tartar, concluding their sentiments with the speech of an honest Briton at the memorable battle of Agincourt: Damn them, if they do come, there is enough of them to fight, enough to be killed, and enough to run away."[84] This suggests no lack of resolution. Rather, it displays an absolute conviction on the part of Murray's garrison that they would achieve victory, regardless of the cost in blood and sweat.

In warfare, the side that emerges victorious is usually not the one that does the most things right, but the one that does the fewest things wrong. Murray's leadership throughout the winter of 1759–1760 and the spring of 1760 was superb. Yet his single error in choosing to leave the superior ground of the Buttes à Neveu on April 28 proved to be nearly fatal. However, the ensuing fight inflicted such catastrophic casualties on de Lévis's army, particularly among its officers, that the French leadership was unable to exploit the advantage that they had derived from Murray's error. And de Lévis also made numerous errors throughout the spring campaign: first in his flawed allocation of resources for the attack on Quebec, and then during the siege when his major effort seemed to be desperately yearning for the arrival of a French fleet. His leadership thus serves to demonstrate one long-standing, but all too often ignored, military maxim. Specifically, hope does not constitute a viable principle on which to plan and conduct an effective and successful military campaign.

CHAPTER 4

"WE MIGHT THANK OUR HUMANITY MORE THAN OUR ARMS"

Murray's Advance up the Saint Lawrence River

Although Brigadier General Murray's Quebec garrison had suffered terribly during the long, cold winter of 1759–1760 and had then been roughly handled on the Plains of Abraham by de Lévis, the Royal Navy and army reinforcements that augmented the garrison in early May permitted Murray to move up the Saint Lawrence River as the eastern column of Amherst's planned three-pronged invasion of Montreal. Amherst issued his instructions to Murray from his headquarters at New York City on April 15:

> I therefore intend to advance on them . . . from Quebec up the River St Lawrence . . . will depend entirely on you, by pressing on the Enemy with all the Troops you can spare from the Garrison of Quebec, which place cannot require any great force for its defense & Security, when you have a Fleet in the River, your Troops advanced between Quebec & the Enemy & that the Attacks are at the same time carrying on by Lakes Champlayn & Ontario. You will therefore make such disposition of the Troops under your Comand as you shall judge most expedient for pressing & annoying the Enemy on your side, by distressing them and taking any opportunities that may offer of attacking them, by forcing them back, by advancing your Corps . . . as near as possible to Montreal.[1]

Because of the inevitable delays in communications, Murray received these instructions only when Lieutenant John Montresor of the engineers personally delivered them five weeks later on May 19.[2] Murray was given no specific timeline in his written instructions, although Amherst entrusted Montresor with supplemental verbal guidance.[3] Murray made no mention of any schedule in his response to Amherst of the same date. Because of the difficulties of direct communications caused by the French forces on the Richelieu and Saint Lawrence Rivers and the fact that ice isolated Quebec for nearly six months of the year, Amherst issued Murray no further instructions for the remainder of the campaign.

Although the French spoiling attack considerably delayed Murray's mission, it did not prevent his column from moving forward. Murray informed Amherst on May 19, "The moment I can, which will be soon, I will move up the River."[4] Murray's garrison, however, was in no condition for an immediate advance. They had endured a severe winter with considerable attendant illness, sustained a major engagement and subsequent defeat, and resisted a siege for nearly a month. Many men were mere skeletons, and officers and soldiers alike were exhausted by their arduous labors during the siege.

An immense refitting effort had to be undertaken. A large number of British store vessels carrying reinforcements of healthy men and officers, provisions, medicine, new uniforms, replacement equipment, and additional ordnance materials and munitions arrived at Quebec. Murray was disappointed by the meager funds sent for his war chest, for he complained to Amherst: "We have received the £20,000 sent in the Hunter[;] it is a poor sum for a Garrison which has had no pay since the 24th August."[5]

Murray's column would be transported by the fighting vessels and transports of the Royal Navy. The daunting force at Murray's disposal gave him complete naval superiority. This permitted Murray to maneuver up the Saint Lawrence River almost at will. The numerous heavy cannon on board the Royal Navy warships provided Murray with formidable firepower. The mobility afforded by the transports and their smaller boats gave Murray the opportunity to outflank any serious opposition that the French could present and destroy any fortifications that they could construct. The incessant challenges, however, of shallow water, obstacles, tides, currents, and contrary winds that sailing vessels faced on the Saint Lawrence River always inhibited Murray's advance.

Because many soldiers of the winter garrison remained unfit for active service due to illness, wounds, or injury, Murray was forced to leave behind a fairly large force in Quebec. Murray also needed to ensure the safety of Quebec so that it could not be captured by an aggressive French raid while the majority of his combat power was engaged on the river. On June 15, Murray's reports showed 2,463 sick and wounded in Quebec, while the garrison consisted of 1,700 men fit for duty from various regiments, with the whole under the command of Lieutenant Colonel Simon Fraser of Fraser's Highlanders. "These with the sick and convalescents," Murray noted, "will make in all more than three thousand men in that garrison."[6]

Murray embarked 2,451 officers, sergeants, corporals, and rank and file onboard his naval vessels on the Saint Lawrence River.[7] Because the ranks of his regiments had been so badly depleted, Murray was forced to organize composite battalions containing men from different regiments that had been consolidated into companies for the purpose of the campaign. These ad hoc battalions were then organized into two brigades.[8]

The officers who commanded Murray's army were superb. Colonels Ralph Burton and William Howe were highly skilled soldiers who had served with considerable success throughout the 1759 campaign in particular. Burton and Howe, actually the lieutenant colonels of Webb's 48th Regiment of Foot and Anstruther's 58th Regiment of Foot respectively, had both been appointed as colonels for duty in North American operations only.[9] A light infantry battalion, combined with Captain Moses Hazen's ranger company into a separate advance guard, was commanded by Major George Scott of the 40th Foot, one of the leading officers of the rapidly evolving British light infantry in North America. Scott had commanded a light infantry battalion made up of volunteers from Amherst's army, which had earned renown at Louisbourg in 1758. He was probably the most capable light infantry leader in the British army at the time.[10]

The Royal Navy contingent consisted of the sloop HMS *Porcupine*, the smaller HMS *Racehorse*, a forty-four-gun frigate HMS *Penzance*, the thirty-two-gun frigate HMS *Diana*, the armed ship *True Briton*, nine floating batteries (artillery gunboats of various designs), and numerous sailing transports. The *True Briton* was a converted merchantman that had been pierced for twenty-six guns, including a primary armament of twenty 24-pounder cannon, and would serve as the Royal Navy flagship.[11] In addition, considerable numbers of bateaux accompanied the flotilla, along with twenty-two flat-bottomed boats specifically designed for amphibious operations. These boats had been left in Quebec following Wolfe's campaign the

TABLE I

Column of Brigadier General James Murray, Operating from Quebec to Montreal on the St. Lawrence River

Right Brigade
Colonel [local rank] Lieutenant Colonel Ralph Burton,
Royal American Regiment (60th Foot)
Brigade Major: Captain Barry St. Leger, Webb's 48th Foot

1st Battalion Grenadiers	Grenadier Companies, Amherst's15th Foot, Lascelles's 47th Foot, 3rd Battalion Royal Americans, Otway's 35th Foot, Anstruther's 58th Foot	Major Agnew, Anstruther's 58th Regiment of Foot
1st Battalion	Amherst's 15th Foot and Webb's 48th Foot	Major Irving, Amherst's 15th Regiment of Foot
3rd Battalion	Otway's 35th Foot and 3rd Company Royal Artillery	Major Morris, Otway's 35th Regiment of Foot
5th Battalion	Lascelles's 47th Foot and Fraser's Highlanders (78th Foot)	Major Spittal, Lascelles's 47th Regiment of Foot

Left Brigade
Colonel [local rank] Lieutenant Colonel William Howe,
Anstruther's 58th Foot
Brigade Major: Lieutenant Alexander Hay

4th Battalion	Kennedy's 43rd Foot, 2nd Company Royal Artillery	Major Oswald, Royal Artillery
2nd Battalion	Bragg's 28th Foot, Anstruther's 58th Foot	Major Corry, Bragg's 28th Foot
2nd Battalion Grenadiers	Grenadier Companies, Bragg's 28th Foot, Webb's 48th Foot, Fraser's Highlanders, Kennedy's 43rd Foot	Major Addison, Otway's 35th Foot

previous year, and had survived the rigors of the winter ice. Bateaux, flat-bottomed boats that were typically rowed but could be sailed with a favorable wind, served as the workhorses of any army on the water. They transported both men and matériel, could be relatively swiftly constructed by any carpenter, were simple to operate, and could be used in comparatively shallow water.[12] HMS *Sutherland*, a fourth-rate frigate carrying 50 guns, had been part of the relief fleet that arrived at Quebec in May. The *Sutherland* was sent as far west as Deschambault to protect Murray's line of communications along the river.[13] Unlike Amherst's and Haviland's columns, Murray's force consisted exclusively of British regulars, with the sole exception of Hazen's single company of rangers. The only significant provincial representation was in the fleet, which contained a number of New England transport vessels.[14]

At the same time, Murray continued to gather information from a variety of sources. Murray's intelligence network, established at considerable effort in the fall, had paid dividends throughout the spring campaign. Murray continued to gather intelligence while moving up the river. Among his primary sources of information were escaped British soldiers who had been previously captured by the French. These soldiers were generally reliable and accurate, but they could not provide high-value information, which the French would not have shared with them. Other sources included enemy deserters, who were of questionable veracity; Canadian civilians, who tended to be familiar only with local events; and an occasional Indian, whose reports had to be judged against their radically different cultural perspective, and who possessed little or no military knowledge. Murray had also hired some actual spies, principally merchants traveling to Montreal. Murray gathered intelligence whenever the opportunity offered itself, and he augmented his established network by landing rangers and light infantry as scouts. On August 1, he put a party of rangers on the north shore, specifically charged with capturing a prisoner for intelligence. They succeeded, although Montresor noted that he "gave some account but rather imperfect."[15]

Murray was opposed by relatively small French detachments. Given the need to maintain major garrisons at Montreal, Île aux Noix, and Fort Lévis, de Lévis could ill afford any further diminution of his already strained military strength. The French defenses along the Saint Lawrence River were located at three places: two on the northern shore, and one on the south. The defensive position farthest east was the main French lines facing Murray at Jacques Cartier River twenty-five miles west of Quebec and north of the Saint Lawrence. The French had also constructed fortifications at Three Rivers, the third largest city in Canada, located approximately halfway between Quebec and Montreal, again north of the river. Three Rivers was located northwest of a prominent river junction, where the Saint Maurice River flows into the Saint Lawrence River from the north, and the Becancour River joins the Saint Lawrence River to the south. On the southern shore of the river, additional minor defenses were constructed at Sorel, where the Richelieu River enters the Saint Lawrence. Dumas commanded these three posts throughout the winter from Deschambault, where the Richelieu Rapids constituted the major obstacle to navigation on the Saint Lawrence River. Dumas, however, regularly traveled between the various posts, and when he received information that Murray was moving in mid-July, he shifted forward to Jacques Cartier.

The strength of Dumas's force varied considerably from day to day, as soldiers were transferred frequently. Dumas also had to deal with desertion among his French regulars, and what could best be described as catastrophic abandonment on the part of the Canadian militia. He noted in early June: "It will I think be very difficult not to say impossible to bring the militia of the district of Quebec and of Three Rivers as far as Montreal. How can these people be induced to abandon their families at the moment the enemy is rendering himself master of their homes?"[16] He further reported in late June regarding the deterioration of the morale of the Canadian citizens: "The people of Saint Croix [a township due south of Jacques Cartier on the south bank of the river] refuse to mount guard. I have threatened them that I will burn their property. They have replied that they may as well be burned out by us as by the enemy, who would not fail to burn everything if we fell back. All this is very embarrassing and I believe we shall have much trouble in taking the militia of the north and south shores to Montreal."[17]

Governor de Vaudreuil wrote in late May that Dumas's garrison was "fixed at 1,200 men, of whom 300 are Canadians."[18] There were several small naval vessels, of absolutely no consequence because they were completely outmatched in firepower and capability by Murray's fleet. Dumas noted of his vessels: "I greatly fear . . . that the feluccas [narrow lateen-rigged sailing vessels of Mediterranean origin] will not be of much service. They are not very fast and they make a good deal of leeway . . . they can dispute the passage of nothing but barges."[19] Dumas lamented that he possessed inadequate forces and had to leave large portions of the Saint Lawrence valley undefended: "I have nobody to send to the south shore, although it is very necessary to have some one there."[20]

Murray strove to keep his small army informed of their participation in this campaign, as recounted by quartermaster Sergeant Johnson: "General Murray . . . immediately assembled the whole Garrison, without the Walls of the City, and acquainted us with the whole plan; and which we perceived was to end with no less than the total Subversion of Canada.[21] Murray's soldiers responded enthusiastically, and even the sick and frail were determined to accompany him. Sergeant Johnson again remembered, to the great credit of the beleaguered soldiers of this long suffering army:

A vast number of the above Convelescents, made every application they were able to be partakers of the Glory, which they said they should lose by not being present at the finishing Stroke of this Great Work; alleging that as they had borne the burden and heat of the Day; that in the Evening, when they should be present to receive their Wages, that they were to be shut out, and Strangers, who had borne no share of the toil, should come in before them, and receive the honour due to them only; Nay, as well as the Men, several of the Convelescent Officers made the same Allegations.[22]

No matter how sympathetic Murray may have been to the spirit and ardor of his soldiers, some were to be disappointed. He was insistent that only healthy, fit soldiers capable of enduring the rigors of the campaign would leave Quebec. Murray's ships weighed anchor at 6:00 P.M. on July 14, 1760. The first day the fleet traveled a short distance, anchoring off Saint-Croix on the south shore and Point-au-Trembles on the north.[23]

Murray faced a considerably different tactical dilemma than either Haviland or Amherst. Although the other two officers had longer distances to traverse, they both had conventional military challenges to overcome. Amherst and Haviland had to perform reconnaissance to locate the precise alignment of the French defenses. They had to execute a movement to contact, fix, and defeat the French advance guards (covering forces, in modern parlance), and then carry out formal sieges. Murray, on the other hand, was not opposed by any significant French military forces. Rather, he faced the long-established French settlements between Quebec and Montreal and the densest French habitations in Canada, which had provided considerable strength and support to the French during the long, bitter war. The French and Canadian population on his flanks and rear had previously proven to be both hostile and militarily effective. Murray's lines of communication would be continuously endangered by an active insurgency of raids and ambushes. Thus, Murray had to perform what today would be known as counterinsurgency, as he faced the people of Canada rather than the French army.

Murray moved slowly and cautiously down the river. In 1760, the Saint Lawrence River above Quebec was treacherous with numerous shoals and shallows, and past Quebec was entirely unfamiliar to the British naval masters. Accordingly, the advance was slow as the channel had to be sounded and plotted the entire distance to Montreal. Captain Knox recorded a typical event on July 30, when the *Porcupine* ran aground just below Three Rivers, that showed just how challenging movement along the uncharted river actually was:

> The sloop of war put out a large anchor a considerable way a-head, hoping thereby to warp off; but by the breaking of the cable she was compelled to remain fast until the next day, and thereby lost a favourable wind. On the 1st instant the Porcupine made a second attempt to warp off, and broke another cable; she then took out her guns and part of her ballast, by which means they towed her into deep water, without any difficulty or damage to her bottom, having grounded on a loose sand.[24]

James Cook, master of the seventy-gun HMS *Northumberland*, gained recognition and commendation this summer by preparing the first Royal Navy hydrographic chart of the Saint Lawrence River from the North Atlantic Ocean to the Richelieu Rapids at Deschambault.[25]

Murray's priority was focused not on combat actions against the French army and their fortified posts, but in converting the Canadian residents to neutrality along the passage of the entire river. Most of the farms and communities extended no more than two miles back from the water.[26] Settlement patterns in New France were focused on access to the river, and thus water transportation, and property tended to be linear, with a minimum of water frontage and a farm that extended for some distance either north or south of the river. As a result, from Quebec to Montreal both banks of the river were densely populated.

Because of the width of the Saint Lawrence River, which was a minimum of two miles wide between Montreal and Quebec, the French artillery was incapable of interdicting the river. The English navy simply hugged the channel of the river opposite the French batteries to avoid their gunfire. On July 15, the first full day of the expedition, Murray sailed as far as Jacques Cartier. Captain Knox described the French defenses there: "This fortress is situated on a bold commanding eminence, its works consisting of fascines, earth and stockades, with felled trees laid [as an abatis] from the summit of the height to the water's edge, extending a considerable way above and below the fort."[27] Formidable these defenses might have been, but here the river was approximately three miles wide, and the French artillery could not range across the full breadth of the water. Lieutenant John Montresor, now serving as chief engineer of Murray's force, described the ineffectiveness of the French defenses at Jacques Cartier on July 15: "When arrived oppose to that Cape that forms the River of Jacques Cartier the Ennemy fir'd about twelve shot from a Work on the top of the Precipice which they garrison'd during the Winter. The Metal being light it was of no aspect, only one shot at full range coming near us. They have one Gun that's directed across that River."[28] Knox similarly recalled, "The garrison fired several shots, and threw some shells at our fleet, but the river being broad here, and the channel running close by the south shore, we were beyond their reach."[29] To attempt to garner intelligence information on the French strength and intentions at Jacques Cartier, a battalion of grenadiers were landed to scout the French positions, and "to amuse the garrison."[30]

The next day Murray's fleet continued majestically upstream, passing Deschambault, where the French defenses, under the personal eye of the masterful Dumas, engaged the fleet and succeeded in inflicting some very minor damage on the British ships. One gun was dismounted on board the *Porcupine*, one officer of the Highlanders was killed, and five sailors and soldiers were wounded. Several other ships were struck with shot, but it caused no damage. The fleet exchanged shots with the French, but proceeded without any further obstruction, anchoring for the night at Grondines.[31]

Captain Knox simply referred to it as "a brisk cannonade," which the fleet passed with little real inconvenience.[32]

That evening, two hundred regulars and fifty rangers landed on the south shore using flat-bottomed boats launched from the flotilla. A small French post, consisting of about sixty regulars and Canadians, was attacked and dispersed in disarray. A French marine officer was badly wounded and two prisoners taken without loss on the British side.[33] The landing party did not interfere with the inhabitants, who had vanished from sight immediately upon their arrival. Captain Knox recalled, perhaps a bit wistfully, "as they made no resistance, we did not molest them in any respect, though we had it in our power to deprive them of black cattle, pigs, sheep and vegetables, in which they abounded."[34]

When the Canadians finally emerged they were the first inhabitants to take Murray's oath of neutrality during his operations, and surrendered their militia arms to the British army. Several of their community and family elders told Captain Knox: "It was with the greatest reluctance on their part that we meet with any opposition from them; that they hope the contest will be decided in our favour this year, that they may remain in peace and quietness, moreover, they were rejoiced at our landing, as it furnished them with an excuse to return to their habitations, and cease all further hostilities." Canadian resolve was already diminishing. The hungry Captain Knox finally got his refreshment: "These people, contrary to their expectations, seeing themselves amicably received, immediately produced their butter, eggs, milk, &c. and trafficked with our troops, taking salt pork in exchange."[35]

On July 19, "the intire parish of St. Croix surrendered to-day and delivered up their arms."[36] Murray's fleet was delayed here for several days by contrary winds, a typical occurrence on the Saint Lawrence River. The river was wide compared to others in the Canadian interior, but it was still too narrow to permit the British men of war to tack efficiently, particularly with French artillery ranged on the north shore. Accordingly, when the winds blew against him, Murray had little recourse except to wait for them to change. When this occurred, Murray usually dispatched landing parties to the south shore to continue his indirect, bloodless war against the resolve of the Canadian inhabitants. Captain Knox described on July 25 precisely how the oath of neutrality was administered to the Canadian inhabitants of the parish of "Saint-Antoine" (actually the Parish of

Saint-Antoine-de-Tilly, on the southern bank of the Saint Lawrence River, about halfway between Quebec and Jacques Cartier):

> as the form of swearing is solemn, it may not be improper to par-
> ticularize it. The men stand in a circle, hold up their right hands,
> repeat each his own name, and then say—'Do severally swear,
> in the presence of Almighty God, that we will not take up arms
> against George the Second, King of Great Britain, &c, or against his
> troops or subjects; nor give any intelligence to his enemies, directly
> or indirectly; So Help me God.'[37]

This method of warfare that Murray was implementing proved to be extremely effective, even in the few days since the fleet had sailed from Quebec. Murray, fluent in French as were most professional British officers of the age, frequently went ashore to talk to the inhabitants. Upon his landing, seventy-nine citizens of the Parish de Lotbinière (on the south shore, about half way between Jacques Cartier and Three Rivers) took the oath of neutrality, and Murray then addressed them. His words, spoken in their own language, rang true: "Who can carry on or support the war without ships, artillery, ammunition or provisions? At whose mercy are your habitations, and that harvest which you expect to reap this summer, together with all you are possessed of in this world? Therefore, consider your own interest, and provoke us no more." Murray turned and lectured the village priest, considered to be the bulwark of French authority and presence in most Canadian communities: "The Clergy are the source of all this mischiefs that have befallen the poor Canadians, whom they keep in ignorance, and excite to wickedness and their own ruin." Murray then recounted how he had punished Jesuits and other priests who had proved to be recalcitrant, and warned: "Beware of the snare they have fallen into; preach the Gospel, which alone is your province, adhere to your duty, and do not presume, directly or indirectly, to intermeddle with military matters, or the quarrel between the two Crowns."[38] With scores of heavily armed, grim, rigidly disciplined British regulars at his side, and the sails of his ships crowding the river, the priests and the Canadian civilians took Murray's suggestions to heart.

From the beginning of his occupation of Quebec, Murray had been planting the seeds for this counterinsurgency effort by being considerate of the French habitants as well as threatening them. He had gone so far as to mandate respect for Catholic religious processions, publishing in garrison standing orders on November 3, 1759: "When any of their Processions are made in the Publick Street it is Ordered that Officers and Soldiers Pay them the Complement . . . because it is a Civility Due to the People who have chose to Leave [live] under the Protection of our Laws and Gouvernment[.] Should this Peace of Civility be Repugnant to the Conscience of any of those [soldiers, they] must Retire when the Procession Approaches."[39]

Murray also exploited Canada's failed economy through the judicious distribution of silver and gold coins, although his own war chest was by no means robust. On one occasion, he rewarded a French deserter who had willingly shared valuable information with a silver dollar (most likely Spanish). The man looked in astonishment at something that he had not seen in years, "This is no French money! A few of these properly applied would induce even the Officers, as well as soldiers, of the miserable French army to follow my example."[40]

The French had unwittingly made the situation even worse for themselves. Throughout the winter, Governor de Vaudreuil had warned the Canadian habitants of the cruel and unjust treatment that they were certain to receive at the hands of the British: "You know too well by experience the aversion of the English for everything Canadian. You have had the saddest proof of the rigour of their government." He went even further, stating that: "the issue depended upon the question whether they should be free men or slaves in bondage to the hard and exacting English." Instead of encountering cruelty, the Canadian citizens found charity, forgiveness, and generosity, and their faith in the word of their French governor was swept away.[41]

Fighting contrary winds the entire way, Murray required a full week to finally reach Three Rivers, arriving there on July 26.[42] As at Jacques Cartier, the French had constructed fairly formidable defenses at that strategically located town. Montresor wrote:

On entering ye Lake we observ'd a great number of people in Arms on ye South Shore near ye River Nicolet. By the Number of troops, the Works they had thrown up and preparations the Enemy had made one would have imagin'd they expected to have been attack'd. Having thrown up a Redoubt round the Windmill to the West of the Town, with 2 Embrazures & a line of Communication from it to the town and an appearance of lines covering all the westward avenues to a large redoubt lately constructed in the Rear

of the town on a rising ground near it and greatly commanding it
& appearing to command yᵉ upper town thᵒ at a great Distance. On
the Cape that forms the 3 Rivers the Enemy had constructed a kind
of Breastwork, this spot as represented in yᵉ plan is the Properest
Situation for the fort[.] [T]here Seems to be an old Stockaded one
[fort] near yᵉ Convent. . . . Observed 2 Embrasures in yᵉ upper town
of a Fascinage [i.e. made of fascines] & one Gun of small calibre,
the soil appearing very sandy. Number of troops that apear'd there
were about 2500, one thousand at least by their Cloathing seemed
to be regular troops. On the fleet passing about 200 rushed out of yᵉ
Works up the River and about 70 horsemen mounted.[43]

Montresor's estimates of French troop strength were flawed, as
Dumas had barely half such numbers at Three Rivers.

Upon performing a cautious reconnaissance of the French works,
the British unexpectedly discovered how French resolve was collapsing. On the morning of July 26, Captain Knox reported: "Two armed
boats went up this morning to the Three River to sound . . . a body
of Canadians having drawn up with their arms on the height above
them; but they were not molested, a person called out in our language
'What water have you, Englishman.' And being answered, 'sufficient
to bring up our ships, and knock you and your houses to pieces; if
you dare molest us, we will land our troops, burn your habitations,
and destroy your country.' Whereupon an Officer, as is supposed,
replied 'Let us alone, and you shall not meet with any annoyance.'"
Two canoes shortly pushed off from shore, loaded with a quantity of
"greens and salading." Making a gift of food to one's enemies does
not suggest a particularly aggressive, combative frame of mind. This
was confirmed that same day when a French deserter came in from
Montreal, attesting "that the French army are greatly dissatisfied and
mutinous, that the Canadians are abandoning their posts."[44]

Three Rivers was heavily fortified, but the French efforts
would go for naught. Murray simply bypassed these fortifications.
By August 7, de Lévis despaired that he had any real possibility of
defeating Murray, claiming that "We have no means of stopping
them." General de Lévis also acknowledged the effectiveness of
Murray's policy toward the Canadians: "The people of the country
are terrified at the fleet. They fear lest their houses should be burnt.
We are at the crisis of our fate. "[45] By early August, Murray had
broken de Lévis's will to resist. In the contest between the resolve
of the two military leaders, Murray had proven the stronger, more

resilient, and more determined man. It should not, however, be suggested that Murray avoided combat. In fact, whenever Murray came upon any small French post, he aggressively assailed it.

On the evening of July 16, Murray had launched his first such attack. On August 10, another strong raiding party was ordered to the south shore, as reported by Montresor: "Orders were given this evening for the first Brigade of the Grenadiers consisting of 5 Companies & the Light Infantry and Rangers to embark in Boats tomorrow morning to land on the South Shore." This was a typical excursion into the French parishes (townships) on the southern shore of the river. Here, "at ye village of Batiscaut [probably Bécancour opposite Three Rivers] according to Brigr Genl Murray's orders that ye Inhabitants also deliver'd in their arms to them."[46]

On August 10 another battalion was landed near the Saint Francis River, "to endeavour," Knox noted, "to get some intelligence of the army under Brigadier Haviland."[47] This effort proved at least partially successful, according to Montresor: "Took some Prisoners that gave an acct that Isle aux noix was taken by our troops under ye command of Coll Haviland on Sun. ye 10th Inst. And that Monsier Buerlamac Commanded the troops at ye mouth of ye Sorel."[48] Montresor also interrogated Canadians whenever the opportunity presented itself. Depending on unverified prisoner or citizen accounts, who were likely to tell their captors whatever they thought was expected to gain concessions, was an extremely unreliable means of gaining intelligence. This information, however, and the occasional unreliable report from an Indian, were the sole sources that Murray had to depend on.

On August 13, a party of rangers was placed ashore to scout on the Island of Saint Ignace (misidentified by Engineer Montresor).[49] A French deserter who surrendered to the rangers there provided information on the French defenses at Sorel.[50] Murray continued to exploit his intelligence sources. On August 15, Montresor reported: "I examin'd a Canadian this evening" and the next day he similarly interviewed a number of Canadians who had appeared to take the oath of neutrality.[51] On August 17, "this day a Deserter escaped from the Enemy of the Regiment of Marine who agreed with the accounts the Canadians gave us."[52] This statement of Lieutenant Montresor is important, for it demonstrates that the various intelligence sources were specifically being weighed against each other to judge their validity, a relatively sophisticated approach to intelligence gathering.

On August 21, two Canadians were taken prisoner by grenadiers and light infantrymen who had landed at Sorel, and similarly interrogated by Montresor.[53] On August 26 a prisoner was taken on the north shore of the river near Îsle Sainte-Therèse who furnished Murray with information "that mentioned Maj^r Genl Amherst was at Isle Aux Gallots."[54] The next day, August 27, light infantry were landed on the Îsle Sainte-Therèse for the purpose of reconnaissance, "to Scour the Island."[55] A "soldier of the seventeenth regiment, who says he was made prisoner last year and has now made his escape" reached Murray's column. This soldier provided detailed information on the progress of Amherst's column.[56] On the last day of the month, as his column neared Montreal, Murray conversed with "a British female captive at Varenne" (the Ville de Varennes on the south shore of the river, across from the Île Sainte-Thérèse), who provided him with information on the strength of the French garrison of Montreal that was timely and certainly welcomed.[57]

All the way down the river, Murray disembarked armed detachments to visit each village, and to require the inhabitants to take an oath of neutrality and turn in their militia weapons. Murray gave his word that if the inhabitants did so, their property would not be harmed, and they would be left in freedom. If they opposed him, Murray promised that they would be killed or captured, and their homes burned. With a formidable flotilla filling the river, and a powerful striking force wandering Canada at will, unopposed and unhindered by the French army, the Canadian inhabitants were more than willing to accede to Murray's orders.

Engineer Montresor led one such detachment ashore on August 4: "This Morning I received orders from the General to administer the Oath of Fidelity to the Parish of Gentilly (a township on the southern shore of the Saint Lawrence River, just east of Three Rivers) and to permit them to Keep their arms which was done this Day and Passports Given by me to each man."[58] Montresor documented a similar success at the Parish of "St. Ignace" (actually Saint-Ignace-de-Loyola, north of the Saint Lawrence River, and directly across from Sorel) on August 15: "some Canadians of ye parish of St Ignace were sent on board ye Porcupine by the Rangers that had surrender'd that had abandon'd their plantations and conceal'd themselves in ye woods, they were return'd and order'd by placard to appear the next day with all the men of ye Parish and to bring in their arms under no less penalty than setting fire to the whole parish." Murray's gambit was successful, and the next morning: "About 150 Canadians came in from the Islands of St Ignace, Dupas, St Aimé & Castor and took ye oath and rec^d Passports." Montresor wrote his father following the campaign:

> One [Canadian officer] made answer that we might thank our humanity more than our arms for so great an acquisition [of Canada] in allusion to Mr Murray's Expedition up the River, where above 7000 men deserted to him and several Regulars (manner of his placards & manifestos) the whole brought in their Arms took the oaths of Fidelity and were well treated which prevented any of the Canadians appearing in arms when we were before the Town [of Montreal].[59]

On August 12 Murray faced the first formidable opposition at Sorel on the southern bank, where the Richelieu River enters the Saint Lawrence. Montresor observed that Sorel's defenses were based around its church, "which was fortified round by a rough Breastwork mann'd by about 150 Regulars besides Canadians."[60] Captain Knox similarly recounted that "they have thrown up other works at the church and windmill; and a little higher a square piqueted fort, where I can observe they have mounted a number of swivels."[61]

For the next few days, Murray brought up a small brigade of reinforcements consisting of Colonel Rollo's 22nd and Major General Peregrine Hopson's 40th Regiments of Foot, commanded by Colonel Andrew Rollo, the fifth Lord Rollo and chief of Clan Rollo of Scotland. These regiments had been dispatched by Amherst earlier in the year from Louisbourg, but their arrival had been delayed. Lord Rollo was an experienced senior officer in his fifties, who had fought at the Battle of Dettingen in 1743 and had commanded a succesful expedition to capture Dominica in 1759.

According to Montresor, Murray had also run low on firewood for the fleet, and had to delay while he sent protected timber parties to his rear to gather more. There was also another brief period of unfavorable winds that caused Murray to suspend major operations along the river.

In the meantime, Murray tried to resolve the challenging problems of communicating with Amherst and Haviland through an intervening French army. On August 13, Murray decided to risk an effort to communicate with Colonel Haviland on Lake Champlain: "This night were detach'd express through the woods to our Troops upon Lake Champlain one serjeant and 3 Rangers with dispatches from Brig^{r}Genl Murray."[62] This was a perilous mission indeed.

Finally, on August 21, the weather cooperated, and Murray launched a major attack on the defenses of Sorel, which stood in his way. He embarked the light infantry and grenadier companies from the 22nd and 40th Regiments of Foot, augmented by other detachments from these regiments to form a battalion of approximately 300 men. He placed the experienced Major Scott in command of the whole. Under cover of darkness, they rowed ashore at 11:00 P.M. in two converging columns, and once ashore they wrecked the parish of Sorel. Lieutenant Montresor specifically observed this destruction, "which was effected by setting fire to the Houses in N° [number] about 32. Each party leaving one house standing to fix a Placard or Manifesto on.[63] This was hard warfare, and Murray deeply regretted having to take such a stern and unrelenting measure. Sadly, he explained to Pitt: "I found the inhabitants of the parish of Sorrel had deserted their habitations and were in arms. I was therefore under the cruel necessity of burning the greatest part of these poor unhappy people's houses. I pray God this example may suffice, for my nature revolts when this becomes a necessary part of my duty."[64] Captain Knox, standing at Murray's elbow, observed that this action "affected the General extremely, but the obstinate perserverance of the inhabitants in arms made it necessary."[65]

Although distasteful, this attack had the desired effect. The brutal measure of leaving a single house standing, with a manifesto prominently tacked to it, was certain to engender fear and obedience. This grim memento clearly expressed Murray's resolve to those Canadians who still supported the colonial government: if you return to your home and live peaceably, you will not be harmed, but if you take up arms for Canada, you will have no home to return to. It was highly effective, and in short order the already unsteady Canadian militia abandoned the French cause in droves. By demonstrating British power and resolve in Sorel, while at the same time offering the olive branch, Murray effectively stripped the support of the Canadian population from the French army.

To reinforce his intentions, Murray also insisted that his soldiers behave properly ashore, particularly once the inhabitants had sworn their oath of neutrality and disarmed their militia. On August 15, Murray "declared that, if any soldier presumes to plunder, or offer any violence to the women on the island, he will be instantly hanged." Similar orders were issued by the Royal Navy.[66] The result was that "the inhabitants of the south coast come on board our ships without reserve, supplying us with vegetables, poultry, eggs, and whatsoever else they can spare, in exchange for salt pork and beef."[67]

Although Sorel had been disposed of, once again the fleet found itself delayed by "perverse winds" and "the rapidity of a strong current being against us . . . not being able to make any way."[68] On August 27, the fleet "worked up to the village of Assumption" (the village of L'Assomption and the parish of Saint-Pierre-du-Portage-de-l'Assomption, on the northern shore of the Saint Lawrence River approximately two-thirds of the way from Sorel to Montreal). Here, Murray began making his force ready for the final advance on Montreal. He ensured that every man was issued with thirty-six good cartridges and three flints. Large working parties were detailed to go ashore to prepare gabions and fascines, which would be critical supplies in the event that a siege of Montreal became necessary.[69] By now the British army was operating at will on the Île Sainte-Thérèse, northeast of Montreal Island.

On the 31 of August, the light infantry and grenadiers continued the advance, landing at daybreak at Varennes, on the south shore of the river opposite Pointe-Aux-Trembles and Montreal Island. Montreal was now nearly in sight. The French resistance was negligible, Captain Knox recording "the enemy fired some scattering shots at them, and ran off." By the next day, Murray's counterinsurgency continued to pay dividends, "the whole parish of Varenne have surrendered, delivered up their arms, and taken the oaths; their fighting-men consisted of five companies of militia; two other parishes, equally numerous, have signified their intention of submitting tomorrow."[70] Murray's force was by now nearly irresistible, Captain Knox recalled on September 3: "The regulars [many of whom had married Canadian women and intended to become permanent settlers in Canada at the end of the war] now desert to us in great numbers, and the Canadian Militia are surrendering by hundreds." Murray issued manifestos to the inhabitants, warning them "that if they will surrender and deliver up their arms he will forgive them; if not, they know what they may expect, from the examples which he has hitherto reluctantly given them." Knox was impressed by the effect that Murray's proclamations generated: "This evening four hundred of them belonging to the parish of Boucherville [across the Saint Lawrence River from Montreal] came to Varenne and delivered up their arms."[71]

The Jacobite officer with a decade of service to the French Army, the Chevalier Johnstone, assessed at first hand the efficacy of Murray's operations:

> General Murray conducted himself as an officer of great understanding, knowledge and capacity, and left nothing to do for General Amherst, he employed five weeks in coming from Quebec to Montreal, which is only sixty leagues, and did us during his march more harm by his policy than by his army. He stopped often in the villages; spoke kindly to the inhabitants he found at home in their houses—whom hunger and famine had obliged to fly from our army at Montreal; gave provisions to those unhappy creatures perishing for want of subsistence. He burned, in some cases, the houses of those who were absent from home and in the French army at Montreal, publishing everywhere an amnesty and good treatment to all Canadians who would return to their habitations and live there peaceably. In short—flattering some and frightening others—he succeeded so well, that at last there was no more possibility of keeping them at Montreal.[72]

Murray followed a consistent approach throughout his journey up the Saint Lawrence River. As French defensive positions were encountered, he simply bypassed them, rendering them impotent. French resistance was limited to a few, relatively ineffectual cannon shots, harassment rather than legitimate military obstruction. Murray's progress was slow and deliberate, as he landed strong detachments ashore at every parish (or township), swore the inhabitants to neutrality, and disarmed the Canadian militia, on which the French depended for resistance. Murray succeeded entirely in coopting the militia. He left behind him a population that had become predominantly neutral, if not actively supportive of King George, as economic and commercial incentives were offered. Murray's unhurried pace was imposed on him more by the natural obstacles of the Saint Lawrence River itself than by any French opposition. The river was uncharted by the Royal Navy, and he was working upstream against a strong current. Numerous shoals, rapids, sand bars, and rocks slowed his advance to a crawl, even when the winds were not contrary. Still, this afforded Murray ample opportunity for counterinsurgency, which he did with considerable skill and success.[73]

Murray's performance as garrison commander of Quebec over the winter of 1759, his defense of the city against the French resurgence in the spring of 1760, and his command of the column operating up the Saint Lawrence River against Montreal in the summer of 1760 had been superb. Murray had been forced to establish the Quebec garrison with great urgency in the fall of 1759, with no prior arrangements and facing the onset of winter. His garrison suffered from insufficient shelter and firewood and inadequate rations during the harsh Canadian winter. Still, Murray successfully pacified the French Canadian countryside in the immediate vicinity of the city. He established an effective system of patrols, posts, and intelligence operations in the area surrounding the city. He constructed rudimentary outerworks in front of Quebec's defenses and implemented effective measures for the protection of the city while maintaining high morale in the garrison. His maneuvers, which culminated in the Battle of Saint-Foye, were well conducted, with the single flawed decision to launch an attack against the French that resulted in his defeat on the Plains of Abraham. But Murray expeditiously recovered from that debacle, restored effective discipline within his garrison in short order, and the safety of Quebec was never in jeopardy. His conduct of the defense at the siege of Quebec was flawless, and he had swiftly established superiority over the French forces outside his wall. A few weeks later Murray's operations along the Saint Lawrence River sealed the fate of Canada more than any other factor. Murray had proved to be one of Amherst's most skilled, successful and valuable subordinates on this campaign.

CHAPTER 5

"THE ATTACK ON THE ÎSLE AU NOIX WILL BE YOUR CARE"

Winter and Spring on Lake Champlain

Murray's column was Amherst's eastern wing. While Murray moved up the Saint Lawrence River, Amherst's central column moved north down Lake Champlain and the Richelieu River. Although Murray had faced relatively weak and disorganized French resistance, the British southern column had to overcome a formidable defensive position before it could advance into the heart of Canada.

Îsle aux Noix, the French "Island of Nuts," is a large island located nearly in the center of the Richelieu River, six miles south of the small village and fort of Sainte-Jean and nine miles north of Lake Champlain. Approximately a third of a mile north of the island, the Rivière du Sud (South River), a tributary, enters the Richelieu River from the east. The island is roughly one mile long and a quarter mile wide, approximately 210 acres in size, and is extremely low lying. It is nearly perfectly flat, and contains no prominent topography. The water table is quite high, practically at ground level. When it rains, the island is poorly drained, soil conditions are typically muddy, and the rainwater tends to collect in pools across the island. Throughout most of the year the island is wet and damp, and evening and morning fogs and mists are common. The island has almost no trees, but does possess low brush and a few shrubs. During the summer, the island has very little shade and becomes blazing hot as the sun reflects off the river. Îsle aux Noix had not been settled until 1753, when Pierre Jourdenet, a former French marine from the Compagnie De Lorimier, was permitted to establish himself there for the annual rent of "a bag of nuts" from the hazel trees that populated the island.[1]

Beginning in the summer of 1759, the French had transformed the barren plain of the island into a strong fortress. If there had ever been any nuts on the Île aux Noix, they had all been consumed by the French army by the fall, and the hazelnut trees had been cut down for fortifications. To prevent the British from negotiating the Richelieu River, French engineers constructed two heavy log booms reinforced with strong chains, extending from the southern end of the island across both channels.[2] According to Captain Joseph Bayley, a provincial officer from New Hampshire serving with the British army, the French had "fastened 5 logs abreast with iron staples & [chain] links 1 ½ inches in diameter, the whole anchored every 10 ft. in ye ground [in the river]. The length of the boom is about 80 yds."[3]

The Chevalier Johnstone, now with the Île aux Noix garrison, recalled: "He barred the two branches of the river which formed the island with staccados, or chains of big trees, linked to one another at their ends by strong rings and circles of iron. This prevented the English boats from Lake Champlain to pass the island in the night."[4] Contemporary French maps consistently indicate the presence of these two log booms and chains.[5] A map prepared by Captain T. Walker of the Royal Americans (60th Foot) in 1760 also clearly depicts these two log booms.[6]

By the middle of the eighteenth century, military art, science, and engineering, were well established and extensively studied.[7] Numerous professional treatises were available to military officers and engineers to guide them in the use of terrain, the construction of fortifications, and nearly every conceivable aspect of military operations. A number of these treatises discussed the use of chains, booms, and other obstructions to prevent an enemy force from traversing a river.

Regrettably, knowledge regarding the use of these river obstructions is no longer common. In large part, this is because modern West Point historians have created the impression that the famous chain stretched across the Hudson River at West Point in 1778 was the first of its kind.[8] It was nothing of the sort. Rather, such chains and booms had been widely used for centuries and were common in the eighteenth century. The obstructions the French army installed across the Richelieu River at Île aux Noix were extremely significant because they prevented the powerful British fleet from moving around the island and made any amphibious assault an extremely difficult proposition.

Some background on the use of these river obstacles may be valuable. One readily available military study that addressed this subject was *A Treatise on the Art of War* (1677), by Roger, Earl of Orrery: "If the river adjoining be navigable, or not always fordable . . . a competent distance above your standing camp, you must have a boom or cable under water, or chain ready to draw across the river, and to cover and well defend them at both ends."[9] Monsieur Ozanam, "Professor of Mathematics at Paris," prepared *A Treatise of Fortifications Containing the Ancient and Modern Method of the Construction and Defense of Places and the Manner of Carrying Sieges*, which was translated into English in 1727. Ozanam noted: "If the river runs through a town . . . to hinder surprises, the entrance must be shut up with an iron chain, sustained by little boats or logs of wood, which every night must lie quite cross the river.[10]

John Muller, Professor of Artillery and Fortification at Britain's Royal Military Academy at Woolwich, in his classic *A Treatise Containing the Elementary Part of Fortification, Regular and Irregular* (1746) addressed river defenses: "But if the river is above 100 toises [640 feet] large . . . chains and booms may be laid to the shore in the night, and in time of danger."[11] Another of Muller's works, *The Attac and Defence of Fortified Places* (1757) also suggested that "a boom, or several chains, should be fasten'd cross the entrance of the harbour."[12]

Although the concept of stretching a heavy log boom or similar obstacle across a large body of water seems to be an advanced engineering project for 1759, such techniques had been in use for centuries. The first documented use of chains and log booms to obstruct the free navigation of rivers was across the Golden Horn at Istanbul, installed in the fifth century A.D. The chain was anchored on both ends by large fortified towers of which one, the Galata Tower, survives. This chain and the city fortifications successfully protected Istanbul from attack until it was conquered by Crusaders on April 13, 1204.

Another chain blocked the harbor at Girne (Kyrenia) on the Island of Cyprus as early as A.D. 1300. The chain was anchored by two large fortified stone towers and extended across the mouth of the harbor. One of these towers, "The Chain Tower," remains at Kyrenia.[13] One of the towers is said to have protected a large stone pillar to which the chain was anchored, and the other stone tower protected a windlass that enabled this chain to be raised or lowered. The length of this chain was approximately three hundred feet.

A third chain was emplaced to obstruct the harbor at Padua, Venice, beginning in 1516. This thirty-six-meter-long chain was anchored at a strongpoint in the fortifications that encircled the town, the so-called Bastione della Saracinesca (The Chain Bastion).[14] The Grand Harbor at Malta was also defended by a hand-forged iron chain stretched between Fort Saint Angelo and Fort Saint Elmo. This chain was approximately two hundred meters in length, and was "permanently anchored. There was a windlass on the Fort Saint Angelo side, and on the L'Isla/Senglea side the [chain] was embedded in rock. In times of crisis, the windlass was tightened and the chain was raised. In peaceful times, the windlass was unwound, and the chain rested on the bed of the creek. When the chain was raised, it was buoyed up in the centre by being tied to boats or logs, this would stop it from sagging in the middle, and thus permitting a small boat from sneaking over the top of it."[15] This chain and its harbor defenses withstood a siege by a Turkish army in 1565. When Turkish forces attempted to land at the chain to outflank it, they were decimated by a hidden artillery battery guarding the chain. During the siege of 1565 the Turkish forces "had secured their ships in these two harbors [in their rear] and had barred the entrances with chains and stakes."[16]

Finally, a fifth chain blocked the harbor at Famagusta, Cyprus. This chain is depicted on a map of a 1571 siege of the city by the Turkish army.[17] As with the other chains, it was anchored to heavy defensive towers on either end. As these examples document, by the middle of the eighteenth century, such river obstacles had been in use for centuries.

During the previous years in the defense of Canada, similar river obstacles had been employed by French military engineers at both Quebec and Fort Carillon at Ticonderoga in 1758–1759. During Amherst's attack on Fort Carillon in the summer of 1759, the French defenders drove log pilings into the La Chute River between Lake George and Lake Champlain to obstruct it. The nature and extent of these log pilings is not known, although their location was recorded in a 1777 British map of Fort Ticonderoga and vicinity.[18] The French also constructed some type of minimal log boom across Lake Champlain.[19] This boom appears on one map of the 1759 Ticonderoga campaign as "a work made to prevent our cutting off the enemy's retreat."[20] This could not have been of particularly substantial construction, since on July 26, 1759, Amherst dispatched Rogers's Rangers in boats with saws to cut the boom: "I had ordered Major Roberts to go to night and cut the boom."[21]

Although it would not figure in the military operations around Quebec in 1759, the French army constructed a boom of logs bound with chains and anchored in place to block the mouth of the Saint Charles River, immediately to the east of Quebec.[22] Military maps of the operations around Quebec referred to this obstacle simply as "the boom." One observer noted of the Saint Charles River defenses on June 3, 1759, "There was no sight better than these entrenchments defended at intervals by good redoubts furnished with many cannons, two ships moored at the entry to the small [Saint Charles] river with ten cannons, as well as a chain of masts that make it impossible to force entry, and the last defense is our batteries on the commissariat dock." [23] Thus, the Richelieu River at Île aux Noix was obstructed by a long-used feature of military engineering.

The center of the island's fortifications was a fort that served as the primary interior defensive position. A series of outerworks encircled the circumference of the entire island. Surrounding the fort proper were four redoubts that afforded a defense in depth, and would have to be overcome before the main fort could be assailed. An oddly shaped set of earthworks with various salient and reentrant angles and a rough bastion facing south were primarily designed for defense by infantry and configured to prevent any British landing from the water. A crude center citadel guarded the garrison's major buildings and the center of the encampment. The defenses were not built according to any established tenets of military fortification, and were apparently dictated by the configuration of the island and the severely constrained time and resources available for the construction of the fort. The fortifications employed seventy-seven pieces of artillery. Fourteen of these were relatively small iron swivel guns that would have been effective only in repulsing an infantry assault. The largest of the guns were three 16-pounder cannon.[24] Additional logistical facilities included a large wood yard due south of the main fort. The woodyard was necessary since what little firewood to be found on the island had long since vanished by the winter of 1759–1760. There were also two wharfs on the eastern side of the island, several storehouses, officers' houses and barracks, and gardens for the garrison.

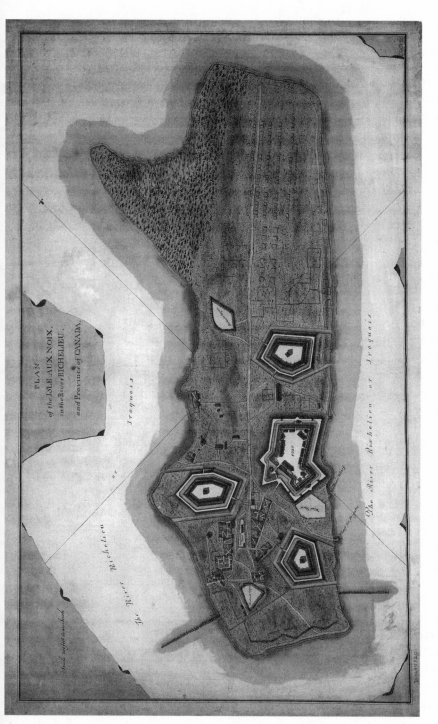

"Plan of the Isle aux Noix, in the River Richelieu, and Province of Canada. [Signed:] T. Walker, Capt., 6oth regt." Map No. 256, Peter Force Map Collection, Geography and Map Collection, Library of Congress, Washington, D.C.

The entire island was surrounded by a strong wall of large sharp-ened pickets emplaced vertically to prevent any British force from launching a surprise amphibious assault. An American provincial officer who operated against the island, Captain Jacob Bayley from Massachusetts, observed of the strength of these defenses: "The island is exceedingly strong . . . There is no such thing as to storm the island on the upper side. It is picketed 2 rods into the water & a vast deal of boards thrown without the pickets."[25] Another American provincial who occupied the island in August 1760 described it: "As to the Cituation of the Isle Au Noix it is cituate & Lying very Low in the Center of the Lake & has a very Strong Fortress on it & is very strongly Piqueted in all Round & The Island very Low & Swampy Greate Part of it & Chiefly Cleard up."[26] The French commander Bougainville succinctly noted that he "had strongly entrenched" the island.[27]

The French garrison consisted of between 1,000 and 1,500 sol-diers, as many as Canada could spare for the Richelieu River val-ley. The Chevalier Johnstone reported, "M. de Bougainville was sent in the spring to command at Isle aux Noix, with eleven hundred men, of which number were the Regiment of Guienne and Berry."[28] Given the natural strength of the position, its recently constructed entrenchments, the dual river booms blocking the river, and the large number of artillery pieces, a force of this size should have been more than adequate for its defense.

The fortification, apparently never formally named, was com-manded by thirty-one-year-old Colonel Louis Antoine de Bougain-ville, who had served under the Marquis de Montcalm in Canada since 1756. Although relatively young to be entrusted to such a great responsibility, he was an experienced commander by this time, his military capacity had been well proven, and he was a popular leader. In any event, by 1760 Canada was beginning to run out of seasoned combat commanders, and his youthful vigor and energy would prove to be a leadership asset during a sustained siege.

So long as Lake Champlain remained ice-locked throughout the long Canadian winter, it was difficult for the rangers at Crown Point to launch scouts as far north as Îsle aux Noix. But with the seasonal melting of the ice in late April and early May, Major Robert Rogers could initiate reconnaissance missions directed against the French garrisons along the Richelieu River to determine their strengths in anticipation of the summer movement against them. Rogers's first expedition was in early May, and resulted in scouting but no combat action. Upon his return to Crown Point, Rogers was hastily summoned by Amherst to Albany for consultations. Amherst had by this time been informed of Murray's defeat in front of Quebec, and he determined to launch Rogers and a strong force of rangers against Île aux Noix in an attempt to divert the French focus away from their siege of Quebec. General Amherst recorded in his journal: "[May] 26ᵗʰ. I ordered Mr. Rogers with 300 men to surprise St. Johns & destroy the Magazines at Chambly and the West of the River while 50 of the 300 were to destroy Wigwam Martinique on the East side. This may alarm the Enemy & may force some of their Troops away from Quebec. 'Tis all I can do till I get more Troops here to forward to the advanced Garrisons."[29] Amherst issued Major Rogers detailed instructions, and Rogers swiftly returned to Crown Point to put Amherst's orders into effect.[30]

Lieutenant Colonel William Haviland had spent the winter of 1759–1760 at Fort Crown Point as Commandant of Forts Crown Point (still under construction) and Ticonderoga (under repair from damage sustained during its capture that summer). Blakeney's 27th Regiment of Foot, which Haviland commanded in field service, and two companies of rangers commanded by Captains Noah Johnson and James Tute (also spelled Tate) comprised the Crown Point garrison. The late General Forbes's 17th Regiment of Foot was divided, with six companies at Fort Ticonderoga, and the other four companies at the newly constructed and still incomplete Fort George at the southern end of Lake George. [31] One of the New York independent companies of British regulars, commanded by the experienced Captain William Ogilvie, was stationed at Fort Number 4 on the Connecticut River to the east of Crown Point.[32]

Captain Noah Johnson was an experienced officer who had served with Major Robert Rogers since joining the rangers in 1755 as an ensign. Captain James Tate was a less seasoned Ranger officer, only having served through the 1759 campaign as a lieutenant before assuming company command. Captain Johnson would be killed in a skirmish with the French near Île aux Noix on June 5, 1760. Captain Tate had been captured by the French in a skirmish near Crown Point on March 31, 1760, and was not available for service on the campaign.[33]

Rogers's two ranger companies at Crown Point were too small to provide the three hundred extra men that Amherst had specified.

Captain Thomas Davies, "A south view of Crown Point" (1760). Courtesy of Library of Congress, Prints and Photographs Division, Washington, D.C.

Accordingly, upon his arrival, Rogers asked Haviland to assign additional soldiers to his command, and he provided two companies of light infantry. Still, Rogers felt that he needed more men to bring his force up to strength. The winter of 1759–1760 at Crown Point was severe, and Haviland's garrison had been depleted by illness, including smallpox. Haviland demurred at Rogers's request for more men, as he did not believe that he could safely further reduce his garrison.[34]

On June 1, Rogers's force, smaller than he would have preferred, departed down Lake Champlain aboard the pair of British sailing ships that had operated on Lake Champlain since the previous summer. Rogers had about 250 men, comprising his two companies of rangers and the two light infantry companies from Forbes's 17th and Blakeney's 27th Regiments.[35] Enroute, Rogers detached Ranger Lieutenant Robert Holmes with fifty men to attack Wigman Martinique, in accordance with Amherst's orders. At the same time, he sent Sergeant Thomas Beaverly (or Beverly) with three men, carrying a secret dispatch from Amherst through the woods to General Murray at Quebec. This small team of rangers was dispatched on foot on a deep penetration patrol through woods infested with hostile Indian warriors and French Canadian militia, simply to transmit a one-page letter. This shows the straits to which Amherst was driven to send timely communications to Quebec.

A fragment of an orderly book from one of the ranger companies has survived from this June raid. Although it does not provide any tactical or operational details, it does contain detailed instructions for the conduct of the raid:

> In Case of an Attack on the front, the Right and Left Companys are to Endeavor to gain the flanks of the Enemy, and the Main Body to form the front;
>> On this occasion the advance Guard Comes in and Joyns the Senter;
>> The Rear Guard faces to the Right about and Maintains its Ground;
>> If Attacked in the Rear to face to the Right about and form the same as the Front—and the Rear Guard Comes in and Joyns the Senter, the advanced guard becomes the Rear;
>> If attacked on the right Wing, the advance and Rear Guards becomes Flanking Partys and will Endeavour to Gain the Right and Left Wings of the Enemy;
>> No firing without orders, nor fires to be made, no unNesisary alarms;
>> Nor no Retreating with out orders they were to Stick by one another and Push the Enemy Close then nothing can hurt them; and
>> No Plunder to be taken as it may incumber their March and prove of Bad Consiquence.[36]

These succinct tactical instructions were taken directly from Major Rogers's considerably more verbose "Rules of Rangers," which he had taught to selected British regular officers at the direction of Lord Loudoun at Fort Edward in November 1757. This orderly book fragment, limited as it is, confirms that Major Rogers did indeed use these rules during his woodlands operations.

Rogers landed about twelve miles south of Île aux Noix on the western shore of Lake Champlain, with the intention of skirting the large French garrison located there so that he could reach Saint-Jean and Chambly. His efforts to do so were uncovered by the French, and a brutal skirmish occurred on the edge of the Richelieu River in what Rogers described as a "bog." Ensign John Wood from the light infantry company of Forbes's 17th Regiment of Foot was killed, and one other officer was mortally wounded. Sixteen rangers were killed, and two light infantry and eight rangers were wounded. Rogers claimed that he had recovered fifty French muskets and had killed forty of the French force. Although he overestimated French casualties, both forces had been bloodied.

Rogers briefly retreated to Lake Champlain to reorganize his command and sent his casualties back to the hospital at Crown Point aboard one of the ships. He received reinforcements, both timely and welcome, of thirty accomplished Mohican warriors, the newly formed Stockbridge Mohican Indian Company. Thus augmented, Major Rogers "about midnight" on June 9 landed 220 men on the western shore of Lake Champlain, opposite the modern Isle La Motte, probably in King's Bay north of the Great Chazy River. This time Rogers successfully slipped past Îsle aux Noix.

By the evening of June 15 he had come within two miles of the small French fort at Saint-Jean. Carefully scouting the post, Rogers was disconcerted to discover that "the number of the centries within the fort were seventeen, and so well fixed, that I thought it was impossible for me to take the place by surprise." This post had doubtless been alarmed by the earlier engagement south of Îsle aux Noix. Accordingly, Rogers moved away from Saint-Jean and continued farther north. The next small post that he encountered was Sainte-Therèse, three miles north of Saint-Jean and nine miles south of Chambly. Sainte-Therèse was located at the southern extremity of the several miles of rapids that obstructed the Richelieu River between there and Chambly. The post was a lightly defended stockade containing a pair of storehouses and a supporting hamlet. In early September, an American provincial visited it: "a Little Snugg Fortress Before it was Consum'd but there was the Stockad & Pikets Standing, and a Butifull Little Trench Round it." Rogers carefully observed the post in the early dawn light:

> I observed two large store-houses in the inside, and that the enemy were carting hay into the fort. I waited for an opportunity when the cart had just entered the gate-way, run forward, and got into the fort before they could clear the way for shutting the gate. I had at this time sent different parties to the several houses, about fifteen in number, which were near the fort, and were all surprised at the same instant of time, and without firing a single gun.[37]

His rangers captured twenty-four soldiers in the fort, and an additional seventy-eight prisoners in the village, including women and children. Rogers interrogated the prisoners and discovered that the fort at Chamblee was too well garrisoned and alert for him to have "any prospect of success." Accordingly, he burned the fort and village, along with a considerable quantity of hay and provisions stockpiled around the post. He also seized eight bateaux to cross the river and destroyed every other boat and canoe he could find on the west bank of the Richelieu River. Rogers was diligent in his work of destruction: "We also killed their cattle, horses, &c., destroyed their waggons, and every other thing which we thought could be of service to the enemy."[38]

Crossing the Richelieu River to its opposite bank and destroying the captured bateaux behind him, Rogers then moved swiftly to withdraw past Île aux Noix. By June 20, he was far south on Lake Champlain, where he learned that Lieutenant Holmes had not been able to reach his target. Rogers's and Holmes's combined forces then boarded the waiting British vessels and returned to Crown Point on June 21. Although Rogers had not been able to fulfill his precise orders, he had clearly achieved the intent of the raid, "to alarm the enemy" through his heavy skirmish near Île aux Noix and his destruction of Sainte-Thérèse.

Amherst was quite pleased with the accomplishments of Rogers and his rangers, the Mohican warriors, and the British light infantrymen. He wrote to Sir William Johnson on June 21: "Major Rogers is doing very well on the farther End of Lake Champlain, keeps the Enemy in constant Alarm, for the more We can force them to Assemble, by which they must Consume their Provision, is hastening them so much the sooner to their Fall."[39]

Although neither Rogers's intense skirmish with the French nor his raid on Sainte-Thérèse dealt any substantial blows to the French occupation of the Richelieu River valley, and by the time he launched his raid, the French incursion against Quebec had already been defeated, Rogers had still executed an extremely effective operation against the French defense of the river. He had spent the better part of three weeks operating on both banks of the Richelieu River, from Isle La Motte on Lake Champlain to Sainte-Thérèse, and had acquired considerable knowledge of the terrain around the French fortifications at Île aux Noix. The intelligence gained would soon prove invaluable, when Haviland launched his campaign up Lake Champlain.

Haviland would command the combined British and provincial force that would move against Île aux Noix. He was a seasoned officer, a lieutenant colonel who had been appointed a brigadier general for service in North America by General Jeffery Amherst. Born in 1718 in Ireland, he had received his first commission as an ensign in Colonel Thomas Fowke's Regiment of Foot (later numbered as the 43rd Regiment) in December 1739. He had accompanied his regiment on the disastrous campaign to Cartagena in 1741. In 1742 he received command of a company and was promoted to captain in Major General William Blakeney's Regiment of Foot (the 27th Foot, or Inniskilling, Regiment), then stationed as a garrison in Stirling Castle in Scotland. Captain Haviland served as an aide-de-camp to General Blakeney during the 1745 Jacobite Rebellion and fought in various small engagements around Stirling Castle, where Blakeney's garrison successfully guarded the entrance to the River Forth near Falkirk. He must have served with skill and gained recognition, for he was promoted to major in 1750 and lieutenant colonel in 1752. In July 1757 Lieutenant Colonel Haviland brought Blakeney's Regiment to Halifax, Nova Scotia, by way of New York to serve in Lord Loudoun's proposed expedition against Louisbourg.

During the winter of 1757–1758 Haviland had been commandant of Fort Edward, and his garrison command there was marred by angry recriminations and conflicts between him and the Rogers's Rangers. The rangers, although renowned for their skill at patrolling, raids, and ambushes, were also known for their relaxed discipline when in garrison at their isolated camp on Rogers Island. The rangers had a tendency to engage in recreational marksmanship and hunting, doubtless facilitated by the liberal consumption of spirituous beverages. When Haviland arrested some rangers with the intention of whipping them (literally) into discipline, the rangers mutinied and chopped down the fort's whipping post. The incident caused considerable dissension between the rangers and the fort garrison. Apparently the situation was exacerbated by some level of personal animosity and professional jealousy between Haviland and Major Robert Rogers. A few long-distance scouting missions and heavy combat in the midst of a severe Adirondacks winter soon settled things down. Haviland and Rogers remained professional enough to resolve their differences, and they worked quite well together on subsequent campaigns.

In the summer of 1758, Haviland took part in General James Abercromby's unsuccessful attack on Fort Carillon (Fort

Ticonderoga) and the following year he commanded the advance force of General Jeffery Amherst's expedition that successfully captured both Fort Carillon and Fort Saint Frederick at Crown Point. By the spring of 1760 he had considerable military experience, and had seen extensive service in North America. He must have impressed Amherst, for he hand picked Haviland to lead the column up Lake Champlain in 1760. Later, when Haviland served as colonel of the 45th Foot, he was regarded as a "kind father" to his regiment, and it was observed that his years of military leadership was marked by his "overlooking many opportunities of emolument but none of benevolence."[40]

Amherst issued Haviland with instructions for the campaign in a letter written from Albany, dated June 12, 1760: "The Attack on the Isle au Noix will be Your Care, for which I have alloted You such a Corps of Troops, with such a Proportion of Artillery, and such a Number of Batteaux, as I am hopefull will Render that Conquest Easy."[41] Amherst also provided Haviland with intelligence that he had received on the French defenses, noting in his journal on July 11: "I wrote to Col Haviland, sent him a plan I had received from Quebec of the Isle au Noix & a Letter from thence wrote by the Engineer giving a description of it."[42] Although Amherst did not specify his source for this information, it may well have been captured by Rogers in his earlier raids on the Richelieu River valley.

As they were formulating his campaign, Amherst communicated with Haviland using a well-established set of couriers along the Hudson River, Lake George, and the Lake Champlain corridor between Albany and Crown Point. Typically, letters could be passed along this route in three days in favorable weather. On May 13, General Amherst recorded in his journal: "I received a Letter from Col Haviland of the 10th."[43] Additional confirmation is provided by Amherst, as he wrote on May 10: "I had a Letter from Major Rogers of the 7th."[44]

Amherst issued instructions to both Haviland and Murray to make every effort to establish and maintain communications between the separated columns. Amherst further instructed Haviland that "whatever my Operations or the Success of them may be, I shall Acquaint You therewith by Letters, when I think necessary, Which I shall send to You across the Country, and You will do the Like to me, directing Your Messengers to follow the Path that Capt. Tuicket[?] Did last Year from Lake Champlain to La Galette ."[45] Amherst amplified these instructions in early June: "In Case the Enemy by finding themselves forced to give up their Out Posts, Should draw back the Whole to their Center, and there Attempt to make a last Stand, we may be able to press so close on them on Every Side, that We may Joyn if Necessary for the Intire Reduction of the Enemy."[46]

In addition to Haviland's responsibility for the movement up Lake Champlain against the French defensive position at Îsle aux Noix, Amherst charged him with construction work: "And it must be some time before the Troops Allotted to Serve Under Your Command, can possibly be Assembled, as likewise those that are to Assemble at Oswego, that both may Advance at the same time, I would have You make all the Use You can of the Intermediate Space in finishing the Works at Crown Point; Rebuilding the Barracks at Ticonderoga, and Compleating the Works at Fort George."[47] Since the previous summer, Amherst had intended that Fort Crown Point serve as the defensive fortress against any possible French incursion from Canada, and Ticonderoga as merely one of several posts on the line of communications from Albany to Crown Point. Full reconstruction of Fort Ticonderoga was never contemplated, and only the barracks were to be restored to provide quarters for supply convoys moving in both directions.

While constructing Fort Crown Point proper, Haviland placed considerable emphasis on the various dependencies there, particularly the fort's garden. Although to modern observers this activity may appear superfluous, sustaining a productive garden at Crown Point was absolutely critical to ensuring the health of the expedition dispatched from Crown Point as well as to sustaining the winter garrison there. Haviland specifically noted that he had "been very busy fencing the garden" and had also sown a considerable quantity of turnip and hay seeds that Amherst had forwarded.[48] Haviland also stated that he had established a smallpox hospital, which was located a good distance from the fort to ensure that the infected soldiers could be safely quarantined from the garrison.[49]

Although Haviland had his hands full preparing his column for the movement down the lake, the construction at Fort Crown Point remained a major priority. Major John Hawks, a field grade officer with the Massachusetts provincials, maintained an orderly book at Crown Point for much of 1760, and he consistently reported daily fatigue parties of 500 to 700 men engaged in this labor.[50] Peter Kimball, a carpenter from Massachusetts, was retained at Crown

Point throughout the summer and fall to help construct the fort. Kimball's succinct journal documented incessant work being done every day except when poor weather intervened, from sunrise to sunset.[51] Haviland reported to Amherst regularly on the progress of the works, on July 6 noting that: "I think the Fort goes on well for our Numbers. The Grenadier Fort [Grenadier Redoubt] has given us great trouble as most of the Meadow work gave way, it is now almost mended so that the Barracks will be soon begun upon."[52] On August 7, shortly before he departed for Île aux Noix and the reduction of Canada, Haviland rendered a final report:

> Every one here thinks the Works goes on very fast for our Numbers, as to myself, I spend so much time there, I scarce see the Change for a days work, indeed a great part of our Labour is Buried in Casemates; which I hope will be soon over, we have had great delays for want of proper Timber, but are now getting a good Supply. The Prince of Wales's Bastion in a day or two more will be Rampart high, the Princess of Wales's Bastion is getting up very fast, Prince Edwards Bastion will have its second Coat of Casemate timber finished in three or four days, the long Curtain and Princess Emelia's Bastion are all nearly Covered once and part of the Curtain doubled, and this day the foundation of the Barracks is begun between the Kings Bastion and the Princess of Wales's.[53]

Amherst provided Haviland with a strong column for his advance up Lake Champlain and the Richelieu River. The core of Haviland's strength was provided by Forbes's 17th and Blakeney's 27th Regiments of Foot. Both regiments had arrived in North America in the spring of 1757 and had participated in the aborted expedition against Louisbourg that summer. They returned for the successful siege of Louisbourg in 1758 and accompanied Amherst in his capture of the French Forts Carillon and Saint Frederick on Lake Champlain in 1759. Lieutenant Richard Montgomery, who would later achieve fame in the American War for Independence, served as Adjutant of Forbes's 17th Foot. The light infantry and grenadier companies from the two regiments were detached and organized as a separate four-company battalion, commanded by Lieutenant Colonel John Darby of the 17th Foot, in accordance with the typical field arrangement that placed the elite light infantry and grenadier companies into a special battalion that could be used for particularly hazardous, demanding, or important duties.

Five companies of rangers were assigned to Haviland, per-sonally commanded by Major Robert Rogers. These included the two ranger companies that had spent the winter at Crown Point and been formerly commanded by the ill-fated captains Tate and Johnson. These two ranger companies were relatively well seasoned. Major Rogers also brought his own veteran company of rangers. The two additional companies were formed for the campaign, and may not have been as effective as the other companies. They were com-manded by Captain James Rogers and Captain David Brewer, offi-cers in whom Rogers had considerable confidence. Captain Rogers was the younger brother of Major Rogers. Captain David Brewer had been an ensign of rangers as early as 1756, and had served as a ranger company commander since 1758. The five ranger companies were supplemented by a company of seventy Stockbridge Mohican Indians. Stockbridge warriors had served with Rogers since 1755, and in large part they had trained his rangers in the skills and tech-niques necessary to excel in woodlands and riverine small warfare. The Stockbridge Mohican Company was commanded by "Captain Solomon," who was known by his assigned English nickname since his Mohican name of Uhhaunwaumot was so difficult for the British to pronounce and spell. Captain Solomon had previously served with Rogers as a lieutenant, and was probably selected because he spoke fluent English.[54] These companies had all participated in the June raid along the Richelieu River, and would be operating on relatively familiar ground. The irregulars were supported by the battalion of grenadiers and light infantry commanded by Lieutenant Colonel Darby, thus giving Rogers a strong and capable body of disciplined regulars to back up his irregular forces. Haviland's advance guard thus comprised experienced rangers and Native American warriors, and was commanded by a master of the art of irregular warfare. Rogers's force of rangers and Indians would prove to be adept at cov-ering Haviland's advance.

Haviland carried with him a powerful artillery detachment, under Lieutenant Colonel Thomas Ord of the Royal Artillery.[55] Ord was one of the most experienced Royal Artillery officers then serv-ing in North America. He had entered military service as a cadet gunner in 1731, and been commissioned as a first lieutenant on December 1, 1741. He had fought at the Battle of Fontenoy in the War of the Austrian Succession on May 11, 1745, and had gained combat experience on the plains of Europe, serving under the Duke of Cumberland. He had earned a reputation as an excellent officer, commanded an artillery detachment as a captain in Newfoundland from 1748 through 1754, and was then hand picked by the Duke of Cumberland to join the army under Major General Edward Braddock, which moved against Fort Duquesne at the Forks of the Ohio in March 1755. As commanding officer of Braddock's train of artillery, he had gained invaluable experience in transporting artillery through the wilderness conditions of North America. He survived Braddock's defeat on the banks of the Monongahela River on July 9, 1755, where he was reported as being present on the field of battle without being wounded.[56] Ord was subsequently transferred to Albany and the Hudson River. He commanded the British artillery in both the 1758 and 1759 campaigns against Fort Carillon. He received regular promotions in recognition of his service and knowledge, even though according to Lord Loudoun, he was "very industrious, but has no execution."[57]

Ord was responsible for a powerful complement of approximately forty cannon to be carried up the lake, including both field pieces to support the infantry battalions and a train of heavy siege guns. During the 1759 campaign on Lake Champlain, Amherst's army had employed six 24-pounder cannons, four 18-pounder cannon, ten 12-pounder cannon, seven 6-pounder cannon, and three 3-pounder cannon. The artillery train contained six eight-inch howitzers, two five-and-a-half-inch Royal howitzers, one thirteen-inch mortar, four ten-inch mortars, and eight five-and-a-half-inch Royal mortars.[58] Haviland carried a nearly identical train of artillery with him up Lake Champlain in August 1760. Ord's train of artillery contained several pieces of specialized equipment necessary for the heavy siege guns that Haviland carried forward to reduce Isle aux Noix.

Haviland's comparatively small force of British regulars was augmented with a large assemblage of provincial forces raised from the New England colonies. This included a regiment of New Hampshire provincials commanded by Colonel John Goffe. He had been with the New Hampshire militia as a captain in 1746, and had served actively with the New Hampshire provincials as a major since 1756. Goffe had been recently promoted to colonel, and this was his first regimental command. A regiment of Rhode Island provincials was commanded by Colonel Christopher Harris. A considerable number of Massachusetts provincials also accompanied Haviland. One regiment was commanded by Colonel John Thomas. He had previously

TABLE 2

"An Abstract of Guns, Mortars and Howitzers for Service of the Campaign by way of Crown Point (May 19, 1760)"

Brass Ordnance [cannon] mounted on carriages		
Heavy	24 Pound	6
Heavy	12 Pound	3
Light	12 Pound	6
Light	6 Pound	4
Brass Mortars in Beds		
13 Inch Iron	2	
10 Inch Brass	2	
5½ Inch Brass	8	
Howitzers Mounted		
8 Inch Brass	4	
5½ Inch Brass	2	
Block Carriages	2	
Covered Wagons, Compleat	4	
Tryangle Gins, Compleat	2	
Carts, Forge	4	
Carts, Sling	2	

Source: "Abstract of Guns, Mortars and Howitzers for Service of the Campaign by way of Crown Point–Albany, 19ᵗʰ May 1760," enclosed in Amherst Orders to Haviland, June 12, 1760, "Amherst Correspondence with Colonel Haviland" WO 34/52 f. 48–50 (old PRO 285), Amherst Papers, Microfilm Reel 38.

Note: A block carriage was essentially the running gear of a wagon without a bed used "to carry guns in the field, which are too heavy to be transported upon their own carriages." The "triangle gin" (as it was correctly designated) was a framework of sturdy poles with block and tackle used to mount barrels upon carriages. A sling cart was a large wagon frame with wheels five to six feet in diameter, used to transport gun barrels over rough terrain for short distances, by hoisting the heavy barrels in slings beneath the frame. Muller, *A Treatise of Artillery*, 133, 143–145.

served as a field officer in the 1759 campaign against Carillon and Saint Frederick, so he was a relatively experienced officer serving on familiar ground. Another regiment was commanded by Colonel Asa Whitcomb, and a third was commanded by Colonel Abijah Willard. Colonel Willard had been a captain of Massachusetts provincials at the 1745 Siege of Louisbourg, and had served as a colonel commanding a regiment in the 1759 campaign. All these regiments were known simply by their commander's names. These Massachusetts provincial battalions were formed into a brigade commanded by Brigadier General Timothy Ruggles. General Ruggles also served as the second in command of the expedition. General Ruggles was another experienced officer, having served under Colonel William Johnson at the Battle of Lake George in 1755. He had also commanded a provincial regiment in the 1758 Campaign.

Haviland complained about the delay in the arrival of these provincials at Albany and Crown Point, and they were dispatched piecemeal by companies up the Hudson River–Lake George–Lake Champlain corridor transporting materials from Albany as swiftly as they arrived. They received little opportunity for focused company or regimental training. Many of the soldiers and officers, however, had served on previous campaigns, and the quality of the American provincials was on the whole excellent. Given their likely duties, they were fully capable of performing the logistical and transportation labor, and military construction, on which Haviland's column depended. Although these tasks generally were devoid of military glory and were both arduous and tedious, they were absolutely critical. The services of the provincials had proven integral to British successes in previous campaigns that had traversed the wilderness.

Haviland's column had to be carried by a sizeable fleet down Lake Champlain, as there were no roads north of Crown Point in the summer of 1760. This fleet had been constructed the previous summer and fall at Fort Ticonderoga by Amherst, and consisted of two sailing vessels, the 155-ton brig *Duke of Cumberland*, and the 115-ton sloop *Boscawen*. The *Duke of Cumberland* was armed with twenty 4-pounder and 6-pounder cannon and twenty swivel guns. She was crewed by seventy seamen and sixty marines. The *Boscawen* was outfitted with four 6-pounder cannon, twelve 4-pounder cannon, and twenty-two swivel guns, and was crewed by sixty seamen and fifty marines.[59]

To supplement these traditional sailing ships, three unique vessels called *radeaux* had also been constructed, with the largest being christened the *Ligonier*.[60] Although the *Ligonier* itself has never been located, a boat of this class that sank in Lake George in 1758 has been discovered, facilitating study of this unique type of vessel. A radeau was hexagonally shaped, with a flat bottom and no keel but a large rudder. Its flat bottom meant that it drew little water, a considerable advantage when operating on Lake George or Lake Champlain. They were constructed of three-inch-thick oak boards, sharply angled to deflect shot, with the upper portion angled in to provide additional protection to the crew. A radeau was virtually invulnerable to small arms or swivel cannon fire and antipersonnel rounds such as canister and grapeshot. It carried large cannon capable of delivering devastating firepower, and since it was essentially a giant floating raft, it had enough cargo capacity to convey the massive quantity of ordance required to conduct a siege. Unfortunately, radeaux also handled like gigantic rafts, and they were for all practical purposes impossible to maneuver, except with the wind. They were fitted with a pair of simple square-rigged masts and a full contingent of oars to enable rowing, albeit with limited speed and capabilities. Two of these radeaux were apparently relatively small vessels, while the *Ligonier* was a veritable floating fortress, for it was a massive vessel, "84 feet long & 20 feet broad on the platform, where the guns run out she is 23 feet & to carry six 24 pounders."[61] A sketch of the radeau done by British Royal Artillery Captain Thomas Davies in 1759 depicted it with two masts, each with a square sail, and ports for thirty-four oars. It also appears to have had some raised decks, possibly to facilitate protected storage of ordnance.[62] It is known that the other two radeaux were smaller, although detailed descriptions and dimensions of them have not been located.

Three row galleys were also constructed, a hybrid type of vessel derived from ships widely operated on the Mediterranean Ocean. The row galley was a vessel with a keel, rigged with lateen sails, and equipped with no fewer than twenty-two oars, so that it could be readily rowed or sailed in nearly any wind. It drew relatively little water. The galleys typically mounted one large cannon, an 18-pounder or 12-pounder, in the bow, with two smaller 4-pounder cannon located broadside and astern, and mounted sixteen swivel guns. They had a relatively large crew of 250 sailors and marines.

Construction of this fleet moved ahead slowly and required all of August and September 1759. It was not until October 11 that the fleet could sail down Lake Champlain. The fall's foray was successful. The four major French vessels were swept from the lake, with one sunk and the sloops *Musquelonguy, Esturgeon,* and *Brochette* captured. This was accomplished too late in the campaign season for Amherst to exploit the success, for snow was already on the hills surrounding the lake. A British advance could resume in the spring without appreciable French opposition since Canada lacked the resources to construct a replacement flotilla. Amherst's 1759 fleet, augmented with the three captured French sloops, would again transport and support Haviland's force in August 1760. Amherst's 1759 shipbuilding at Forts Ticonderoga and Crown Point and his subsequent operations on Lake Champlain had provided Haviland with overwhelming naval superiority.

Particular preparations had to be made for the nautical transportation of the large and critically important train of artillery. This was to be transported down Lake Champlain using one large and two small radeaux, "Eight French Batteaus" that were presumably larger than the typical bateaux, and "three prows" that served as flatboats, since cannon and horses could not be loaded onto the bateaux.[63] This Royal Artillery train did not include additional cannon brought up from Fort Edward and New York City to equip the fleet, which could be employed in land operations if need be.[64] In addition to the field pieces that were broken down and transported aboard the flotilla, the larger cannon were installed as armament aboard the ships. These cannon could be readily unloaded upon arrival at Île aux Noix. Colonel Haviland directed that *Boscawen* be employed as a Royal Artillery storeship.[65]

Rogers's Rangers used primarily whaleboats, with a few canoes.[66] Several hundred bateaux were dedicated to carrying the soldiers and the majority of provisions and other equipment. Haviland's fleet was a motley assemblage indeed, with two English sailing vessels, one large radeau, two small radeaux, three row galleys, three captured French sailing vessels, eight large "French bateaux," three prows, and scores of bateaux, whaleboats, and canoes.

Haviland's force consisted of approximately 3,400 soldiers, predominantly provincials. Haviland probably had odds in his favor of somewhere between three to one and two to one over the Île aux Noix garrison. These advantages were not overwhelming, but his naval superiority permitted his army to maneuver at will in near-perfect safety, and considerably increased the firepower that he could employ against the French fortifications.

Amherst selected a date for the advance to begin, writing to Haviland from his "Camp at Oswego" on July 29, 1760: "I propose to be gone from hence by the 10th of next month [August] at far-thest, perhaps sooner, but You may rely on the former, and therefore I would have You proceed down the Lake on that day or as nearly as You can do it." [67] Now that Amherst was at Oswego, his mes-sage had to travel down the Mohawk River valley and then up the Hudson valley route, which slowed communications considerably. To insure that such a critical letter was not lost in transit, Amherst dispatched duplicates by a separate courier. Haviland mentioned that he had received Amherst's letter of July 29 only on August 8, with the duplicate arriving at Crown Point on August 10.[68]

Lemuel Wood, a soldier with the Massachusetts provincials, noted of their preparations (with less than correct verbiage): "Sater Day the 9 this Day we all was in a Combustion in making all things Ready for to go to St Johns."[69] In the event, Haviland's column was slightly delayed by adverse winds. Although Haviland had no way of knowing this, Amherst was similarly delayed by the same wind con-ditions. Conditions at Crown Point were better on August 11, and at dawn the journey began.[70]

Haviland made meticulous preparations for his campaign, including measures to protect the valuable provisions on which his army depended. A Massachusetts provincial regimental orderly book instructed that barrels of hard bread "must be Covered Carefully with tents to prevent Its being Damaged in Case it should Rain they are Likewise to take what boards they carries in their Battows in Order to Make a Shed in the next Incampment for the Bread."[71]

When Haviland's strong and capable army embarked at Crown Point on the morning of August 11, it had been as well prepared for action on the Richelieu River as it could have possibly been. It was well that Haviland had taken these precautions, for difficult and demanding service lay ahead.

CHAPTER 6

"THE ENGLISH FLAG IS FLYING ON THE ÎSLE AUX NOIX"

Siege on the Richelieu River

L ate on the evening of August 10, the winds shifted to blow from the south toward Canada. Such an event could easily have been interpreted as a favorable omen for an invasion of Canada by way of the Richelieu River, but it is doubtful that the hardworking British regulars and American provincials had the leisure to savor the moment. Rather, the propitious fortune of nature went unremarked, and Haviland's motley assemblage of vessels set forth on Lake Champlain the morning of August 11, only one day behind Amherst's specified date.

The transit down Lake Champlain, from Crown Point to the Richelieu River, was extremely challenging because of contrary winds and severe weather. A number of provincials who participated in the campaign left behind meticulous records, which described the miseries of the journey down the lake. Captain Jacob Bayley, a company commander with the New Hampshire provincials, discussed the organization of Haviland's fleet for the nautical movement to the north: "Embarked in three columns, the Rangers form a front of the whole. The right column consisted of Regulars, with a small radeau in the front, column of Rhode Island and New Hampshire with Legionary [*Ligonier*] radeau in their front. The 3d and last column were Massachusetts men, with another radeau in their front. Proceeded in this manner. Wind contrary."[1] Private Woods noted: "The wind was very strong against us."[2] Sergeant David Holden, an Orderly Sergeant for one of the companies with the Massachusetts Provincial Regiments, carefully counted the size of the fleet: "The Number of Vessals and Boats the fleet Consisted of is as follows viz. One Brigenteern 4 Sloops, 3 Rideaaus [radeaux],

3 Prows, 2 Large Boats, 263 Batteaus Large & Small, 41 Whale Boats, 12 Canoes."[3]

Early on August 11, shortly after the fleet embarked, the wind turned northerly and gathered strength. This made progress slow and painful, particularly for the three poorly sailing and balky radeaux. Captain Samuel Jenks with the Massachusetts provincials recalled: "the wind blood [blowed] prety fresh a head." The first day the fleet was only able to row six miles into the wind, reaching the vicinity of modern Potash Bay, a sheltered anchorage with good beaches on the eastern shore.[4]

The next day was no better. The wind continued unrelenting from the north. On August 12, Haviland's fleet struggled a mere seven miles to Button Mold Bay, another sheltered anchorage on the eastern shore of the lake.[5] Captain Jenks specifically noted that the large, boxy *Ligonier* was experiencing considerable problems rowing into the wind and waves.

On August 13, the northerly winds kept blowing, and it was another slow, frustrating day. Battling the winds the entire way, Haviland's fleet managed to make about ten miles to what is today known as Willsboro Bay, a large protected cove with a stretch of good beach tucked into the western shore of Lake Champlain behind the peninsula of Ligonier Point.[6] It was a horrific day's work. Their crews exhausted by two straight days of continuous rowing, the three radeaux fell behind. The wallowing *Ligonier* was the slowest of the three.[7] Eventually, six bateaux of the Massachusetts provincials were sent back to her assistance. Lieutenant John Bradbury was unfortunate enough to command this detachment: "Set off at 9 oclock the wind Stil against us. Rowd 3 miles ordered Back with 6 Battoes to help tow the Legganear. Kept her in tow till 10 o'clock at night then cast & joines the Regement. Slept till Light in the Battoes."[8] Lieutenant Bradbury's concise account fails to convey the grueling labor that the Massachusetts soldiers had to endure. They spent twelve continuous hours pulling the awkward radeau into a blustery wind capped with white-topped waves crashing around them. The men were soaked to the skin in the process, and they spent the night aboard their wet and uncomfortable craft.

Colonel Haviland must have believed that things could get no worse, but the events of August 14 proved him wrong. Lieutenant John Frost recorded that day's debacle: "About ten of Clock in fore noon, there was a Very great Storm of rain, high Wind. We Lost ten or more men that were over Set and Drownded. One man to day was Shot by the means of a gun going off accidently. A very Unlucky day inDead."[9] Captain Bayley similarly recalled: "The wind increased & blew very hard, so that the whole fleet was in danger. . . . Several men were drowned this day by a boat breaking in two, 8 men drowned of 11, 3 were from our regiment. Several helmsmen were knocked overboard and drowned."[10] Lieutenant Bradbury's fear remains vivid in his diary entry, even 250 years after the event: "The seas Ran very high and we Narrowly escaped being either floundered or dashed to pieces against the rocks. One Canoe of the Rangers Cast away & 7 men Lost."[11] Captain Jenks echoed, "We were obliged every one to shift for themselves & a prodigious sea and hard wind . . . there is several battoes missing, I fear in bad circumstances."[12] Given the horrific and terrifying weather, the fleet made little progress this day. They anchored for the day at Schuyler's Island, near the western shore of the lake and only five miles north of Willsboro Bay.

Finally, once the storm passed, the wind turned southerly, and the men could put away their oars and hoist sail. On August 14 the convoy reached the Isle La Motte, a large island far down Lake Champlain, just a few miles south of the Richelieu River—a voyage of no fewer than 35 miles in a single day from Schuyler Island. When the wind was favorable, even the flat-bottomed bateaux and radeaux could make surprisingly good speed.[13] Upon landing, the provincials realized that they would shortly see the action they had enlisted for. They "Cleand our fire Locks & Completed the men with ammunition."[14]

At first light on August 16, Haviland's fleet embarked from its overnight encampment on Isle La Motte, again with favorable winds. They sailed and rowed about ten miles to the north, entering what some soldiers referred to as the "narrows" of the Richelieu River. Colonel Haviland and his soldiers were glad to put Lake Champlain, with all its trials and tribulations, behind them. Now they could finally commence active operations against the French fortress of Île aux Noix. As Haviland's force approached the island, he consulted with Major Robert Rogers, who had scouted in the vicinity of the French post as recently as June. Haviland ordered his army to land on the eastern bank of the Richelieu River.

Both sides of the river are flat and swampy, poorly drained with numerous small tributaries. American provincials described the eastern side of the river as wooded. There was no high ground to be found on either side of the fort within the range of eighteenth-century artillery. In 1760, civilian settlement had not yet reached Îsle aux Noix, as French habitation remained north of Saint-Jean. Although the island was near the middle of the channel, a small cove to the southwest of Îsle aux Noix, today known as Anse à l'Esturgeon (Sturgeon Cove), brought the eastern shore considerably closer to the French defenses. Haviland, possibly on Major Rogers's recommendation, put his army ashore to operate against Îsle aux Noix from the east. There was one significant water obstacle that Haviland would have to traverse, a creek that is today known as the Ruisseau Faddentown (Faddentown Stream). This stream flows from the south in the same direction as the Richelieu River, generally parallel to it and about a third to a quarter of a mile to the east. Once level with the southern end of the Îsle aux Noix, the stream turns at a right angle to the west and drains perpendicularly into the river. Thus, this stream inhibited any British advance on the French fort, and would have to be bridged before any effective siege could be carried out. Both the east and west channels of the Richelieu River were too deep to be bridged or forded. The eastern channel today is seven meters deep, with the western channel five to six meters deep.[15] Water flows north from Lake Champlain to the Richelieu, and eventually to the Saint Lawrence River, in a relatively strong current, approaching three to four miles per hour in some seasons. The current and depth of the Richelieu River created an impassable moat surrounding the fort. Thus, Haviland's advance would depend on close and continuous coordination between his fleet to control and maneuver along the watercourses, with strong artillery batteries placed on the eastern bank of the river to reduce the French earthworks.

Over the next two weeks, Haviland's siege efforts would be focused on seven specific phases. First, he had to effect an amphibious landing, possibly against French opposition, on the eastern shore of the river. Once ashore, his infantry had to advance to clear the eastern shoreline of any French irregulars defending the ground. When his beachhead was secured, Haviland would have to establish his infantry in a line of circumvallation to defend the rear and northern flank of the British camps and artillery batteries against any French attack. This accomplished, Haviland's army could set up campgrounds, hospitals, and supply depots. It would then begin landing the staggering quantity of artillery, munitions, and ordnance stores necessary to sustain the siege. A formal park of artillery would be emplaced to serve as the headquarters for the artillery and engineers. In order to construct batteries across the river from the French fort, a road between the logistical base and batteries was needed. It would have to include at least one bridge across the Ruisseau Faddentown. Then, and only then, could the siting, design and construction of the artillery batteries to reduce the French fortifications on the island proceed.[16] Given the obstacle of the Richelieu River, which made French incursions or sorties being launched from Île aux Noix problematic, there was no need for the British to construct the traditional line of countervallation to defend their siege works against French infantry attacks.

The greatest impediment to Colonel Haviland's operations was not the presence of the French defenders and their artillery, but the nature of the ground. It was damp and marshy, with a high water table. Transporting heavy artillery, and the tons of stores and baggage necessary for the army, would be extremely difficult given the abysmal trafficability of the soil. The heavy rain that fell on August 14 had not improved the situation. For the siege to succeed, the American provincials would have to build and maintain fords, bridges, and hundreds of yards of roads and trails. At the same time, Haviland's men had to perform considerable improvements to the camp itself, such as constructing drainage ditches to remove water from the campground to avoid debilitating sickness from erupting within the camp. The establishment of adequate camp hygiene procedures was critical to preserving the health of the army.

Early in the afternoon of August 16, Haviland's force landed on the eastern shore of the river. Captain Jenks recorded: "We formed for landing in about a mile & ½ from the enemy's fort, with all our battoes a brest, to land on the east shore. As soon as the signall for landing was made, we all rowd right to shore & landed in extreme good order without any molestation at all. The Ligoneir redows & prows [three row galleys] kept a fire on the enemys fort & vessells, to favor our landing."[17] Lieutenant Bradbury wrote: "Set off at 4 oclock arrived within 2 miles of the fort at 3 oclock and Landed without opposition. The vessels began to fire on the fort & continued till night very moderate."[18] Sergeant Holden documented: "About 3 o'Clock this morning we all Embarkt & Set Sail for Île au Noix which was about 10 miles & Came & Landed on the Est [East] Shore about 1 o'Clock within about 2 miles of the Fort without any greate matter of mollistation. The french fired Several Shotts at our Rideau & Sloops & our People fir^d Some at them."[19]

Although there are no surviving records that document precisely where the landing was made, the most likely location was immediately south of what is today known as Pointe Hillman. Depending on where a soldier actually disembarked, this would equate with the one- to two-mile distance that most soldiers reported. The river bank here permitted the landing of several hundred bateaux. Because of the course of the river and the protrusion of Pointe Hillman from the eastern bank of the river, artillery fire could not have been directed against a landing site on this beach from the French fort. Point à l'Esturgeon also stood between Pointe Hillman and Îsle aux Noix on the western side of the river. Haviland's soldiers, however, could still have seen the radeaux and row galleys engaging the French fortress from the river to the south of the island.

There was no French opposition to the landing. Incredibly, the French had no scouting or reconnaissance parties ashore, and failed to challenge the British on the ground south of the island. The French had regularly shown their skills fighting in the woods using Natives and Canadian militia. They could easily have inflicted heavy casualties, disorganization, and disruption during the difficult amphibious landing. This absence of French opposition cannot be accounted for. It is likely that the French garrison was caught by surprise, doubtless believing that the recent bad weather would have precluded a British advance.

The first step of the landing was for the advance guard to establish itself ashore. The five companies of rangers, the single company of Stockbridge Mohican Indians, and the combined light infantry and grenadier battalion would then sweep through the landing site, the proposed location of the encampment, and over the land opposite the island to ensure that there was no French opposition. The only extant source from any member of the advance guard, the *Journal of Major Robert Rogers*, concisely described this activity: "We soon came in sight of the French fort, and about ten in the morning Colonel Darby, with the Grenadiers and Light Infantry, and myself with the Rangers, landed on the east-shore, and marched and took possession of the ground opposite the fort on that side, without the least opposition."[20] Once safely ashore, Haviland's main body established a rudimentary camp immediately to the east of the landing beach, and defensive works for the camp site were begun.

A strong guard force (piquets, in the military parlance of the time) was posted against any possible French incursion.[21]

Captain Jenks was not pleased with the ground that he encountered in Canada: "We marcht up & formd a line & set out our pequits. The land we marcht through exceeding wett & mirey. I went sum times almost up to my middle in mud & water . . . We then set about making a breast work which was completed in a little time, as the men are in high spirits."[22] Lieutenant Bradbury, sick with what he described as "purging" (meaning that he was likely nauseated and vomiting) still performed his duties: "took Command of the picket guard Set the Sentries & Lay on our arms. But not Disturbd."[23] Sergeant Holden had similar experiences: "We Encampt & made a Brest worke, half the men up & the other to Lay on their Arms this night."[24]

The soldiers, soaked from their voyage north in heavy rains on the lake and wading ashore, spent a miserable night first night in Canada. Captain Jenks grumbled, "I lodged last night on the ground without my blanket, only a few bushes to cover me & as wett as could well be."[25] Lieutenant Bradbury recalled the "extreem cold" of that night.[26]

The next day the British started construction of a one-and-a-half mile road leading to the eastern shoreline opposite the French fort. They began landing the mountains of provisions and matériel necessary to sustain the siege and they improved their camp. They also began the emplacement of batteries to be employed against the French island, all the while maintaining alert piquets in case of a French incursion.[27] Captain Jenks, having spent the previous night sleeping underneath some shrubs, took actions to improve his situation: "The rest of the day spent in fixing a shed to lodg under."[28] Lieutenant Bradbury was employed most of the day operating on the river to the south, but returned to the encampment that evening: "orderd up to the Brestwork to join our Companies & Dismissed the picket Lodgd under a few Bushes in a Swamp."[29] Sergeant Holden similarly reported of the day's labors: "Keept on fortifying, Clearing a Rhode &c."[30] Captain Bayley was also engaged in this road construction: "Cleared a Road within 500 yards of the French fort without disturbance."[31] Private Lemuel Wood was a member of this working party: "the Cheafe of the armey went and took Pursesion of the Point Next to the fort and Cleard a Road for the Canon."[32] On this day, the army began assembling the material and equipment needed for the coming siege.

To support the various construction activities over the sodden and marshy ground, thousands of fascines and gabions had to be constructed. General Orders were issued that "All the Men that under Stand Making fascines are Emediately [immediately] to be Set to that work the Commanding officer of each Corps will Order One Serjeant from Each Regiment to See that the Men are not Idle they will be paid Agreeable to G[l] [General] Amherst Orders Provided the facion are well made. Orders will be Given when & where they are to be Delivered. There is to be 1000 that is 9 feet long, 2000 16 feet Long, 500 20 feet Long, 8 inches Diameter."[33] Fascines are large bundles of sticks and twigs, bound very tightly together and about six inches to a foot in diameter. As long as natural materials were readily available (never an issue in the thickly wooded areas to the east of the Richelieu River), even a small working party of soldiers could make fascines as rapidly as one per minute. Fascines were impervious to musketry, and when staked together could form a breastwork or parapet resistant to artillery fire. They could also be used for engineering projects such as causeways for roads across a swamp, or bridging small streams. Gabions were large woven baskets that could be filled with dirt to form defensive parapets. Colonel Haviland's army would require staggering quantities of such materials, and during the coming days their manufacture would become routine.

On August 17, one of the two small radeaux was sent perilously close to the island. The purpose this maneuver is difficult to ascertain. Colonel Haviland claimed "It was reported the french had Abandoned the Island, as they had ceased firing all night. Ordered a Raddoe commanded by Cpt. Glegg and three prows to look into the fort."[34] This was partially confirmed by Sergeant Holden, who recalled: "Pretty Calm this morning about firing."[35] Yet the naval action of the day before covering the amphibious landing had clearly revealed the presence and alertness of the French defenders. It does not seem reasonable that Colonel Haviland simply assumed that the French had departed their fortifications and left the road to Montreal wide open, without the British having taken any actions yet to force them to depart.

Most likely, the small radeau was intended to perform a reconnaissance of the booms across the river to determine their size and strength, as passing these obstacles would have greatly simplified operations by the stronger British flotilla against the French. If the British could gain naval ascendency north of Île aux Noix, they could prevent the French garrison from either being reinforced or retreating, and would force their surrender *en masse*. The booms, constructed of floating logs, would have been nearly invisible from the south, and only a close inspection could have revealed their strength and size. A scouting mission appears to have been the most logical explanation for endangering the relatively small radeau in this manner, though it is possible that Colonel Haviland was simply being optimistic, and hoped that the French had abandoned their island fortress almost without firing a shot.

The scouting mission proved to be a complete fiasco. The crafty French gunners remained silent, luring the radeau toward the island, and then unleashed a devastating artillery barrage at close range. Several provincials observed the ensuing debacle from across the river.[36] Captain Jenks, who had soldiers from his company manning the artillery radeau, was keenly interested in the action: "One of our reddows going to reconitre the forts was fired on by the enemy & Capt Glaye of the Royall Artelery was killd & 5 or six more lost their legs. One of these unfortunate men belongs to my company & has his leg cut off; I hear he is like to recover."[37] The attentive Sergeant Holden saw the whole thing: "About 8 o'Clock Capt Clagg Belonging to the [Artillery] Train on board of a Small Artillery Rideau, Bore away Towards the fort whose orders was to go on til fir'd upon, accordingly he Did & By a Six Pounder had Both his Legs Shott off after which the Capt soon Died, 5 more wounded, one of which had Both his Legs Shott off, the other 4 one Legg apiece Soon after one or Two Dy'd."[38] Lieutenant Bradbury received a comprehensive accounting of the earlier radeau action, directly from some of the wounded: "This morning an unfortunate afair hapend; one of the Small Raddoes was orderd to go very near the fort the 2nd Shot they Received from the fort one 12 pounder, come through the fashens [fascines] and Cut off Both Capt Cleg's feet by his ankles, Carried away ye Calf of Christopher Langlys Leg[,] Nathaniel marsh Both his Legs Broke off, Robert townsend the pin Bone of his Knee & Shin Carried away, James union one Leg by his Knee; the Capt & Nathaniel Marsh Died after having their Legs cut off."[39] The Royal Artillery Officer killed was actually Captain-Lieutenant Samuel Glegg.[40] Two other artillerymen and one provincial were also killed, with another three provincials critically wounded. Regardless of what Colonel Haviland's precise intentions had been, this proved to be an expensive method of acquiring intelligence on French capabilities and intentions.

The British wounded were evacuated to a small island in the middle of the river approximately three miles to the south of their landing, earning this island the permanent name of Île de l'Hôpital (Hospital Island).[41] British supplies were also stockpiled on this island. Lieutenant Bradbury of the Massachusetts provincials was engaged in this duty: "ordord to Carry our Battoes Down to an Island 3 miles off and Land our provision & take 3 Days alowance."[42] The island was well suited for this purpose. Being in the middle of the river, it would be entirely safe from any French or Indian raiding parties, and the sick and injured could easily be transported there by the many available British vessels. This would also prevent or slow the spread of infectious diseases by isolating any sick soldiers from the healthy ones in the encampment.

August 18 continued much the same as the previous day, with the British improving their encampment and working on their logistical support. They continued to build roads between their beachhead and the batteries, and they constructed the batteries on the shoreline. Colonel Haviland recorded in his journal for this date: "1,000 men with twelve Carpenters, Officers in Proportion Ordered with Captain Williams to make a road for the Artillery, Redoubts ordered to be erected on the right and left of the bay to cover the boats." French resistance continued to be relatively light, suggesting that the French were deliberately sparing their ammunition for the moment when the British revealed their batteries. The location of the British camp, screened by Pointe Hillman and the heavy woods on the eastern side of the river, prevented the French from identifying targets for their artillery. The making of fascines continued unabated. Captain Jenks remembered of this date: "In the morning was orderd out to cover a party of fashine makers in the woods, about ½ mile from the breast work."[43] Captain Bayley, who was still working on the roads necessary to permit the heavy cannon to be moved into the battery positions, recorded: "Continued clearing the road, began our batteries which were within 400 yards of the French, who fired smartly on us, but without effect."[44] Lieutenant Frost was assigned to the batteries to be directed against the French island and was in perfect position to observe the poor French firing: "I was on fatigue about the battery. Just before night the French Fired three Shot at us ware we were at work. The first was very high. Cut off the trees. The next were Very Low."[45] Sergeant Holden observed: "[French] Fired Several Cannon at the men at woke opposite the fort, But to

Little Purpose. . . . Began to build our Battries for Bumb [bombs] & Cannon.[46] Lieutenant Bradbury "built a Bridg almost opposite the fort" over the Faddentown Stream. The weather that day was rainy, Lieutenant Bradbury complained: "Raney weather and nothing to Shelter us But a few bushes[.] the water and mud half Leg deep."[47]

On August 19 and 20, Colonel Haviland and his soldiers continued their labor as they had the two previous days. The major event was the arrival of a French deserter from the fort at first light on August 20, although precisely how he escaped from the island is unfortunately not documented. Sergeant Holden reported: "A Disartar came from the french and Resin'd himself to our guard this morning about Day brake. He gives us an account that there is about 1500 men in the fort & that they are Short of Ammonission & have but Nine Peaces of cannon in the fort."[48] Lieutenant Bradbury was present on piquet duty when the deserter arrived: "This morning as our guard was Comeing in there came a french Deserter & Deliverd himself to Captain Butterfield Who sent him Directly to the generall."[49] A major effort throughout these days continued to be the manufacture of fascines. The General Orders stated: "As [all that] is wanting to Compleat Our Batteries but fascines it is Expected that Every Man that Can be spared is Emediately Set About them tho they may not be so Good fascions Makers they may assist in bring back wood [to] those Making them."[50]

The weather remained wet on both days, raining "prety much" at times.[51] Lieutenant Bradbury grumbled: "unsettled weather & Rain" and later "had a very uncomfitable Night as it rained very fast the chief of the time."[52] On this date, a breastwork extending across the length of the shoreline opposite the French fort and connecting the British firing batteries was built to provide some additional cover against the intensifying French cannon fire. Lieutenant Bradbury recorded for August 20: "2 Shots from the fort this Day which cut several trees over our heads but Did no Damage." On August 21 he wrote: "This day all the officers in Camp were obliged to turne out to Build a Breastwork to Keep off the Cannon Ball which came from the fort as we are very Near the fort; one man wounded from the fort to-day; 3 or 4 more this afternoon—one of Capt Fellows Serjeants Named Frost had his arm Shot off—fired Briskly from the fort as our Batteries that were not finished."[53] With the French fire on this day becoming increasingly aggressive, Colonel Haviland took measures to ensure that the French could not launch an effective sortie from the fort. In his General Orders on August 21, he instructed: "One Company of Light Infantry or Grenadiers to be Posted . . . by the Battery at Sun Set & to Post Sentry Near the Edge of the Warter untill Near Sun Rise & then the whole to Return to Camp."[54]

The French gunnery proved to be extremely poor. Although the French commander Bougainville would later enjoy a distinguished career, the ineffective artillery fire suggests a serious flaw on the part of Bougainville and the French leadership, as well as the French artillerymen. The French had been at work constructing Île aux Noix for a full year. There were limited locations where the British could establish artillery batteries capable of engaging Île aux Noix. The location of Sturgeon Cove virtually dictated that any British siege would have to be conducted from the eastern bank of the Richelieu River. A resolute and intelligent commander, and any competent artillery officer, should have surveyed the precise range from every cannon on Île aux Noix to the likely British cannon positions. They should have performed ranging shots and prepared the equivalent of modern range cards. Then the French cannon would have been capable of delivering accurate fire on demand, even during hours of darkness when most of the construction for a siege was taking place. For whatever reason, the French failed to perform this elementary preparation. Most likely a shortage of ammunition was the primary contributing factor. Yet even with limitations of ammunition, expending a limited number of rounds to improve accuracy when under attack would have been well warranted.

Ord's artillery batteries were constructed to standard designs that had been taught in military engineering schools in Europe for decades, as permanent batteries and siege batteries were a routine and recurring aspect of eighteenth-century warfare.[55] There were no differences between the siege batteries that Haviland was constructing and any siege battery constructed in North American or Europe at the time. As with other military fortifications, a large number of military engineering treatises provided guidelines and standardized designs for such artillery batteries. These artillery batteries were the single most important aspect of a siege, and British success relied on their design, construction, and employment. In fact, if the batteries were not properly constructed, artillery could not be effectively employed, and the batteries would be vulnerable to destruction by the French guns. They were the most complex, time-consuming and demanding of any construction necessary for the success of a siege. Accordingly, the design and construction of artillery batteries is worthy of a comprehensive analysis.

Ozanam's *A Treatise of Fortifications* stated that twelve feet be maintained between cannon in a battery: "Thus for four pieces of cannon, the breadth of the battery must be about 48 feet." He continued: "The depth of a battery is always 30 feet or thereabouts, 15 feet for the gun, 15 feet for recoil." Ozanam also noted that the parapet covering the cannon should be six feet high, and the embrasures three feet high, "that the enemy may not see what is done in the batteries." Regarding the flooring of the battery, he stated: "The floor or bed of the battery must be made of good oaken planks, nailed across beams, to hinder the wheels of the carriages from sinking into the ground, and that this floor or platform must incline a little, as about one foot . . . to check the recoiling of the pieces."[56]

Extremely detailed specifications for artillery batteries were provided by an experienced Saxon military engineer in 1727 in *The Field Engineer*, translated into English in 1769 by Captain J. G. Tielke. This work assigned two different sizes to artillery batteries, depending on the poundage or caliber of the artillery pieces. For battalion field pieces (3- or 6-pounders), each cannon required a platform sixteen feet in length and six to eight feet in breadth. For larger cannon (12-, 18-, or 24-pounders), each artillery piece required a platform twenty-four feet in length and ten feet in breadth. Tielke further noted: "If the cannon are to be occasionally fired in an oblique direction, the platforms must be broader behind than in front. In general, a difference of four or six feet is fully sufficient," and "In all batteries there should be a small banquette [firing step] on each side of the embrasures, that the men who are employed at the guns may be able to see the effect of their fire." Captain Tielke also provided specifics regarding the construction of the floors and foundations of artillery batteries. He stated that a simple firing platform should consist of three planks eight or nine feet in length, leveled, on which the floor of the platform would be mounted. Tielke wrote that the planks could rest on strong wooden pickets, two to four feet in length. "In either case, pickets should be driven down on each side, for the purpose of fixing them in their proper places." He again distinguished between smaller and heavier artillery pieces: "If the cannon should be very heavy, two strong beams may be buried in the earth." Finally, he provided a third, more substantial method of construction when sufficient time and materials were available. The gun platform should be carefully leveled, "Set three or four beams or sleepers into the earth . . . and then add a covering of boards—fastened either with nails or wooden pegs."[57]

A course of instruction on artillery presented at the Royal Military Academy at Woolwich, London shortly after the American Revolution provided two detailed plans for the platform of an artillery battery.[58] Although not accompanied by any narrative, these two plans (provided below) clearly indicated the supports to the joists (also sometimes referred to as the "sleepers"), the joists that ran perpendicular to the parapets, and the boards that comprised the floor of the firing platform that were laid parallel to the parapet, such as were described by Ozanam and Tielke. Recent archaeological explorations at Fort Ticonderoga revealed a French constructed artillery platform atop the northeast bastion of the fort that was nearly identical to these various specifications and designs.

The batteries that Colonel Haviland was having built on the eastern bank of the Richelieu River directly across the channel from Île aux Noix were constructed to these precise specifications. Had they been constructed differently, the heaviest French cannon would have knocked them to pieces before the British gunners could ever bring their own artillery into play. And this required hard labor on the part of the American provincials, living in the mud and swamps along the river for the better part of two weeks.

Captain Jenks provided a glimpse of the considerable amount of effort that had to go into this effort: "Thursday 21st August To day I am ordred to assist the engineer; I have a party of 150 men, 2 subs [subaltern officers], 4 sergts in carrying timber to the batterys; there is 800 of the provincials of us on fatigue in building batterys to day."[59] Demonstrating the considerable efforts that a siege demanded, this working party engaged a full quarter of the army's strength for this day.

With the construction of the artillery batteries proceeding well along, although according to Lieutenant Bradbury "our Batteries ware not finished," the road and bridge connecting the landing place and the batteries had been completed, and thus the time to land the artillery from the larger vessels of the fleet was at hand.[60] Sergeant Holden recorded for August 21: "Landed Part of our Artillery." Movement of Ord's bulky and heavy artillery, and final preparations at readying the batteries, continued though August 22. Private Lemuel Wood wrote

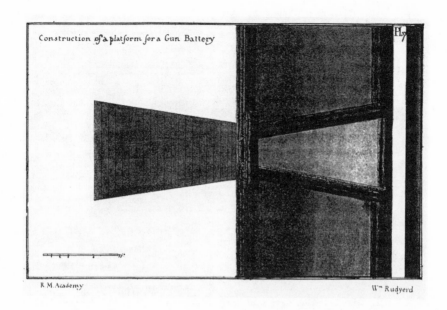

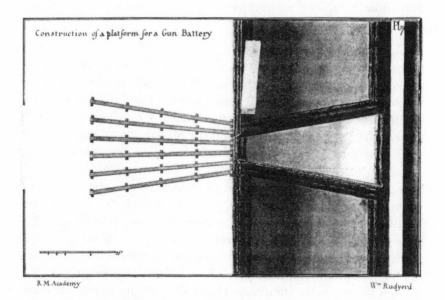

Artillery platform design from Rudyerd, *Course of Artillery* (1793).

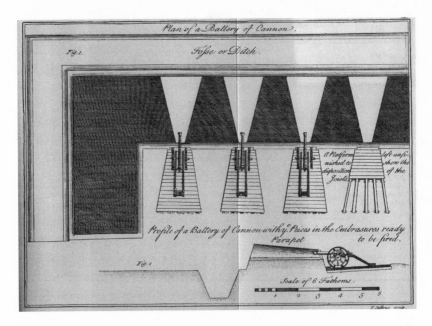

Illustration to accompany artillery battery description, from LeBlond, *A Treatise on Artillery.*

in his journal: "to Day they was all hands a getting up the Cannon on the shoer and to Day the begun a Battre Calld the Royal Battree where they are to Place the Royals Cold the Cowhorns and to Day the french was very still[,] fird none only a few Poping shots."[61] Captain Jenks, actually working on the batteries, was impressed by their construction: "We have got a fine breast work, both in front & rear, & have cut all the trees & cleard them out of our camp to prevent our being hurt by the limbs falling that are shot off by the enemys cannon."[62] This observation by Captain Jenks is important because it shows that the French gunners must have been either poorly trained or badly out of practice due to lack of ammunition. Many provincial soldiers reported that the French consistently fired too high. Captain Jenks also carefully monitored the progress of the cannon as they were transported from the landing to the batteries: "We have landed all our morters & got them up to the bomb-battery & are gitting the cannon on shore & drawing them to the batterys & hope to have three batterys opened by night."[63]

A minor incident occurred on August 22 that revealed how Colonel Haviland had to gather intelligence on the activities and locations of the other two British columns under Murray and Amherst. Because of the distances involved, communications were simply unfeasible between the three detachments. Even if messages could have been transmitted, the information would have been hopelessly out of date by the time it arrived. Rogers' Rangers, who were actively scouting well north of Île aux Noix employing canoes they had carried around the island, captured five French prisoners. Captain Bayley provided an account of the incident that appears to be both accurate and comprehensive, suggesting that he must have been involved in the receipt and transfer of the prisoners: "Took 5 prisoners who informed us that General Amherst was at isle La Galloa [La Gallette on the Saint Lawrence River] last Tuesdays night [Tuesday, August 12ᵗʰ] & was besieging that place, which lies on the river about 80 miles above Montreal & Gen. Murray was at the mouth of the river Sorrel, which is the river we are on, about 50 miles from us & about the same distance from Montreal."[64]

Lieutenant Bradbury reported, somewhat inaccurately: "major Rogers got 3 french prisoners Last night which gave account that general Amherst was near."[65] Sergeant Holden also recorded the incident, although he was more interested in the financial reward that the Rangers had received for their achievement: "3 French Prisoners was broᵗ in that was taken Between Sᵗ Johns & Montreal, for which the men that Took them had 50 Guineas Reward the Party Consisted of a Serjᵗ & 6 men."[66] Lieutenant Bradbury also focused on the reward offered the Ranger party: "Jonathan Door went out with 8 of the light infantry and in 4 days brought in three persons for which Col. Haverlin gave him 32 dollars, besides other things; those that went out with him 8 dollars each. These prisoners say General Amherst is within 50 miles of Moreal [Montreal]." Lieutenant Bradbury also documented the weather for August 24, which continued miserable for the soldiers engaged in the siege from both armies: "Rainy, cold and uncomfortable weather."[67]

Finally, on the afternoon of August 25, the batteries were unleashed with a roar. According to Lieutenant Frost, "About three of clock we open'd ouer Batery, and held on Fireing all night."[68] Captain Bayley provided a somewhat more expansive rendition: "At 3 o'clock the signal was given at which our cannon & mortars, royals & cohorns, consisting of about 30, fired five rounds successively with good effect, beating down all before them, continued all the afternoon & night."[69] Private Lemuel Wood was quite impressed

with the barrage unleashed by Ord's gunners that day: "this morning the Reglauers went to halling the Cannon and first they Placed
the Morters at the Bum [bomb] Battree 4 morters the 2 13 Inch ones
one on the Right and the other on the Left and then the 24 Pounders
[cannon] and Placed them all and on the Right they Placed the Royals
[5 ½" mortars] and at 3 o'Clock the Battree was all opned first the
middle one then the Bum battreee and then the Royall Battre and
we Cept a Continuall fire all the time of our Side and att nite we
threw Bumbs all the time Cannon Ball."[70] Captain Jenks similarly
recounted: "About 3 oclock P.M. all our batterys was opened & gave
the French a fine salute, which Monsieurs did not return; the artelery kept playing constantly & did great execution."[71]

Private Wood's diary reveals that there were three separate batteries: a mortar battery on the left (south), referred to as the "Bomb
Battery," which contained two thirteen-inch mortars; a conventional cannon battery in the center, which contained a number of
24-pounders, most likely the six carried up the lake in the *Ligonier*
Radeau; and on the right, the "Royal Battery," another mortar battery that employed an unspecified number of five-and-a-half-inch
Royal mortars. Lieutenant Bradbury provided dimensions for one
of the batteries, most likely the one that he built himself: "One of
the Batterys 60 feet long & 16 wide is now fit to play on the fort."[72]
A battery of sixty feet in length would have been entirely consistent
with the center battery that employed six 24-pounder cannon, as
described in the military engineering treatises.

As soon as these three batteries were in play, they rapidly began
battering the French works and keeping the French defenders' heads
down. The Chevalier Johnstone recorded the devastation that these
batteries unleashed: "They erected five batteries on the south (east)
side of the river, with a bomb battery, which rendered our trenches
useless, as they had a sight of us everywhere, back, face and side-
ways, and so near us that at the south staccado they killed several
of our soldiers by their musket shots. The sandy ground protected
us from the effect of their shells, which they threw upon us in great
numbers, with a continual fire from their gun batteries."[73]

Under the covering fire of the first three British batteries, another
battery was actively under construction, somewhat farther to the
north and closer to the French works. This was in accordance with
conventional siege procedures that called for advanced batteries to
be opened to cause additional devastation to the enemy's works

under cover of the first set of batteries.[74] Captain Jenks observed of this construction as early as August 22: "This morning we are clearing a road through our camp to draw cannon across below the enemys fort, to erect a battery on a point of land in order to cut off all communications between them & St. Johns."[75] Captain Bayley recorded on Sun., August 24: "Began a new Battery within musket shot of the French."[76] All this was done under continuously miserable weather, Sergeant Holden writing at the end of his entry for this date, "this was a Lowry wet Day."[77]

In addition to beginning the construction of a more effective battery, Haviland also instructed that efforts be made to sever the boom on the eastern channel so that his armed vessels could operate north of the island. The American provincials attempted to cut the obstacle, but the French defenders responded with heavy gunfire, Captain Bayley recalling: "The French fired smartly upon us."[78] Captain Jenks was not directly involved in the operation, but he was close enough to monitor its progress: "I had no sleep last night, for our people was cutting away the boom & the enemy would fire volleys of small arms on them & then our battery would return it with grape shot & the morters were kept going all night, which made it seem that the elements was all fire & smoak."[79]

Sergeant Holden remembered: "Made a Trial Last night to Cut away the Boam that the french had fixd across the Lake from the fort to the Est [east] Shore to Prevent our Shipping going Past the fort."[80] Lieutenant Frost documented the intensity of the ensuing fighting: "This is the Lord's Day, and a most Terebal Day it is In Stead of going to Church, nothing but the Roaring of Cannons and morters; the alarms of war and a Crie for human Blood."[81] Lieutenant Bradbury reported that in conjunction with this effort the batteries "continued firing till after sunset, and then ceased till one o'clock at night when our men endeavored to cut away the Boom. The enemy fired with small arms very smart which caused all our artillery to play on them, which soon stilled them. We continued playing till day. . . .Boom partly cut off."[82] Lieutenant Bradbury was being rather optimistic, as the boom was never removed, because of the intensity of the French fire. Captain Bayley provided a more balanced account: "We did not complete cutting the boom, it being very strong . . . They defended it in the best manner, being sensible that if we got below them they could not go off, but must fall into our hands."[83]

In 1979, archaeologists working from Parks Canada's Fort Lennox Historical Site on Île aux Noix located a burned bateau resting on the bottom of the river, about fifty yards to the east of the island. While it was initially thought to be a commercial boat from the nineteenth century, a closer examination revealed that this bateau had been burned and sunk. The discovery of military artifacts in association with the vessel confirmed that it was a relic of the 1760 siege. The archaeologists proposed that the bateau was part of the small French fleet burned and sunk in conjunction with Rogers' action against the French vessels on the night of August 24.[84] The archaeologists also tentatively identified the bateau as "French," although they provided no evidence for this assertion. There would have been little if any difference between British and French bateaux in design, construction or materials. Rather than being a French bateau, most likely this was a British bateau that had been employed in the unsuccessful attempt to open the log-and-chain boom. To accomplish this, the provincials would have had to go out on the river with saws, axes, and mauls to dismember the boom, and they almost certainly employed bateaux. The smaller canoes would have been better suited to this work, but the few available canoes were committed to supporting the ranger deep reconnaissance patrols operating to the north. One 4-pounder and one 6-pounder cannon ball, two small cast iron projectiles from grapeshot or canister rounds, fragments from a mortar bomb, and three lead musket balls were found in close association with the burned bateau. Rather than being fired from British cannon as the archaeologists surmised, it is much more likely that these projectiles were fired by the French in their successful defense of the boom. The presence of the 4-pounder cannon ball confirms this theory, as the British employed no cannon of this size in their batteries. Additionally, the use of grapeshot would be consistent with the French firing artillery to engage soldiers in boats, exposed on the river as they remained stationary while they attempted to cut through the boom with hand tools. Interestingly, the lead musket balls "have traces of their mould seam as well as of the channel through which lead was poured into the mould." British musket balls were manufactured in England and then shipped in boxes across the North America, and were nearly always perfectly smooth. Musket balls cast by the American provincials, however, would have had these characteristics. The musket balls had a diameter of eighteen millimeters, or .71 caliber, too large for French muskets. They are, in fact, the standard caliber for British Long Land Pattern muskets. These musket balls are almost certainly American, home manufactured, and were most likely carried by the soldiers onboard the bateau and lost when it had to be abandoned. Once damaged, afire, and abandoned, the bateau: "would have drifted with the south-north current, gradually burning and sinking several hundred meters north." This was precisely where it was located nearly 220 years later.

Since the boom remained intact, Colonel Haviland instructed Lieutenant Colonel Darby and Major Rogers with their advanced guard to launch an attack to seize the small French flotilla that remained in support of Île aux Noix.[85] These vessels, which included the large schooner *La Vigilante*, the sloop *Waggon*, and several smaller ships, were located immediately north of the island. With their broadsides supporting the two substantial log and iron booms across the channel of the Richelieu River, they denied the British freedom of maneuver north of the island. The plan that Darby and Rogers formulated was for the grenadiers and light infantrymen to drag two five-and-a-half-inch Royal howitzers and one 6-pounder cannon into position to engage the French vessels. Under cover of their gunfire, a determined party of rangers would then take to the water, swarm onboard, and seize the ships. It was an audacious plan, exactly the sort that would appeal to the rangers, grenadiers, and light infantrymen.

With a fortuitous westerly wind, a key factor in the timing of the attack, Darby and Rogers swiftly put their plans into execution in the late evening hours of August 24. Rogers described his force as two companies of regulars under Darby, two companies of his own Rogers' Rangers, and the stalwart company of Stockbridge Indians. Major Rogers left a detailed account of the operation:

> We carried with us two howitzers and one six-pounder and silently conveying them along thro' the trees, brought them opposite the vessels, and began a brisk fire upon them, before they were in the least apprised of our design, and by good fortune, the first shot from the six-pounder cut the cable of the great rideau, and the wind being west, blew her to the east-shore, where we were, and the other vessels weighed anchor and made for St. John's, but got all aground, in turning a point about two miles below the fort. I was, by Col. Darby, ordered down to the east-shore with my Rangers,

and crossed a river about thirty yards wide [the Rivière du Sud], which falls into Lake Champlain from the east. I soon got opposite the vessels, and, by firing from shore, gave an opportunity to some of my party to swim on board with their tomahawks, and took one of the vessels; in the mean time Col. Darby had got on board the rideau, and had her manned, and took the other two; of which success he immediately acquainted Col. Haviland, who sent down a sufficient number of men to take charge and man the vessels.[86]

The alert provincials manning the artillery batteries and encampment observed the rangers going in. Captain Jenks, who marched with his Massachusetts provincials to support the advanced guard at the onset of the action, provide a detailed account of the raid's aftermath:

About 9 oclock we heard a great number of small arms fireing down the lake side & sum cannon. Imediately all the pequits [piquets] was turnd out to assist Major Rogers, who it seems had engaged the French vessels. . . . In a few minutes a regular officer brought us the joyfull news that the French great redow, thir brigg & sloop had struck to us; we then marcht down to the point of land where the cannon was & saw the vessells al laying there under English coulours. We have not lost a man in this affair, altho the action was very sharp & no batery for the cannon to lay behind. Monsuirs has no vessel now on the lake except a row galley & battoes. We have killd a field officer of their who was on board & have taken their commodore & about 20 men prisoners.[87]

Lieutenant Bradbury specifically recalled "the wind drove her toward our shore, the rangers kept up such a fire on them after shooting the Captain's head off, the others were glad to surrender on any terms."[88] Captain Jenks' account is particularly valuable, as he documents that the three British guns fired from "the point of land," indicating that they were positioned on the modern Pointe du Gouvernement [Government Point] south of the junction of the Rivière du Sud (South River) with the Richelieu River. This aggressive assault swept all the major French vessels from the Richelieu River north of Île aux Noix, and dealt the French defense of the island a major blow.

With this action, Rogers and Darby sealed the fate of Île aux Noix. The British now had three artillery pieces positioned in such a manner that they entirely enfiladed the island's defenses, and could sweep the island across its length from north to south. Once the British got the captured French ships and their own into operation on the river north of the island, they would possess uncontested superiority on the river, and could maneuver at will around the island. The French position had suddenly, and irrevocably, been rendered untenable.

Acting swiftly, the British put their own men aboard the vessels and began operating them. On the evening of August 25 Captain Jenks observed: "we met our comodore & a large party of sailors going down to man our new fleet."[89] In addition to sailors from the vessels of the flotilla, a large number of American provincials were also drafted to man the captured ships. Sergeant Holden recorded on the morning of August 26: "Orders for a Number of men to go on bord the Prize Vassals Consisting of 165 men officers included to go Volunteires from the Proventials."[90]

By August 26 the British batteries were pounding the French defenses. On this date the newest battery, located closer to the French fort and to the north of the other batteries, lent its firepower to the barrage. This brought a total of five British batteries pummeling the French works at point-blank range across the river. Lieutenant Bradbury commanded the guard detachment at the Royal Battery from midnight on August 26 to midnight on August 27. It consisted of himself, one subaltern officer (an Ensign Taylor), and 34 rank and file. During that twenty-four-hour tour of duty he kept careful count and recorded that "they threw 300 shells in the fort."[91] This was an astonishing and brutal application of firepower from only one of Haviland's five batteries, and it shocked and stunned the French defenders. The Chevalier Johnstone on the island recalled being under "a most violent cannonade, without a moment's interruption."[92] The soldiers of both nations continued to suffer as the unseasonably cold and rainy weather continued, with Lieutenant Bradbury documenting "fowl weather."[93]

The heavy bombardment continued on August 27, and on this date the French managed to get in an extremely lucky shot. It passed through the embrasure of the British batteries and placed a shell directly into one of the magazines. The ammunition went up with a thundering roar as Lieutenant Bradbury watched in horror: "An unlucky shot from the enemy set our magazine on fire which blew one provincial 40 feet in the air and burned his life out, killed one regular wounded others."[94] Lieutenant Frost told a similar tale:

"And about two of Clock in the afternoon met with a bad axident: we had ouer magaezien of one battery blown up by means of the French fireing hot shot. We lost six men."[95] Sergeant Holden, in a position to observe the ensuing inferno, recorded: "A Ball from the Enemy Came through one of our Amberzoers [embrasures] & into a Magazean Where was many Shells & Cartridges & Sat it on fire and Blew it up Broake about 20 Shells which Killed 2 men & wounded 2 more very bad, one of those that was killed Belonged to the Massachusetts, the other to the 17th Regt. The french Played very Smartly with their Cannon all this day."[96] Captain Jenks was farther away and not able to directly observe the detonation: "About 3 oclock PM. We was alarmd by a sudden explosion. At first we thought that the enemy had opened a larg battery, but we was soon informd that a number of our shells & sum powder at the 12 gun battery took fire by sum accident unknown; about 30 shells burst by this means & 3 men killd out right & several others wounded. The enemy have kept a very smart fire all day, but done no damage worth notice."[97]

Captain Jenks recounted a remarkable incident that took place on this date, during the heavy exchange of artillery fire between the French and British: "A soldier of mine going with a dollar in his hand to the sutlers & a nine pound shot strake his hand, which only grazed the skin, but lost of his dollar."[98] Apparently this incident became a camp rumor in relatively short order, as Lieutenant Bradbury reported it somewhat differently: "A man in the siege was going along to the sutlers with a dollar in his hand, a cannon ball came and struck the dollar away and cut his fingers off."[99]

By this point the French situation was truly becoming desperate, the devastating British cannon fire would shortly render the island untenable, if in fact it had not already done so. With the loss of naval supremacy north of the island, any retreat would have to be effected nearly immediately. As soon as the British got their fleet into operation north of the island, they would make such an effort impossible. The Chevalier Johnstone, a confidant of Bougainville's, remembered that "it was a very critical conjuncture, having only two day's provision for the garrison, which had subsisted until the arrival of the English troops by means of fishing-nets . . . with seven or eight oxen which had been kept as a reserve and killed by the enemy's cannon." A messenger arrived at this critical juncture with letters from Governor de Vaudreuil and General de Lévis. Johnstone described their contents: "M. de Vaudreuil's letter contained a permission to M. de Bougainville to capitulate or retire from the island if it was possible. M. de Lévis' letter was a positive order to defend that post to the last extremity. De Bougainville, notwithstanding his genius, good sense and learning, with personal courage, and who lacked only taste for the study of the art of war to distinguish himself, was nevertheless put to a nonplus how to act from the contradictory letters he received."[100] Johnstone suggested to Bougainville that the garrison was sorely needed at Montreal, and that they should retreat while they still had the opportunity. Bougainville realized that Johnstone was correct, that the fortress of Îsle aux Noix could not hope to hold out much longer in any event. Retreat was only possible within a very short period, and every French soldier would shortly be needed for the defense of Montreal and the final battle for Canada. Accordingly, he ordered a withdrawal on the evening of August 27, to be conducted under cover of darkness.

To hide their preparations for withdrawal, the French increased their fire to a crescendo, expending their remaining ammunition. Bougainville "ordered M. le Borgne, an officer in the colonial troops [French marines], to remain on the island with a detachment of forty men, to keep up a smart fire from our battery, which consisted of seven or eight pieces of cannon, during the time we were employed in passing the river, in order to hinder the English from hearing us in our operations, and to continue firing whilst ammunition lasted, and to conceal our retreat as long as it was possible to do so."[101] Johnstone documented the performance of the French retrograde maneuver under cover of darkness: "We began to cross the river in two lighters, with some small boats, about ten at night. They plied continually to and fro until midnight, when all had crossed the river without the enemy perceiving or even suspecting our operation. All was executed without the least noise, disorder or confusion. "[102]

Some British soldiers clearly suspected that the French were contemplating a withdrawal. Captain Jenks wrote his journal an entry for August 27 that proved remarkably prescient: "The enemy have kept a very smart fire all day, but done us no damage worth notice. All this we take as their last words."[103] Lieutenant John Bradbury was on piquet duty at the batteries as the realization came that the French were gone. He made no mention of any indication that the French were embarking, demonstrating that the French withdrawal was as well performed as Johnstone had indicated.

Bradbury learned about the French retreat when a number of deserters came in: "Aug. 27. At two o'clock this night, there came a French deserter which gave an account that the French had left the island; at four o'clock there came 15 or 20 more which gave the same account. [August] 28. This morning the regulars and rangers took possession of the island & fort."[104] Sergeant Holden verified the numbers of the French defenders that surrendered: "About 20 french Regulars Came & Resin'd themselves."[105] The Chevalier Johnstone recorded that: "We had eighty men killed or wounded during the siege."[106] British casualties were inconsequential.

Colonel Haviland and his column had effectively swept aside the only substantial French defense between Crown Point and Montreal. They had done this in superb fashion, in less than two weeks of actual operations. The greatest obstacle that Haviland's column had to face was the adverse weather conditions on the mercurial Lake Champlain. The weather had briefly delayed his departure from Fort Crown Point and had substantially hindered his advance. The British fleet had required a full five days to sail the short distance down the lake, a mere ninety-five miles, and this voyage had been made under difficult circumstances.

Once he performed the amphibious landing on October 16, Col. Haviland still faced substantial tactical challenges. The French position at Île aux Noix was exceptionally well sited, strongly fortified, and amply supplied with artillery. The installation of the two booms entirely negated Haviland's ability to exploit his naval strength on the Richelieu River. The water barrier of the two channels of the Richelieu River made it impossible for the British artillery to establish breaching batteries directly underneath the walls of the fort, and made an infantry assault on the works decidedly difficult. Because of the pair of sturdy log booms, an amphibious assault was only feasible on the most heavily defended southern portion of the island.

Once Haviland was ashore, he moved swiftly to establish an effective siege. His first batteries opened fire on August 25, nine days after his landing. This was a significant accomplishment given the immense quantity of ordnance, rations, and matériel that had to be landed and then manhandled into position. The terrain on the eastern side of the river was boggy and traversed by numerous small streams. Arduous labor was necessary to construct defensive lines, artillery batteries, and magazines. Haviland's tactical maneuvers once his batteries opened up were outstanding. By sending his rangers and light infantry farther to the north, he enfiladed the French position. He also seized French vessels that could operate north of the island. Almost simultaneously he severed the log boom on the right channel of the Richelieu, opening up the river to his own vessels. After less than seventy-two hours of this operation, the French abandoned the island and retreated to Montreal. It had been, by any conceivable standards, an exceptionally well-executed siege. European masters of siege craft such as Vauban and Coehorn would have been impressed.

Bougainville's plan had been to retreat to Saint-Jean under cover of darkness, and then perform a cross-country march to Longueuil across the Saint Lawrence River from Montreal. From Longueuil, his force could readily reinforce the principal French army remaining in Montreal.[107] In the darkness, his local Canadian guides became confused and led the French army astray for no less than twelve hours. It was an absolutely miserable march, the Chevalier Johnstone remembered: "having marched . . . from midnight until twelve at noon, over fens, swamps, mosses, and sinking often up to the waist in marshy ground, without reposing or halting one minute. Instead of being near Montreal, as we imagined, we were thunderstruck on finding ourselves . . . to be only at the distance of half a league from Isle aux Noix. Our guide . . . had caused us to turn round continually for twelve hours without advancing! My strength was so entirely spent, that it was with great difficulty I could draw one leg after the other."[108] Eventually things were made right by the French leadership, and the exhausted soldiers marched through Saint-Jean to Longueuil over the next several days.

As Bougainville's army waited to be transported across the Saint Lawrence River to Montreal, it was devastated by desertion. Every single one of the Indians abandoned the force. Nearly all of the Canadian militia fled the cause to return to their homes. The French regulars, many of whom had married Canadian women, defected in large numbers.[109] Only a few hundred soldiers of Bougainville's command ever reached Montreal.

The withdrawal from the strong entrenchments at Île aux Noix, and the realization that with this post abandoned the next (and last) French stand would have to be made at Montreal, caused a catastrophic failure of French and Canadian morale. Haviland's successful siege effectively collapsed the southern French defense of Canada.

On the morning of August 29, the British regulars occupied Île aux Noix. With the exception of a few appointed to become the permanent garrison of the island, the American provincials were not permitted to enter the fort. This engendered some animosity on the part of the colonial soldiers, who felt that they had performed most of the heavy labor and withstood the dangers of the siege. Private Lemuel Wood complained bitterly: "our men had not the Liberty of going into it."[110] Lieutenant John Frost became a member of the garrison detachment, along with fifty of his soldiers. On the afternoon of that day he located a "house to Live in" along with his commanding officer Captain Wentworth. The young Lieutenant was not impressed with the island, and when he was relieved from this assignment early the next month he wrote: "Blessed be God that I am Releved from the Isle noix, where I Hop I Shant never bee aGain."[111]

The provincials, having barely caught their breath from the hard labor and dangers of the siege, were almost immediately engaged in preparations for a pursuit. Private Wood recalled: "all our men went to getting the Artillery on Board and they got it all Done that nite."[112] Lieutenant John Bradbury must have been very busy on August 29th, for he only had time to scribble in his journal: "The artillery all embarking on board, the vessels endeavored to proceed to St. John." Sergeant Holden was also engaged in this important activity: "Embark[d] all our artillery that was thought Necessary to Carry along with us."[113]

The French fortress on Île aux Noix had to be occupied, and the damage caused by the siege repaired, so that the fort could support a British garrison. Artillery had to be designated for this new British post, and moved across the river onto the island. The artillery, ammunition, tools, equipment, and rations landed to support the siege had to be repacked and re-embarked on the boats for transportation to Montreal, the anticipated site of the next siege. Finally, the siegeworks on the eastern shore of the river had to be leveled and filled in, to deny ready-made batteries to any resurgent French force.

The British advance toward Montreal appears not to have been particularly well organized, although heavy rains were largely to blame. Lieutenant Bradbury specifically recalled: "Fowl weather and everything in confusion."[114] On the morning of August 30 Haviland's column had planned to resume their advance down the Richelieu River, with Saint-Jean and Chambly their targets.[115] The bad weather delayed their departure, but Lieutenant Bradbury noted that he arrived at Saint-Jean to discover the French fort smoldering by 5 o'clock that day.[116]

The aggressive Major Rogers was responsible for the only combat that occurred during Haviland's pursuit of Bougainville. Haviland had issued Rogers with peeremptory orders "by no means to follow further than the fort [Fort Saint-Jean], nor run any risk of advancing further to Montreal." When Rogers discovered, however, that his rangers were on the heels of the French, he "was resolved to make his dance a little the merrier." Rogers deliberately disobeyed his explicit instructions and ordered his rangers and Stockbridge Mohican warriors to give chase. They quickly came upon the French rear guard and pursued them toward Montreal, inflicting a few casualties and seizing two prisoners.[117] The skirmish occurred approximately six miles west of Saint-Jean. The French rear guard escaped across the Rivíere L'Acadie and burned a bridge behind them, preventing Rogers pursuing any further.[118]

Haviland remained at Saint-Jean for three full days, not departing for Chambly until September 2.[119] The American soldiers were impressed by the rapids, Private Wood referring to them as "the falls."[120] More adverse weather visited the British who by now must have been heartily tired of the Canadian climate: "A very cold Storm of rain."[121] The British tarried at Chambly for several days. Lieutenant Bradbury marched directly from Saint-Jean to Longueil on the morning of September 8.[122] Private Woods likewise departed Chambly on the same date.

With his arrival in the settled portion of the Richelieu River valley, Colonel Haviland took measures to ensure that his army treated the new subjects of King George II with respect and dignity. This was a particular concern since many of his soldiers were New England Protestants who openly disdained the Catholic religion of the French and had a strong animosity to the Canadians who had raided their communities for decades. Haviland accordingly issued General Orders from "St. Johns" on Monday, September 1, 1760:

> As the Army is now going into the Inhabitant part of Country therefore Ordered that none of the Inhabitants are plundered or ill used on any pretence[.] Whoever are Detached, Disobeys these Orders, will be hanged. Milk, butter provisions or any thing else must [be] regularly paid for- this is done to Induce the Inahibitants

to stay in there Villages and good usage will prevent there men from Laying trouble for the Army. No Non Commission Officer or Soldier to be Suffered to pass the out Sentries and itt is Expected that the orders of this day Related to the Inhabitants are Read to the Men that they may not plead Ignorance.[123]

Haviland's orders seem to have had some positive results, and in any case the Canadian residents saw the writing on the wall. The Canadians hastened to not only express their allegiance to King George, but to provide transportation to the British army. Taking advantage of this, the British army had their baggage carried by the Canadians and reached Longueuil and La Prairie "Opisite against mount Real" by dark on September 8. Here, to their immense pleasure, they "had the news of mount reals Being Given up."[124]

CHAPTER 7

"I HAVE COME TO TAKE CANADA"

Amherst's Siege of Fort Lévis

The logistical heart of Amherst's western and central columns was Albany. This city had served as a base for British operations along both the Mohawk River and Hudson River–Lake Champlain corridors since 1755. Albany was well suited to serve such a function, as sailing vessels could navigate the Hudson River from New York City. The British army had been encamped in large number here since 1756, and by 1760 the city contained numerous regularly established quartermaster operations such as guardhouses, storehouses, magazines, stables, wagon yards, wood lots, docks, and shipyards.[1]

From Albany, the line of communication to Crown Point ran north up the Hudson River. It was necessary to portage around rapids at both Half Moon and Fort Miller, where minor fortifications and storehouses were established. Fort Edward, at the northern end of navigation on the Hudson River, served as a secondary logistical base. From Fort Edward a well-established road ran north to the southern end of Lake George, where Amherst had started a new fortification in 1759. Christened Fort George, it was intended to be a permanent stone fortification. Because of the subsequent success of Amherst's campaign that summer, however, work on this fort had been terminated as superfluous. Only the southwestern bastion and the grading of the planned fortification site had been completed. The gorge of the bastion had been closed to turn Fort George into a strong redoubt; and a small barracks, guardhouse, and storehouse had been constructed within the interior of the bastion-redoubt. The cleared, leveled ground around Fort George afforded a ready-made encampment. Smaller timber and earth redoubts such as Fort Gage had been constructed on high ground to the south of Lake George to help secure the encampment. A small fleet, including at least one radeaux and numerous whaleboats and bateaux, operated on Lake George to transport supplies. At the northern end of Lake George, the British had established a landing on the eastern side of the lake and had constructed a well-maintained portage road to a landing at the sawmill on the La Chute River. Here rudimentary defenses, including a blockhouse, had been constructed. Numerous bateaux based at the landing there transported all supplies by water down the La Chute River, then down Lake Champlain to Fort Crown Point, and eventually to the operations against Îsle aux Noix.

West from Albany, supplies and matériel were transported along the Mohawk River corridor. The Mohawk River entered the Hudson River north of Albany at Cohoes Falls, where a portage to the Mohawk was required. Water transportation was further interrupted by a mile-long portage over a single set of rapids, Little Falls, located approximately eighty miles west of Albany. The Mohawk River was then navigable for another sixty miles to the newly constructed Fort Stanwix (modern Rome). From Fort Stanwix a well-established road, christened the Great Carrying Place, led roughly six to eight miles west to Wood Creek, depending on water levels. Wood Creek was then navigable into the large Lake Oneida, for approximately forty miles west. At the western end of Lake Oneida, a small earthen and timber fortification titled Fort Brewerton guarded the eastern end of this portage. From Fort Brewerton water transportation could again be depended on, utilizing the Onondaga River (modern Oswego River), navigable except for major falls about twelve miles short of Lake Ontario, which had to be bypassed by another brief portage.

At the junction of the Oswego River and Lake Ontario, the British had constructed a fortified trading post as early as 1727. The British had continuously improved and expanded this establishment and in 1755 had erected two forts nearby supported by a small fleet. A French army had destroyed the British defenses and captured the garrison and vessels in August 1756. The British had returned in the summer of 1759 during their campaign against Fort Niagara. A strong detachment of the British army had constructed field fortifications there that summer. With the intention of establishing a permanent British presence, Brigadier General Gage had initiated construction of a strong timber and earth traditional fort, and had maintained a garrison throughout the winter of 1759–1760. The army under Amherst's direct supervision would begin their campaign from Gage's new Fort Ontario at Oswego.[2]

Captain Thomas Davies, "A west view of Oswego and Fort Ontario with General Amherst's camp at Lake Ontario in the year 1760." Courtesy of Library of Congress, Prints and Photographs Division, Washington, D.C.

Amherst first had to gather his army together. During the winter of 1759–1760, a large contingent of British regulars had remained in garrison at Albany and its environs, including the 1st Battalion, Royal Highland Regiment (42nd Foot) around Albany; the 2nd Battalion, Royal Highland Regiment (42nd Foot), also at Albany; Major General James Abercromby's (later Halkett's) 44th Regiment of Foot at Fort Niagara and on Mohawk and Oswego Rivers; Lieutenant General Thomas Murray's 46th Regiment of Foot at Fort Stanwix and along Mohawk River; Colonel James Adolphus Oughton's (late Howe's, late Prideaux's) 55th Regiment of Foot at and around New York City; Colonel Frederick Haldimand's 4th Battalion, The Royal American Regiment (60th Foot) at Fort Oswego and on Oswego River; Gage's Light Infantry Regiment (80th Foot) at Schenectady on the Mohawk River; and three New York Independent Companies at Albany.[3] An additional regiment, Montgomery's Highlanders (the 77th Foot), which was actually two battalions in strength, had initially been stationed around Albany. One of the battalions had been dispatched by Amherst to the Carolinas to deal with an Indian insurrection. Accordingly, only a single battalion of Montgomery's Highlanders was available to participate in Amherst's column against Montreal.

Considerable numbers of provincial forces were required to augment this force of British regulars.

Amherst started his efforts to raise provincial soldiers early in 1760, when he wrote to Governor Thomas Pownall of Massachusetts Bay Colony on February 21: "With his Majesty's Commands for the Reduction of all Canada, received last Night . . . You do forthwith Use your utmost Endeavours and Influence with the Council and Assembly of Your Province, to Induce them to Raise with all possible dispatch within Your Government, at least, as large a Body of Men as they did for the last Campaign, and even as many more as the Number of its Inhabitants may Allow."[4] Amherst wrote at the same time to the Governors of Connecticut, New Jersey, New Hampshire, and New York similarly requesting that they recruit regiments of provincials from their respective colonies. Amherst's letter seconded one that Secretary Pitt had sent from Whitehall on January 7 ordering the governors to "furnish a Body of several Thousand Men to join the King's Forces in those Parts, for some offensive operations against the Enemy."[5]

Amherst intended to send the Massachusetts, Rhode Island, and New Hampshire provincials to join Haviland moving down Lake Champlain. For his own column, he retained the New York and Connecticut provincials. There was insufficient time to raise provincials and transport them to Quebec, so Murray's column consisted entirely of British regulars, except for a few provincial rangers. A few sailors from New England operated ships on the Saint Lawrence River with Murray's column as well. Amherst also intended for his own column to be reinforced with large numbers of Iroquois warriors.

The recruitment of Indian allies was performed almost exclusively by Sir William Johnson through his relationship with the Mohawk Nation and the Iroquois Confederation, as he had done with considerable success in 1755, 1757, 1758, and 1759. Following the conclusion of the 1759 campaign, in which he had played a prominent role, Johnson returned for the winter to Fort Johnson, his home on the north bank of the Mohawk River. As early as February 23, Amherst had written to Johnson from his winter headquarters in New York City asking him to "use all Your Influence with the Several Tribes and Nations of Indians . . . to bring as many into the Field as You can possibly prevail on to Join His Majesty's Arms."[6] Johnson swiftly responded on March 7, requesting "the Cloathing,

Arms & other Necessarys I shall begin to provide as soon as I can for the Campaign for which purpose Your Excellency will please to grant me a Warrant for at Least five Thousand Pounds Sterling."[7] Amherst fulfilled Johnson's needs swiftly, on March 16, although he asked Johnson to use his own personal credit until Amherst's war chest had been replenished.[8]

Amherst met personally with Johnson in the Mohawk Valley for several days in May.[9] Johnson persuaded Amherst to visit one of the Oneida villages, where he spent time with several of the Native families and observed the daily routine of the village life, including prayer (many of the Oneidas were Christians), agricultural activities, and weaving cloth. Amherst appears to have both enjoyed and benefited from the visit, and in one case recorded with favor as he observed a family: "The father & mother appeared vastly fond of the little child & allways gave it some of everything we gave them."[10]

Historians have traditionally alleged that Amherst despised Indians, principally because of his actions during Pontiac's Rebellion, then three years in the future. The first to develop this thesis was Francis Parkman, who claimed that Amherst "treated them [the Indians] with indifference and neglect."[11] Within the past decade, Gregory Evans Dowd has reiterated that "Amherst . . . radiated contempt for the Native Americans."[12] Most recently, Colin G. Calloway has echoed: "Arrogant and ignorant of Indian ways . . . Amherst viewed an empire as something to be governed not negotiated and cultivated by giving gifts to Indians."[13] Yet, it is instructive that although Amherst is alleged to have despised Indians, he recorded a lengthy account of his 1760 visit to this village in his journal, appeared to be impressed by the Oneidas, and failed to make a single disparaging remark about them.[14]

At Amherst's request, through the spring and early summer, Johnson recruited Indians, primarily from the Iroquois Confederation. Two of Johnson's agents, Jelles Fonda and Colonel John Butler, personally visited the Oneida and Tuscarora nations of the Iroquois Confederation for this purpose in late June and early July 1760.[15] Sir William Johnson proved successful with his efforts. On August 2 Amherst wrote from his "Camp at Oswego" that: "I am glad to hear Your Indians are in so good a humour, ours here are likewise very quiet, and I can't Say but what they are much more so than I expected; they are upwards of 1,300, it is true that there are more than 600 Women & Children among them; but these are for the most part going home."[16] Johnson himself noted: "I yet was able to proceed from Oswego with upwards of 600 Warriors."[17]

Even such a simple matter as communicating between Fort Johnson on the Mohawk River and Amherst's winter headquarters in New York City using a well-established water transportation network required no less than a full week's transit time. Today this route is only a three-hour drive on the New York thruway. Amherst noted: "On Mon. [March 31] I was favored with Your Letter of the 24th by Your Secretary."[18] Communications between Fort Johnson and Fort Oswego were even more tenuous, particularly during winter when heavy snowfall could close the lines of communication for days at a time, though at any time of the year heavy rains or drought could substantially slow transit times.[19] Johnson wrote to Colonel Frederick Haldimand at Fort Oswego on May 30 that: "Your favour of the 19th I received the 26th in the Evening by one of your Serjants."[20] The last letter in his papers written from Fort Johnson was dated July 4, 1760, and shortly thereafter Johnson moved to Fort Ontario to join Amherst's army.[21]

Although Johnson had proven successful at gaining the support of Indian warriors, enlistment of the provincial soldiers proved to be slow and difficult. Neither Amherst nor Haviland, who both had to rely on the provincials for transportation, logistics, and heavy labor, could proceed until they had arrived. Captain Anthony Wheelock, a British commissary of prisoners observing provincial officers attempting to enlist soldiers in Massachusetts, reported to Amherst on June 8: "The apprehension of military Discipline, the Fatigues of the Service & also the Danger, are strong Objections with the Common People against enlisting, notwithstanding the Great Premium now give—cou'd they be taken on the Footing of Smiths, Carpenters, etc. I believe many wou'd come in." He continued: "But the Common people by the Experience of former Years are cunning enough to keep off enlisting at first & by that means if they enlist at all get greater Premiums & do less Duty by deferring their Enlisting to the last."[22] As a result of these recruitment problems, Amherst found himself seriously delayed. Lieutenant Colonel James Robertson of the Royal American Regiment grumbled to John Calcraft, a regimental agent back in England: "The provincial Troops this Year have been raised late, are very bad, worse than usual . . . they are sufficient to work our Boats and drive our Waggons, to fell Trees, and do the Works that in inhabited Countrys are performed by Peasants."[23] On June 21, Amherst echoed Robertson's concerns to Sir William Johnson: "I am getting every thing on as fast as the Arrival of the Provincial Troops would let me: I should have been glad to be Earlier, but I doubt not in the least but We shall have time Enough to Compleat the Intended Work of this Campaign."[24] On the same date Amherst was even more candid to Pitt: "The sloth of the Colonies in raising their troops & sending them to the rendezvous, made it impracticable for me to move the troops on so soon as I could have wished."[25]

Still, frustrating as their delayed arrival was to Amherst, slowly but surely the provincials reached Albany. They came not as a flood but as a trickle, in individual ships and by lone companies. As they reported at Albany, Amherst dispatched them either up the Mohawk or the Hudson, to safeguard and transport the precious but bulky supplies that had to arrive at Crown Point and Oswego before the expedition could proceed. Another reason for limiting the provincials' stay in Albany was also noticed by the observant Amherst: "June 9th. As most of the New York Troops are come in I ordered the First Regt to march tomorrow. They desert very fast."[26] Amherst carefully recorded the arrival and disposition of these provincials in his daily journal, for their presence and performance was a matter of monumental importance to him. Until the materials of Mars moved, no one would advance on Montreal.

Colonel Nathaniel Woodhull, who commanded the 3rd New York Regiment, provided a detailed account of the loads that his regiment transported up the Mohawk River: "I had in my regiment 52 bateaux, and about 800 barrels of provisions."[27] Woodhull's regiment arrived at Fort Oswego with twenty-seven officers and 458 rank and file, for a total strength of 485. Accordingly, each bateau carried nine men and sixteen barrels of provisions. Each barrel weighed approximately 233 pounds, although there was some variation depending on how well a barrel had been packed. There was also a difference in weight between barrels containing flour, pork or beef. Assuming an average weight of two hundred pounds per soldier, including his musket, clothing, accouterments, and knapsack, each bateau thus carried 1,800 pounds of soldiers and 3,728 pounds of provisions, for a total of 5,528 pounds.

The total strength that Amherst personally commanded from the garrison of Albany for the movement down the Saint Lawrence River to Montreal consisted of nearly 11,000 soldiers. The core of his column comprised eight battalions of British regulars number-ing somewhat under 6,000 trained soldiers. Amherst also employed approximately 6,800 provincials.[28] This was a considerable aug-mentation from the colonies, suggesting that Amherst's complaints regarding the unwillingness of the colonies to support him were not particularly well founded. Amherst was accompanied by the 1st, 2nd, and 3rd Regiments of New York provincials; the 1st, 2nd, 3rd, and 4th Regiments of Connecticut provincials, and an experi-enced and long-serving New Jersey regiment under the command of Colonel Peter Schuyler, a provincial officer of considerable expe-rience and talent. Another regiment of New Jersey provincials was detailed to remain behind at Albany, with the responsibility of pro-viding details to continuously forward supplies up the Hudson and Mohawk Rivers.

Amherst's advanced guard consisted of the battalion of eight companies of Montgomery's Highlanders who had remained at Albany; a composite battalion of the regular regiments' light infantry companies commanded by Amherst's younger brother, Lieutenant Colonel William Amherst; and a combined battalion of the regular regiments' grenadier companies commanded by Lieutenant Colonel Eyre Massey of Murray's 46th Regiment of Foot.[29] The advanced guard also contained two companies of rangers, commanded by two veteran officers, Captain Amos Ogden and Captain Joseph Waite. Captain Ogden, a provincial from New Jersey, had accompanied Robert Rogers on the famous Saint Francis Raid, where Ogden had been badly wounded. Captain Waite had been with Rogers since at least the winter of 1757–1758, had fought at the Battle on the Snowshoes, and had also participated in the Saint Francis Raid where he had comported himself with great credit and honor.[30] The entirety of the advance guard was commanded by Colonel Frederick Haldimand, commanding officer of the 4th Battalion of the Royal American Regiment.[31] This was a robust advance guard, with Montgomery's Highlanders fielding 470 officers and soldiers, the grenadier battalion having 592 officers and rank and file, the light infantry battalion containing 592 men, and 191 rangers, for a total of 1,845 officers and rank and file.[32]

Frederick Haldimand had been born in the Canton of Neuchâtel, Switzerland, on August 11, 1718. He initially enlisted at the age of fifteen as a cadet with the army of Sardinia. Haldimand discovered military service to be to his liking, and passed through a succession of assignments and armies, eventually fighting under Frederick the Great of Prussia at the Battle of Mollwitz in 1741. He then joined the Swiss Guards of the Dutch Republic at Hague, where he rose to the rank of Lieutenant Colonel. There he formed a friendship with Henry Bouquet, another Swiss military man with whom he would serve in North America. In 1754 he transferred to service under King George II, and in 1756 arrived in North America at the head of the 4th Battalion of the Royal Americans (60th Regiment of Foot). Haldimand participated in Abercrombie's assault at Ticonderoga in 1758 where he had received a minor wound, and had been the garrison commander of Fort Edward during the winter of 1758–1759.

Colonel Haldimand went on to participate in the Siege of Fort Niagara in the summer of 1759, and then would be detailed to command at Fort Ontario, where he had withstood a vigorous French attack in the fall. Haldimand continued to command the fort's garrison that winter. He had considerable experience in North America, including directly relevant, independent leadership experience on Lake Ontario. He was a superb selection as commander of the advance guard.[33]

Seven battalions of British regulars comprised Amherst's main body. These included the 1st and 2nd Battalions of the Royal Highland Regiment (42nd Foot), Abercromby's 44th Regiment of Foot, Murray's 46th Regiment of Foot, Oughton's 55th Regiment of Foot, the 4th Battalion of the Royal American Regiment, and Gage's Light Infantry.[34] The main body was augmented by Johnston's approximately 700 Indian warriors, predominantly but not exclusively from the Six Nations of the Iroquois Confederation. Interestingly, the Indians accompanied the main body, rather than serving with the advance guard as would normally be expected. Amherst did not entirely trust Johnson's Natives, and intended to keep them within the main body of his army and thus presumably under somewhat tighter control and regulation. The strength of the main body was a formidable 5,258 British infantrymen; 4,479 provincials, and Johnson's 706 Indians. To this number should be added the detachment of Royal Artillery, 13 officers and 124 artillerymen, 191 provincial rangers, and 190 crewmen of the sailing vessels. Amherst's army contained a total of 10,961 soldiers.[35]

The majority of these regiments had arrived in North America in 1757 and had served on at least two active campaigns. A single battalion of Montgomery's Highlanders had been raised in 1757 and dispatched to North America, with a second battalion raised in 1758 and sent that spring to Pennsylvania. The 1st Battalion of Montgomery's Highlanders had spent 1757 idle on garrison duty at Charleston, South Carolina, but both battalions had participated in the 1758 Forbes campaign against Fort Duquesne and the 1759 campaign against Fort Carillon. The Royal Highland Regiment had served in both the 1758 and 1759 campaigns against Fort Carillon, gaining acclaim during the July assault at Fort Carillon. Oughton's 55th Regiment of Foot had originally been commanded by the youthful Brigadier General George Augustus, Lord Howe, who had trained the regiment to an exceptionally high standard before he had been killed near Ticonderoga in July 1758. The regiment seemed to have bad luck with commanding officers, as its second commander, Colonel John Prideaux, had been killed by one of his own mortars at the 1759 Siege of Fort Niagara. It was now commanded by Colonel James Adolphus Oughton. Abercromby's 44th Regiment had served in North America since arriving with Major General Edward Braddock for his ill-fated expedition to Fort Duquesne early in 1755. Murray's 46th Regiment of Foot and the 4th Battalion of the Royal American Regiment were on familiar ground, as they had participated in the Fort Niagara campaign of 1759. The regular regiments with Amherst were well seasoned for sustained field service through the rigors of a North American campaign season.

Gage's Light Infantry was a particularly distinctive unit. It had been organized in the winter of 1757 by Lieutenant Colonel Thomas Gage, who convinced British commander Lord Loudoun that he could raise a regiment of British regulars to effectively fight as rangers. Loudoun, concerned about the exorbitant expenses of the various companies of rangers, readily concurred. The result was Gage's Light Infantry (designated the 80th Regiment of Foot), a regiment recruited, organized, disciplined, and paid as British regulars, but specifically outfitted and trained to operate as rangers. Instead of the traditional red coats and cocked hats, they wore well-fitted sleeved brown waistcoats, tight fitting black leather skullcaps, brown breeches, and Indian leggings. They were armed with short barreled carbines and carried waist boxes and powder horns. Recruiting extensively in the North American colonies, they apparently had some success. In January 1759 Amherst had noted: "Recruiting goes on very well. . . . Brigadier General Gage's light infantry who wanted a great many men are completed, the Yankees love dearly a brown coat."[36] Members of the regiment were specifically trained to use canoes, bateaux, and whaleboats, employed snowshoes and ice skates during winter, and were able to fend for themselves in the woods. Gage's "leatherheads" had actively participated in the 1758 and 1759 campaigns against Fort Ticonderoga. Members of the regiment had regularly accompanied the famous Rogers' Rangers during various scouting missions, patrols, and raids throughout 1758–1759 and the spring of 1760. By August of 1760 they were an experienced regiment superior to the British light infantry companies, although they were still outmatched in woods fighting by Rogers' Rangers and the Stockbridge Mohican Indians.[37]

Amherst's large and capable Royal Artillery detachment was commanded by Lieutenant Colonel George Williamson, a long-serving artillery officer. Williamson was born in 1704 and entered the Royal Artillery on February 1, 1722, before the establishment of the Royal Artillery Arsenal at Woolwich, at a time when junior artillery officers had to learn all their skills quite literally "on the job." He was later commissioned ensign on November 1, 1727, second lieutenant on October 1, 1731, and first lieutenant on December 1, 1737. Serving with the garrison at the fortress of Minorca from 1731 to 1746, he was promoted captain on July 1, 1740. Williamson participated in the campaigns in Flanders during the War of the Austrian Succession from 1746 to 1748, gaining the rank of major on June 22, 1747, and acquired considerable active field experience in the process. Ten years later he became a lieutenant colonel. He had arrived in North America early in 1757 in time to participate in the abortive movement against Fortress Louisbourg. Colonel Williamson had commanded the Royal Artillery at the Siege of Louisbourg in 1758 and had commanded Wolfe's artillery at the Siege of Quebec in 1759. Williamson was relatively old, fifty-six at the time of the campaign, but he had considerable artillery command experience in North America, and he was both energetic and aggressive.[38]

Amherst carried an impressive train of artillery with him: six 24-pounder cannon, eight heavy 12-pounder cannon, two ten-inch mortars, four eight-inch mortars, two light 12-pounder cannon, two 6-pounder cannon, five 3-pounder cannon, two five-and-a-half-inch Royal howitzers, four five-and-a-half inch Royal mortars, and ten four-and-two-fifth inch Coehorn mortars.[39] In addition to the guns themselves, more than three hundred tons of ordnance stores were shipped in no fewer than two hundred bateaux.[40] To reduce the baggage of the army, even the officers carried the bare minimum. Lieutenant Farqharson of the Royal Highlanders wrote home that "our bedding generally consists of a blanket & bearskin which when spread on the ground makes a very good bed; the hair of it is pretty long and soft, and keeps us from the cold earth so that we sleep as sound as on a bed of down."[41]

Amherst's advance would be preceded by a strong naval flotilla constructed the previous year at Fort Ontario. This included two sailing vessels and five row galleys operated by American provincials, with the cannon manned by the Royal Artillery. The ships had been assembled under the supervision of Philadelphia shipwright Peter Jacquet, using companies of provincial artificers to perform the actual construction.[42] According to Williamson, "We had 5 Row Galleys . . . on 4 of which I mounted 4 heavy Brass 12 Pounders & in the 5th an 8 inch Howitzer."[43]

The two sailing vessels were originally christened the *Mohawk* and *Apollo*. In an impressive ceremony at Fort Oswego on August 1, the *Apollo* had been given a new name, as Amherst carefully reported:

> To please the Indians I desired them to christen the Snow and took all the Chiefs on board in the afternoon, as they had told Sir Wm. Johnson they would like to have her called ONONDAGA. I had a large flag made with an Onondaga Indian painted on it. This was hoisted just as I christened the Snow by breaking a bottle at the head. Then Gages Regt fired a volley. The Fort fired a gun & the R Highlanders fired a volley & the ONONDAGA answered it with 9 guns. All this pleased the Indians extremely & I had made them some speeches by Sir Wm Johnson. Gave them some Punch & they were greatly delighted with the whole, promised to be fast friends & said they were ready to go with me. . . .[44]

What the Indians actually thought of the christening must, unfortunately, remain a mystery.

The newly rechristened *Onondaga* and the *Mohawk* were both three-masted merchant vessels designated as "snows." The *Onondaga* carried four 9-pounders, fourteen 6-pounders, and one hundred seamen. The *Mohawk* carried sixteen 6-pounders and ninety seamen.[45] Amherst noted: "The Mohawk and Apollo appear to be much larger & finer Vessels than the Enemys."[46] These two vessels were under the overall command of Captain Joshua Loring, an American-born Royal Navy officer assigned specifically for this purpose, who would serve as commodore of the fleet during operations on the Saint Lawrence. An experienced ship's master from Massachusetts, Loring had previously commanded a privateer in operations against the French Fortress Louisbourg in 1744, had served as a Lieutenant with the Royal Navy from 1745 to 1749, and had then served as the senior naval officer with considerable success on Lake George and Lake Champlain in 1759 under Amherst's direct observation.[47] Loring showed every indication of being both experienced and well qualified to serve as a naval commander on the inland lakes. He was the only Royal Navy officer with the fleet. The two vessels were actually commanded by Lieutenant Charles Robertson of Montgomery's Highlanders, and Lieutenant Patrick Sinclair of the Royal Highland Regiment.[48]

The five row galleys were all commanded by Royal Artillery officers, Captains David Standish and Samuel Strachey, and Lieutenants John Williamson, Thomas Davies, and Nathaniel Connor. Captain Strachey had been appointed to the Royal Military Academy in 1742, and had been commissioned two years later. He had fought in Flanders in the War of the Austrian Succession, had commanded a company of Royal Artillery in North America since 1757, and had directed the train of artillery at the siege of Fort Niagara the previous year. He was the senior officer among the row galley commanders. Captain Standish had joined the artillery as a matross, the lowest rank in the Royal Artillery in 1744. He must have demonstrated considerable skills, as he was commissioned as a lieutenant-fireworker from the ranks in 1755. Lieutenant John Williamson had also joined as a matross in 1752, and clearly showed potential. He was admitted to the Royal Military Academy in 1755, and was shortly thereafter promoted to lieutenant-fireworker. Davies and Connor had both been appointed to the Royal Military Academy in 1755, been commissioned as lieutenant-fireworkers, and had immediately been dispatched to the seat of war in North America.[49] All these officers had seen service throughout the Seven Years' War in North America, and had received promotions to higher rank, suggesting that they had proven their leadership and technical skills.

Although this was a relatively powerful fleet that considerably outgunned the small French nautical force, the French possessed the advantage of having operated along the Saint Lawrence River and

Lake Ontario corridor for years. Here, Gage's hesitancy in advancing the previous year caused the British considerable problems, for the British had squandered the entire summer and fall of 1759 without acquiring any knowledge of the innumerable islands and channels of the Saint Lawrence River. Before the British fleet at Oswego could reach the French at the junction of the Oswegatchie River, they would have to traverse what is today known as the Thousand Islands of the western Saint Lawrence River. Lieutenant Alexander Farqharson of the Royal Highlanders was impressed at his first view of the locale: "The end of the Lake, and what I have yet seen of the River is beautifully diversified with innumerable fine agreeable romantic Islands, some of which are very extensive & contain the greatest soil in the world, others are small & rocky covered with birch, a kind of wood that I revere almost to devotion."[50] The glory of the landscape, however, was doubtless lost on the British pilots. They had to maneuver their clumsy sailing vessels around these obstacles without running aground and damaging or destroying one of the precious few craft. They had to navigate uncharted channels with constantly changing winds altered by the myriad of large and small islands. To transport his army, Amherst utilized 166 whale boats and 656 bateaux.[51] To support his logistical chain along the Mohawk River corridor, Amherst maintained additional bateaux along his lines of communication, manned by the New Jersey regiment and supervised by the experienced Colonel John Bradstreet. The rear guard and line of communications Amherst delegated to his most senior subordinate, the experienced but undistinguished Brigadier General Gage.

Born in England, as a youth Thomas Gage (1719/1720–1787) attended the prestigious Westminster School, affording him the highest quality education available at the time. Such men as Richard Howe, John Burgoyne and George Sackville (later Lord George Germain) also attended Westminster. In 1736, at the age of sixteen Gage purchased a lieutenancy in General James Cholmondeley's Regiment of Foot in 1741, and then purchased a promotion to captain-lieutenant in another regiment of foot commanded by Colonel John Battereau in 1742. He was promoted to captain during the War of the Austrian Succession, during which he served with the British forces in Flanders as an aide-de-camp to the Earl of Albermarle at the Battle of Fontenoy. He was among the officers of the British army dispatched home to defeat the Jacobite Rebellion in 1745–1746. He then returned to Flanders, where he continued serving between 1747 and 1748. Although he thus had considerable active campaign experience, all this service had been as an aide to Lord Albemarle, and he had not exercised any troop command or field leadership.

In 1748, Gage purchased a major's commission in Colonel John Lee's Regiment of Foot stationed in Ireland from 1748 to 1755. In 1751 Gage was promoted to lieutenant colonel of Colonel Sir Peter Halkett's regiment (formally designated as the 44th Regiment of Foot). In 1755, Gage accompanied Major General Edward Braddock to Virginia. On July 8, 1755, at the Battle of Monongahela, Gage commanded Braddock's advance guard, which was routed by the French and the Indians. After Gage lost control of the panicked and disorganized advance guard, it crashed through Braddock's Army as it was deploying, in the process dooming his general, his army, and the campaign. Gage failed miserably. He was fortunate that both Braddock and Halkett had been killed, providing two ready-made scapegoats for the defeat.

In August 1756, Gage participated in the unsuccessful attempt at the relief of Fort Ontario at Oswego. Again, Gage's force retreated in panic down the Mohawk River after the French captured this fort. Brigadier General Webb received all the blame, and though Gage was his second in command, he avoided responsibility for yet another abject failure. In 1757, Gage participated in the planned attack on Louisbourg, which was never completed. This was another failure, and the British commander in chief, the unpopular Lord Loudon, was relieved of his command.

In 1757 Gage formed his regiment of Gage's Light Infantry and became colonel of that regiment. In 1758, he participated in the attack on Fort Ticonderoga, where he was slightly wounded. Gage did not have a leadership role in this particular debacle, and being valiantly wounded in a glorious attack is always good for one's professional reputation. Gage had thus served in a variety of posts in North America between 1756 and 1758 without garnering any honor or achieving any particular distinction.

By 1759, Gage had been promoted to brigadier general, and dispatched by Amherst to Lake Ontario to assume command after Brigadier General Prideaux had been killed at the siege of Fort Niagara. He relieved Sir William Johnson, nominally a colonel as Indian Superintendent. Amherst specifically instructed Gage to maintain the momentum of the summer offensive by advancing down the

Saint Lawrence River. Gage was to capture the advanced French post at Fort de La Présentation at the junction of the Oswegatchie and Saint Lawrence Rivers, near modern-day Ogdensburg, New York. Instead, Gage squandered the summer and fall in inactivity at Fort Ontario. Gage's failure earned Amherst's enmity. Accordingly, although Gage was Amherst's most senior subordinate, Amherst relegated him to bringing up the rear guard in the 1760 campaign, with the principle responsibility of managing the logistical trains and supplies. In the vernacular, Amherst assigned Gage to command the army's salt pork.

One of Amherst's challenges was obtaining accurate and timely intelligence of the French defenses. Amherst primarily depended on Indian scouts, as they regularly traveled between their homes and the French community at Fort de La Présentation at Oswegatchie. On May 24, Amherst noted with approval that Sir William Johnson had ordered two parties of Indians there "for Prisoners and Intelligence" and noted that he "shall wait their Return with Impatience." Johnson dispatched another party to Oswegatchie on May 25, and followed this up with yet another Indian scout that he sent there in early August.[52] Amherst urged Johnson: "Small Parties kept constantly out will be of great Use in giving Intelligence."[53] On August 13 Jelles Fonda, one of Sir William Johnson's agents who accompanied him on the campaign, documented how Sir William Johnson and his native charges complied with these orders: "In the morning I heard from our Indians that the Indians who was gone to Swegatchie [Oswegatchie, or Fort de La Présentation] was Returned and Said should keep themselves Nuetral when we should Come there." They also provided precise intelligence regarding the French vessels on the river. Amherst and Sir William Johnson received scouting reports on conditions at Oswegatchie from a Native scout who returned on August 15. The next morning "we sent two Indians to Swegatchie with Some of the Light Infantry."[54]

It took Amherst the month of July and into the first week of August to concentrate his entire column at Oswego. Early in the summer, his efforts had been obstructed by high water in the Mohawk and Hudson Rivers. Amherst scribbled in his journal for June 7: "A great flood in the River will have stopped everything that was going up."[55] Making the situation worse, this flood was followed by drought, and throughout the summer he was hindered by exceptionally low water along the Mohawk River, Wood Creek, and Oswego River. Amherst's younger brother, Lieutenant Colonel William Amherst, was fully occupied along this route attempting to push the critical supplies up to Lake Ontario. He complained about the challenging conditions that his hardworking soldiers faced:

> July 9th. The navigation from the Oswego Falls . . . is very bad for the boats, destroying numbers, the greatest part of the way being rifts & the current running strong.
>
> July 14th. The river is so very low that stores & provisions come in very slowly, and 'tis with the greatest difficulty that any are forwarded.
>
> July 21st. The navigation of the Wood Creek (from the dryness of the season) being so bad, delays the troops in joining here very much. Some of the smallest batteaus make trips from hence to the Falls, where they load lightly with Artillery stores, and return here & this is the only means at present to get them forward, our new batteaus with the usual loading cannot get forward.[56]

At Fort Ontario, the British army focused on preparations. Amherst was unwavering about instituting effective discipline within the army. Both the provincials and the British regulars were notorious rum hounds. Heavy drinking rarely produced any benefit, and Amherst acted swiftly to stop it. Shortly after his arrival, on July 22, the regimental orderly books contained the following rather pointed instructions: "No spirituous liquors will be permitted to be sold there [the market]; no soldier will be permitted to drink in the sutler's hutts; all the candles to be put out at 9 o'clock."[57]

Amherst held a number of courts martial at the fort and actually found it necessary to hang several of his soldiers. On July 29, 1760 a grisly scene was enacted, as Amherst recorded in his journal: "I was obliged to have a man hanged who was a notorious offender. He had deserted several times."[58] Amherst issued precise instructions to Colonel Haldimand, who as garrison commander at the fort was responsible for carrying out the sentence of the court martial. First, believing that an executioner assigned for his army would serve to intimidate the recalcitrant soldiers, Haldimand commuted the sentence of capital punishment of John Jones of the First Regiment of New York Provincials, so long as Jones served under the provost marshal as executioner for the entirety of the campaign. Haldimand assembled the piquets, and the prisoners under sentence of death were marched to the center of the massed army. A chaplain was summoned so that the condemned could "make their peace with God." After "they have gone through the Exercise of their Devotions" James Ginnans, of Colonel Fitch's regiment of Connecticut provincials, was hanged in front of the rank and file of the army as an object lesson. Then the remaining prisoners, or, as Amherst referred to them, "the other nine Malefactors," were pardoned, but not before first being paraded in front of the gallows. It was his intention that this harsh example of military discipline "will be sufficient Warning to them never to Desert again, and likewise put an end to any more Desertions during this Campaign." The corpse of the unfortunate James Ginnans was left dangling from the gallows until retreat, when he was cut down and buried under cover of darkness. This was to be done by "a party of the Regiment he belongs to" in order to embarass his late unit and comrades.[59]

Regular courts martial were held and, by modern standards, brutal punishments inflicted. The army was still being organized in late July and early August, it had never previously worked as a single command. It contained men from England, Scotland, and three different North American provinces. If this army was to function effectively, organizational cohesion and efficiency had to be established. Amherst was not shy about instilling discipline. Inspections of weapons, uniforms, and equipment were ordered for nearly every day. Amherst was particularly insistent that the provincials' weapons, which were of notoriously poor quality, receive proper maintenance. Inventories were made of flints and cartridges, and additional cartridges were manufactured as necessary. Bateaux were assigned to specific units, equipped, and appropriately marked. Biscuit or hard bread was baked that could be carried without spoiling on campaign.

Amherst also insisted that every battalion fire at least several rounds of live musket ball at marks and in ranks to accustom the soldiers to actual service. His instructions, as with everything that Jeffery Amherst did, were precise and meticulous. First, each regiment was to fire by platoons from right to left, drawn up in ranks three deep as was customary in Europe, each man firing two rounds. After this, the regiment was to form in ranks two deep, a tactical alignment that resulted in a more flexible formation better suited to the rugged terrain and woods of North America. Each regiment then fired two more rounds by platoons. When the regiments were aligned in three ranks, Amherst directed the front rank to kneel.

When fighting in two ranks, the men were to be tightly closed up. Amherst, however, adapted this formation to the wilderness, and ordered that the front rank also be trained to kneel. Finally, after the live firing, Amherst required that each regiment demonstrate its proficiency in various tactical maneuvers that he expected would be employed on a battlefield: "The Regiments may be ordered to wheel by Platoons, to march from the Center by files, to advance their Front & Flank Platoons & march the Rear and Flanks Platoons to the rear, the Battalions are at all times to be prepared for this."[60]

Nearly every day, at least one battalion was engaged in firing live ball. The light infantry and grenadier battalions fired on July 25, the three New York regiments on July 29 and again on July 31, and the Royal Americans and Abercromby's 44th Regiment of Foot on August 1.[61] Amherst carefully monitored these exercises, ordering additional practice as necessary. On August 2 he recorded in his diary: "Abercrombys fired two rounds of ball, as they did not fire so well yesterday as they ought to have done."[62] The frugal Amherst specified that the regiments were to fire into earth-filled gabions, so that the musket balls could be recovered and the lead saved.[63]

When Amherst observed marksmanship practice, he was concerned that "the cartridges for the carbines were so large I had them tried of different quantities as some almost knocked the men down." Accordingly, he instructed the Royal Artillery to manufacture the cartridges to different sizes, based on experiments performed under his supervision at the fort's impromptu firing range.[64]

The soldiers were never idle. If drill and necessary preparations for deployment did not occupy them, Amherst assigned them to large working parties under the supervision of engineers to finish the works at Fort Oswego. Although it was unlikely that the French could mount any sort of attack on the fort with his army operating directly against them on the Saint Lawrence River, the French had launched an unsuccessful assault on the fort the previous summer. Amherst wanted to strengthen the fort so that it provided him with a secure supply depot to his rear.

Amherst considered religious instruction to be important for the spiritual health and good discipline of his soldiers, and when possible he held church services every Sabbath.[65] On Sunday, August 3, before the provincials of Amherst's army embarked religious services were conducted by their battalion chaplains, standing on the rising parapets of Fort Ontario. Ensign Joseph Booth, with the

1st Regiment of Connecticut Provincials, recorded for that date: "Mr. Backet Preacht from 31 Psalm 13:14."⁶⁶ "Mr. Backet" was actually the Reverend George Beckwith, a Congregationalist Minister from Lyme, Connecticut who had served as a chaplain with the Connecticut provincials since 1758, and would be the Chaplain for the 1st Regiment of Connecticut Provincials for the entirety of the 1760 campaign. These two verses read, according to the 1733 version of the King James Bible then in use in New England: "For I have heard the slander of many: terror is on every side: while they took counsel together against me, they schemed to take away my life, But as for me, I trust in you, Oh LORD, I say, You are my God." Although Ensign Booth did not so record, it is likely that the Reverend Mr. Beckwith expanded his sermon to include the fifteenth verse from the thirty-first psalm: "My times are in Your hand; Deliver me from the hands of my enemies and from those who persecute me. Make Your face to shine upon Your servant." Military chaplains frequently employed the Psalms for the texts of sermons because so many of them constituted an appeal to God's providence and deliverance from enemies. The New England provincials, most of them devout Congregationalists, found these verses from the Psalms to be deeply inspirational as they headed down the Saint Lawrence River to oppose their French antagonists in battle.⁶⁷

During his preparations for the final campaign against Montreal, few if any details escaped Amherst's meticulous eye. As his army prepared itself for the movement forward, Amherst exhaustively studied the military problem that faced him. Amherst's first order of business was to clear the small French fleet that was operating from Fort Lévis. This "fleet" actually comprised only two vessels, the schooner *Iroquoise* and the brig *Outaouaise*, but if not interdicted, they could wreak havoc on the defenseless British flotilla of bateaux and whaleboats moving down the Saint Lawrence River. A third French schooner had been under construction at the small shipyard at Point Baril on the Saint Lawrence River, nine miles upstream (west) from Fort de La Présentation (near the present Canadian community of Maitland, Ontario). This fortified French shipyard had been established after the capture of Fort Frontenac in August 1758 by the British. The small work yard was protected by earthworks and a palisade. This shipyard had been abandoned by the French army at the same time they had left Fort de La Présentation, when Fort Lévis was established as the major defensive position obstructing

the river. The unfinished hull had been moved under the protection of the new fort. This vessel would never be completed by the
French, and played no role in the campaign.

Both working French vessels were approximately eighty feet
in length. The brig *Outaouaise* was described as being armed with:
"One 18 Pounder, 7 12-Pounders, 2 8-pounders 150 Tons & 100
Men."[68] The complement of the *Outaouaise* was two officers, thirty-
four sailors, and sixty-five "Marines," presumably French regulars
and marine infantrymen serving as musketmen and firing the cannon. Similar details on the schooner *Iroquoise* are lacking, although
its crew was also described as being 2 officers and 34 men, which
suggests that it was similar in size and armament to the brig *Outaouaise*.[69] A civilian sailing master, Rene-Hippolyte La Force, had
been appointed by Governor de Vaudreuil to be master of the *Iroquoise*, and served in this capacity throughout at least the 1759
campaign. Another "Canadian gentleman" Joseph Boucher dit La
Broquerie, had been appointed master of the *Outaouaise*. La Broquerie was highly experienced on Lake Ontario, having captained the
French schooner *Huron* during the 1756 campaign, and prepared a
chart of the lake in 1757.

The French vessels first appeared off Fort Oswego on Lake
Ontario on July 6. At this time, the two British snows were at Fort
Niagara, carrying supplies to that installation. Amherst immediately dispatched whaleboats and additional seamen to Fort Niagara
to augment their crews "so that Capt. Loring may get out both
Vessels." The French ships returned on July 10, and remained near
Fort Oswego for two more days. Frustrated, on July 12 Amherst
attempted a clever subterfuge. He "ordered Major Baron Munster
with 200 men & 10 batteaus to go out of the harbour & proceed
towards Niagara, in hopes to induce the French ships to try to cut
them off." The French, under the leadership of the experienced La
Broquerie, failed to take the bait. Finally, on July 14 the two British
craft arrived from Fort Niagara. Amherst immediately augmented
their crews and embarked two ranger officers with thirty of their
rangers in three whaleboats to enable the British vessels to carefully
scout for the French fleet. On July 20, an aggressive Amherst urged
Captain Loring to action, as the French vessels were again located
near Oswego: "Take the best Station You can so that the Enemy's
vessels may not pass You.[70] To facilitate Loring's efforts against the
pair of French vessels, Amherst sent a small detachment in bateaux,

transporting additional provisions to the British fleet so that they would not run low on rations. Gleefully, Amherst recorded: "This is a fine opportunity. I think they cant escape him."

Unfortunately for Amherst's prediction, that is precisely what the French did. The sad tidings were received at Fort Oswego on July 24, as noted by Lieutenant Colonel William Amherst: "An officer came here from the vessels with a letter from Capt Loring. They had met with the French vessels on the 22nd: they escaped ours & got into the river. They will never afford our shipping again so favorable an opportunity of taking them."[71] Loring himself reported to Colonel Amherst: "I am extreamly sorry that I am obliged to acquaint your Excellency that the Enemy not withstanding my Utmost Endeavours to intercept them have escaped me." The captain blamed contrary winds "the wind coming to the Eastward" and "having no wind worth mentioning" and fog so thick that "we could not see the Land Tho we were very near to some of the islands, which obliged us to come to anchor."[72] General Amherst echoed his brother's sentiments: "In the evening Lt Kennedy arrived from Cap Loring with the news that he saw the Enemy Vessels yesterday morning & they got from him into the river Saint Lawrence. So he will see them no more & a fine opportunity is lost."[73] The French vessels had easily eluded the British fleet, and Amherst was forced to write Loring the following day: "I am this moment favoured with Your Letter of Yesterday's date by Lieut. Kennedy; I Grieve that the Enemy's Vessels have Escaped You, If You could have cut them off from their Harbour the Conquest would have been very Easy; I doubt not in the least but You have Used Your best Endeavours to Effect it, and I am Sorry they have not been Attended with Success."[74] It would be the first time, but as events would demonstrate that summer, not the last time that Loring's leadership disappointed Amherst.

On August 6 Amherst issued Captain Loring with unequivocal orders: "You will observe [to weigh anchor] to morrow at break of day, or so Soon as You possibly can, and immediately with His Majesty's two Snows, the Onondaga & Mohawk, under Your Command proceed to Frontenac. . . . You will therefore make it Your business to attack, take, Sink, Burn or destroy them.[75] Loring again failed to sink the French vessels, which retreated in haste up the Saint Lawrence River to the sheltering guns of Fort Lévis. However, in the process, the schooner *Iroquoise* ran aground near the Three Sisters Island or in the Brockville Narrows (near modern Brockville, Ontario), and was severely damaged. It was moved to Fort Lévis, where it was subsequently scuttled.[76] The loss of the *Iroquoise* left only the *Outaouaise* to be dealt with, but this success had been garnered by fortune, rather than through any skill on Loring's part.

Amherst's army moved in three separate elements: the advance guard commanded by Colonel Haldimand, the main body including the artillery under the direct supervision of Amherst himself, and the rear guard led by Gage.

The advance guard departed first, leaving Fort Oswego on August 7. They were accompanied by Loring's two vessels, proudly displaying their flags bearing an Onondaga and Mohawk Indian respectively, and the five Royal Artillery row galleys. The light infantry and rangers employed whaleboats, the remainder of the column used bateaux. They experienced a severe thunderstorm that afternoon, typical for Lake Ontario during summer, which caused considerable damage to a number of their boats. Lieutenant Colonel Amherst attested that "the wind continued high & a great surf on shore. We repaired what boats we could & collected the provisions out of those that were staved, which are to be left here with a detachment till the army comes up or sends boats for them. The boats that were missing came in at night." Amherst received a letter from Colonel Haldimand the next morning: "complaining . . . that he had suffered a great deal in the high wind. Several batteaus were stove, a great deal of pork & flour lost, one whaleboat lost and 9000 cartridges spoiled. Some firearms lost."[77]

The battered, damp soldiers continued on, thankful to leave the treacherous Lake Ontario behind them. Upon entering the Thousand Islands, they had considerable difficulty navigating. Lieutenant Colonel Amherst noted that they had been equipped with charts, but that they "passed a great many Islands, the plan we had with us not laying down one & differing in many respects." The advance guard had to send out scouting vessels to even ascertain where on the river they were on August 10. On the evening of August 12 Colonel Amherst simply noted in befuddlement: "We rowed back into a nest of islands in the channel." The next day, while waiting for scouting parties sent to reconnoiter Fort de La Présentation to return, Amherst decided to take "the opportunity of our laying here to practise my Corps to march and form in the woods. We lost our way & did not reach the Camp till after dark, through swamps & the thickest wood we could meet with." The struggling advance guard finally reached a point west of the French fort by the evening of August 16, camping on the south shore of the river. They were then joined by Johnson's Indians who, unsurprisingly, had not gotten lost in the Thousand Islands.[78] It had not been a particularly propitious week for the advance guard.

Amherst got the main body moving on August 10 from Fort Oswego. The embarkation does not appear to have gone smoothly, and on this date only the regulars and the Royal Artillery were able to take to the water, with Gage's Light Infantry Regiment in the van. The Indians, who had been issued with whaleboats instead of using the canoes that they had arrived with, filed to the right of the Royal Artillery, guarding Amherst's vulnerable right (east then south) flank, which was closest to land and thus more likely to be attacked. Amherst noted "The Indians in the whaleboats made strange appearances." Although the Indians had brought their own canoes, eighteenth-century canoes were relatively flimsy in construction and would not have been suitable for use on a rigorous campaign on Lake Ontario. Thus, the Indians were issued with whaleboats, which must indeed have "made a strange appearance!"[79]

The departure was also slightly delayed by the Indians' illicit negotiations with the soldiers to obtain rum. Although Amherst strictly prohibited such transactions in General Orders, these stringent rules were not always rigorously adhered to. When Jelles Fonda, Sir William Johnson's agent, arrived at Oswego he "found all the Indians drunk." He noted that the Natives finally got away from Oswego a day late, on August 11, but only "after the Indians was Sober."[80]

To avoid confusion, the boats were all marked on the starboard bow with the regimental designation and identifying number of the boat.[81] However, all of Amherst's meticulous preparations could not prevent the flotilla from being struck by yet another late afternoon thunderstorm, causing his boats as much trouble as his brother had experienced only three days previously in a similar tempest. Amherst recorded: "In the evening the wind began to increase & I could not get forward quite so far as I intended to. Some of the batteaus did not get up & some were damaged by the coming in the night. As the wind increased a batteau of the Artillery & one of Montgomerys [Highlanders] were quite sunk but nobody drowned; a man of Gages drowned by falling overboard."[82] Lieutenant Farqharson with the Royal Highland Regiment remembered "two or three provincials [bateaux], who in the night, were drove a shore on a rocky beach, during a high surf. We stood out a very high sea on the day we sett out; some Battoes very near foundered, and the baggage of a few of the Officers got wet."[83] That day the main body reached "the place we lay in is called by the French Riviere de Sable & I believe is about 30 miles from Oswego." Captain William Hervey of Abercromby's 44th Foot recorded: "put in at Sandy River."[84] Although eighteenth-century charts of Lake Ontario are rare and extremely inaccurate, this was likely the modern Sandy Creek, somewhere in the vicinity of the North Pond, which would have provided a sheltered anchorage and landing place for Amherst's flotilla.

Having a number of bateaux founder and drown several of his soldiers before they had even seen a Frenchman did not constitute a particularly auspicious start to Amherst's campaign. There was nothing to do for it but repair the bateaux and whaleboats as much as possible and proceed on. The next day, the army's start was delayed by the need to mend the various damaged boats. Once the boats were launched, the soldiers battled against the adverse winds. On August 11, the main body only rowed eight miles to what Amherst called "Prescott Bay" (the modern location cannot now be verified). The next day the flotilla made better time, and proceeded fifteen miles to what Amherst referred to as "Mouse Bay" noting that he camped on "the penninsula called Camp de Mons de Villiers in 1756." This would have been in the vicinity of the northern portion of the modern Henderson Bay, slightly to the south of Sackett's Harbor. On August 13, Amherst continued to make good progress, stating that evening: "I encamped in Robertsons bay which I imagine must be nearly 30 miles from my last Camp." This would be either in the vicinity of the contemporary Mud Bay, or the nearby Basin Harbor on Grenadier Island, both common eighteenth-century anchorages. The following day, Amherst recorded that the main body "rowed about 15 miles & encamped on Haldimand's island, arriving in pretty good time." What was known in 1760 as "Haldimand's Island" might be the modern Carleton's Island, or alternatively could refer to the larger Wolfe Island. The smaller island to the south of Wolfe Island was formally named in 1779 by then governor of Canada Frederick Haldimand as "Carleton's Island" in recognition of his predecessor, long-term British general and Royal governor of Canada Sir Guy Carleton.

Amherst linked up with Loring and his small fleet on August 15, and made excellent progress, reaching Point Baril by nightfall.

Amherst noted that Loring was still struggling with the channel of the Saint Lawrence River through the Thousand Islands: "The lake with a variety of Islands is so very different from what is laid down in the Chart, that it cannot in the least be a guide. Capt. Loring has not yet found a Channel down. The Swegatchi Indians will now be of Service as two of them are sent to pilot the Vessels."[85] How effective the Indians proved at piloting Royal Navy sailing vessels through the Thousand Islands was, unfortunately, never documented for posterity.

The provincials and the rear guard under the command of Brigadier General Thomas Gage departed from Oswego on August 11, behind Amherst's main body. While the three portions of the army moved forward, a small garrison remained at Fort Oswego. Amherst recorded: "I left Capt Stuart to command at Oswego with 169 men, returned for Garrison duty; 259 in the Hospital, left Capt. Towers Engineer with 20 Carpenters, 6 Sawyers, 4 Smiths, 3 Coal Burners, 16 Teamsters for driving the Oxen & 20 Axmen with proper overseers to continue carrying on the works of the Fort as much as the few numbers of Troops there will let them & prepare the timber & draw it in against they may have more Troops there."[86] There were two Captain Stewarts in the Royal Highland Regiment in 1760, and precisely which Captain Stewart became the commandant at the fort is uncertain.

Loring's small flotilla searched for the French vessels, but their efforts proved to be in vain. The five Royal Artillery row galleys covering the front of the British transport fleet finally made contact late on the afternoon of August 16. The *Outaouaise* was hovering around the recently abandoned Fort de La Présentation, hoping for an opportunity to slip in among the vulnerable bateaux and whaleboats to destroy the irreplaceable British transport. On sighting the British boats moving down the river, the *Outaouaise* fired three signal cannon to alert the garrison of Fort Lévis. Amherst noted: "On the Vessel sailing up the River I expected she would have been at our bateaux."[87] Williamson aggressively maneuvered his five row galleys to interdict the *Outaouaise*. Darkness fell before he could press his attack. The British landed on the north shore of the river near the abandoned French shipyard at Point Baril, and emplaced a small battery of cannon to defend their encampment.

Before dawn the next morning, Williamson's gunboats were moving forward. He recorded:

By Sat. the 16th got down to within 3 miles of Oswegatchie [under-lined in original letter] where we saw one of the French Frigates laying in wait for us; in our way we saw our two ships at Anchor not trusting to go any farther having taken a wrong Channel among many Islands & being to go back part of the way to find the right one, We thought it an unlucky circumstance yet resolved to persevere & not wait for them. We disposed of ourselves in 3 Divisions of Bateaux, one to go ahead with the Grenadiers & light Arm'd Infantry headed by the 5 Row galleys, the other two to fol-low within sight and a Breast one another, the River being broad enough. The General did me the Honor to accept of my offer to attack the French Man with my 5 Galleys: we got to within ran-dom Shot of her but falling dark we defer'd the undertaking until the Gray of next morning the 17th when we continued it so well that in 2 hours & ¼ she struck to my red Flag, which I assure Your Lordship [underlined in original letter] gave great satisfaction to us all Commodore Williamson as it was something new to him. [underlined in original letter] The Howitzer did not Fire above twice some Timbers in the Vessell giving way so that I may say that only 4 Guns took a Top Sail Vessel of One 18 Pounder, 7 12 Pounders, 2 8 pounders 150 Tons & 100 Men we were only 25 of the R. [Royal] Artillery with Capt. Strackey, Lieut. Williamson, Standish, Davis & Connor, I count not the Provincials on Board as they only rowed the Galleys. We had Sergeant Wilkie killed & 2 Provincials wounded. The French had 3 killed & 12 wounded the Troops had not an opportunity to Fire[.] The 300 Grenadiers com-manded by Col. Grant were in motion to board her. As our two vessels were not come down, taking this Prize greatly Facilitated our moving on, and the General as a Complement to my endeav-ours was pleased to Name the Prize the Williamson Frigate. My business was to run from Galley to Galley and direct them how to attack with greater safety. We repaired her for service next day.[88]

The lone fatality was Sergeant Wilkie of the Royal Artillery.[89] One row galley, the vessel mounting the eight-inch howitzer, had been damaged when the sliding carriage in the bow failed. It was knocked out of action, but the carriage could be swiftly repaired. The *Outaouaise* had made a valiant attempt to reverse the course of the campaign, but once the wind failed the French brig had fought under great adversity: "She was going up the River but the wind calmed and the Row Galleys behaved very well; fired 118 Shot. The Vessel fired 72."[90] Still, the French ship was outfought by the aggres-sive British gunboats.

Nearly every officer and soldier with Amherst's army whose documents have survived recorded the event, as this was an extremely significant action. With the capture of the *Outaouaise* the British had gained naval control of the Saint Lawrence River, and their fleet could maneuver with impunity. Amherst could now move directly upon Fort Lévis.

When the British army approached Fort de La Présentation that afternoon, they found it abandoned by the French.[91] Colonel Nathan Whiting of the Connecticut provincials observed that "the Enemy have some time since deserted this place had taken the Roofs off the Houses but not Intirely destroyed them & had hurt the Fort but Little[.] Though it Never was of much strength being stockaded only, And a blockhouse at each angle of the Square."[92] Captain Hervey noted the "old fort made against small arms only."[93] The French had also constructed two sawmills on the Oswegatchie River to the southeast of the fort, which Lieutenant Farqharson visited and assessed: "There runs a creek past it, larger as the [River] Dee [in Scotland], on which there is built two saw mills of very curious workmanship."[94] Johnson's agent, Jelles Fonda, recorded: "When we landed at the Indian Town some Indians Ran off for fear of us and them that Stayed at home Recieved us kindly."[95]

The remainder of that day and the next was spent repairing the badly battered *Outaouaise*, which was re-christened the *Williamson* in honor of Colonel Williamson. The damaged howitzer carriage on the row galley was rebuilt. The other four row galleys engaged in that morning's fight had also sustained damage that needed repair. The scores of bateaux and whaleboats rowed from Point Baril to the peninsula with the old French fort. There were camping grounds, which the French had used four years previously, and the army could forage from the farm fields the Indians had planted and later abandoned.[96] Amherst dispatched two engineers in canoes to "view the Coasts and Situation of the Islands near L'Isle Royalle" so that he could swiftly invest the French island fortress that obstructed the river to his front.[97]

Captain Pierre Pouchot had faced considerable challenges constructing a defensive position on what was then known as Île Oraquointon in the middle of the Saint Lawrence River, approximately three miles downstream from the junction of the Oswegatchie River. Pouchot, a Captain in the Béarn Regiment and Chevalier of the Royal and Military Order of Saint Louis, was a long-serving French officer of great repute. Born in Grenoble, France, in 1712, Pouchot had entered the Béarn Regiment of the French Army at the age of 21. He served throughout the War of the Austrian Succession with considerable distinction and was awarded the Cross of Saint Louis. A senior captain in the regiment, Pouchot had sailed to Canada in 1755 and served in every campaign of the French and Indian War. The previous year he had commanded Fort Niagara, which Pouchot had surrendered following a long siege, only after no further resistance was possible and all hopes of relief had vanished.[98]

The fort that faced Amherst on Îsle Oraquointon was formidable indeed, particularly given its strong defensive position in the midst of the river. Before the construction of the Saint Lawrence Seaway, Chimney Island, as it is known today, was shaped roughly like a tadpole with its tail facing downstream to the east.[99] The main defensive position sat astride the body of the tadpole, oriented to the west and occupying the largest part of the island. The defenses faced in the direction of the anticipated British advance. Pouchot, who designed the majority of the works when he assumed command of the post, described the fortifications (Pouchot consistently referred to himself in the third person):

> The fort had nothing completed except the rampart faced with saucissons [long fascines]. The barracks, storehouses & officers quarters & other buildings pertaining to the fort were finished with wooden timbers placed one on top of the other & covered by planks. M. Pouchot, in order to render the position defensible, caused to be erected on the parapet, which was 18 feet wide, another of nine feet with timbers placed one on top of the other and filled with earth, which he had to have transported from off the island. He created embrasures within the parapet. Beneath the parapet he left a berm 4 feet wide on the outside, which featured a fraise. What remained of the first parapet on the inside was used as a banquette. As a result, the parapet was 11 feet high on the outside & 11 on the inside. The addition was indispensible to provide a certain amount of cover for the interior of the fort, which was overlooked to a height of 24 feet by the terrain of isles a la Cuise & de la Magdeleine. M. Pouchot ordered construction of a gallery with pieces of oak 14 inches square by 10 feet long. It ran along the rampart & was used as a terreplein, while the lower part acted as a casemate. The batteries were positioned on this gallery or platform all around the island. He built an epaulement 4 feet thick out of the earth, most of which was dredged from the bottom of the river, since the island

did not have 2 feet of earth as ground cover on slopes. An abatis of branches was placed over the front of the epaulement, which extended as far as possible into the water in order to prevent long-boats from landing. At the island's tip, this epaulement ended in a redoubt of wooden timbers pierced to allow fire from five cannon. On either side of the Island, two spaces in the shape of a jetty were left to allow the bateaux to tie up.[100]

As Pouchot described, an abatis that extended into the river defended the island against an amphibious assault, at which the British were more than adept. The main works consisted of a parapet with fraising, which surrounded the entire island. This parapet contained two bastions facing to the east, guarding the fort's entrance on the eastern curtain wall. To the front of this parapet, Pouchot established a narrow four-foot epaulement, an earthen reinforcement placed in front of the parapet to furnish additional defensive strength against cannon. At the western end of the island this epaulement was turned into a wooden redoubt that mounted a battery of five guns. However, an epaulement with a width of only four feet would have been of limited utility against heavy battering guns. A ditch ran between the epaulement and the main parapet. One French engineering design depicted this as a dry ditch with palisading, but Pouchot described the ditch as "flooded with water." The ditch may have been dry or wet, depending on weather conditions. Behind the heavy ramparts as an extension of the main parapet, Pouchot had constructed separate batteries, where most of his guns were mounted. These were elevated to create better fields of fire. The usual garrison buildings were in the center of the fortification. Pouchot also mentioned that a glacis was erected to provide additional protection to the fortification to the east, in the direction of the closest two islands. Rudimentary dock facilities were located on the northeastern part of the island.

Colonel Williamson, an experienced British military engineer, was impressed with the strength of the post and described it favorably after inspecting it following its capture. He observed, "The 2 Vessels of the Enemy were behind their Island filled with Water that we might not take them, they had 5 Small Row Galleys with 3 of our Iron 3 Pounders (very good Guns) in 3 of them, the other 2 French 4s, but did not make use of them." He also remarked on the French measures to prevent an amphibious assault against the island fortress: "All round the Island (except 2 Places 20 yards wide each for Boats) had a strong abattis of Branches of Trees running 10 or 14 Feet into the River, this opposition would have made a bloody Landing." Williamson was unimpressed with "a cover'd way badly made, next a Ditch partly wet not deep with a Horizon [horizontal] Stockade in the middle running thus & all round the Fort." Williamson included a simple sketch showing fraizing constructed at an angle toward the British advance. He further noted: "The Fort [was] not well flanked [but] was raised to its Cordon height with excellent well bound Fascines: then fraised all round the stakes sticking out Horizontally." Finally, further rendering Île Aux Noix impervious to an infantry attack, "The Ambrazures [embrasures] looked on every part of the Water to annoy Boats Landing."[101]

Given the shortage of time and manpower and the difficulty of moving materials to the middle of the swift Saint Lawrence River channel, Pouchot had constructed an impressive defensive position. Although Fort Lévis had its weaknesses, it completely commanded the river. Amherst's combat elements could bypass the fort, but his supply convoys would be extremely vulnerable so long as Fort Lévis remained to his rear. Accordingly, Amherst had no choice but to reduce it before his army could progress toward Montreal.

Pouchot's garrison consisted of 338 French regulars, marines, and Canadian militia, including officers.[102] After the surrender of the fort, the English seized twelve 12-pounder cannon, two 8-pounder cannon, thirteen 4-pounder cannon, and four brass 6-pounders. They also took four 1-pounder cannon, essentially swivel guns of use only against infantry. They found "several guns with trunnions broken off." These could only have been the eight cannon that Pouchot had recovered from the ruins of Fort Frontenac and that he had mounted on makeshift carriages. Lacking trunnions, these cannon would have been good for only a single shot. They would presumably have been packed to the muzzle with deadly short-range antipersonnel ammunition, such as lagrange, grapeshot, and canister, which could be fired to repulse the anticipated British amphibious landing.[103] The garrison's numbers were most likely as large as the island could accommodate, and be provisioned for a siege. Given the size of the island, the twelve 12-pounder cannon and two 8-pounder cannon were sufficient to command the Saint Lawrence channel, as the range from Fort Lévis to both the north and south shore was only 4,000 feet (1,350 yards), well within the range of these cannon. The smaller guns were useful only for repulsing a British amphibious landing.

Amherst received the engineers' reports on the morning of August 18. At about noon he re-embarked most of his army. The engineers told him that "the North Coast being within Random Shot only," he would have to pass below the fort, where two islands were located within cannon range. Amherst was also informed that the south shore was in good artillery range of the fort. Three Connecticut provincial regiments, Whiting's, Wooster's and Fitch's, remained behind as a garrison at Fort de La Présentation, with Colonel Nathan Whiting commanding the partially dismantled French fort. Amherst instructed Colonel Whiting: "I must particularly Recommend to You, the Repairs and making of Ovens, and the Establishing a Brewerie to supply the Army with Spruce Beer."[104] In a letter that suggests there was some tension between the provincials and regulars in Amherst's army, Whiting grumbled to his wife: "I remain here with my Regiment as a cover to the Rear & though I should much rather be near the principal seat of action must content myself, as it seems a Settl'd point for the Provincials not to share much in the Principal Honor of the Action, their Honor seems confined to their Alertness & care in promoting & forwarding Such things or matters as the Principall action may depend upon."[105] The provincials were primarily occupied with hauling forward the considerable train of siege artillery, which would shortly be used to reduce the French defenses.[106]

Amherst's intention on the afternoon of August 18 was to completely invest the French fort, so that no additional reinforcements could reach it from Montreal. He also planned to sever the French garrison's retreat route. Amherst described how he organized his army for this important movement: "I ordered Gages [80th Light Infantry Regiment] to be the advanced Guard to the North shore, to row down close to the shore, two boats abreast, followed by three Row Galleys. Light Infantry of Regts, Grenadiers & 2nd R Highland Battn, Montgomery's [Highlanders] and Murrays [46th Regiment of Foot] being the 1st Brigade. These were followed by a proportion of Light Artillery & then Schuylers [New Jersey Provincial] Regt. They cannonaded us briskly from the Fort."[107] Amherst had his army hug the north shore of the river, as this placed them the farthest distance from the French cannon in Fort Lévis.

French Commander Pouchot did everything possible to keep the British from sweeping around his post, as he realized that his situation would be tenuous indeed if the British slipped between his garrison and the heart of Canada:

On the 18th, the enemy set out from La Présentation in a brisk wind
. . . It was a splendid sight. Mr. Pouchot at first imagined that they
intended to mount a major attack in order to land on the island. As
a result, he had positioned 9 guns to bombard the top of the river
& had sited others in the epaulement which could make the balls
richochet eleven times over the water. It is certain that the enemy
would have lost many men before effecting a bridgehead had they
attempted to so do. They decided to slip along the northern shores
with a wide interval between each bateaux in order to avoid the
fort's artillery. M. Pouchot could only harass their passage with
4 guns that could get them in their sights. We fired 150 shots at
them without, as far as we could see, doing much damage because
the brisk wind & the current made them sail very swiftly past the
lines of sight.[108]

French gunner Charles Bonin, manning the cannon on the
ramparts of the island, recalled that "the fire from the fort was
unceasing."[109]

Although Pouchot did not feel that his artillery fire had been
effective, Amherst and his British soldiers who were on the receiving end possessed a considerably different perspective: "They cannonaded us briskly from the Fort, sunk one Row Galley, killed two
men in another Row Galley. The Ball went through but did not hinder from proceeding. One man in a whaleboat had his thigh shot off
& seven were wounded. Some batteaus & several oars struck with
the shot."[110] Colonel Woodhull saw the engagement from the shores
of Fort de La Présentation, and presumably received the wounded in
the hospital that he had established there: "The fort and the vessels
began to exchange shots. As the Bateaux and the Redows were passing the fort, a shot struck one of them, and a ball went thro' another,
which killed two New Yorkers, and another struck a batteau, which
broke a man's leg."[111]

Once the light infantry battalion commanded by Lieutenant
Colonel William Amherst was safely past the fort, a few rather
battered bateaux notwithstanding, they seized control of the two
islands just below (east) of Fort Lévis. These two islands did not possess English names in 1760, but were called by the French the Îsle
à la Magdelaine (now known as Drummond Island) and the Îsle à la
Cuisse (today's Spencer Island). The 1950s construction of the Saint
Lawrence Seaway substantially altered the topography of these two
islands by creating the north channel. Drummond Island, to the

south, was not seriously altered at its southside, where the British firing batteries were emplaced. Today, the view of Drummond Island from Chimney Island is nearly identical to its appearance in 1760. Unfortunately, Spencer Island, the more northerly of the two, was entirely altered. The southern portion of Spencer Island, where the British firing batteries were located, has been entirely removed. There are no vestiges of the Seven Years' War remaining on its surface.[112]

Based on the reconnaissance of his engineers the previous night, Amherst intended to place his siege batteries on these two islands. He installed his brother, Lieutenant Colonel William Amherst, on one of them, and Captain James Dalyell, of the 1st Royals, on the other, although which island was occupied by which officer is indeterminable. Dalyell was a personal favorite of Amherst's and his aide-de-camp. From the Île à la Magdelaine, the batteries would be within 2,000 feet (665 yards) of any point in Fort Lévis. From the Île à la Cuisse, the range was slightly greater; the batteries would be within 2,500 feet (850 yards) of any point in the French post.[113] The French defenses would be within point-blank range of the 24-pounders, the largest cannon that Amherst had brought. In eighteenth-century Royal Artillery usage, point-blank range meant that the cannon could be aimed directly at the French fort without any necessary adjustment in elevation. Twelve-pounders placed on the Île à la Magdelaine would also be within point-blank range (733 yards). Depending on the actual target, some minimal adjustment in elevation might have been required when firing 12-pounders from the Île à la Cuisse.[114]

Having successfully bypassed the fort, Amherst ordered that "Gages [80th Light Infantry Regiment] was to get below the Fort & possess Isle Gallot." This island, called Île aux Galots by the French, is today known as Galop Island. When the Abbé Piquet had left Fort de La Présentation the previous summer, he had transferred his mission and farms to this island. It now contained a number of sturdy log structures, and the British gathered supplemental rations from the French farm fields. In the modern era this island's topography was heavily altered by the construction for the Saint Lawrence Seaway. In 1760 it was 6,000 feet (2,000 yards) from Fort Lévis, within the range of the French 12-pounders, the largest cannon in the French fortress. The farther eastern reaches of the island were well out of range of the French guns, and in any event the attentions

Position of British artillery batteries on Île à la Magdelaine (modern Drummond Island, Canada) from the site of Fort Lévis (Isle Oraquointon, modern Chimney Island). Photograph by the author.

of the French gunners were certainly going to be diverted by the batteries closer to them. The Île aux Galots was also a large enough island to permit the British to establish camps, hospitals, and supply stockpiles to support the siege, all safely out of French artillery range. This was crucial to Amherst's plans because the other two islands were relatively small and so close to the French defenses that they could not safely be used to support siege operations.

Finally, Amherst moved a second brigade "consisting of Oughtons [55th Regiment of Foot], R Americans 4th Battn [60th Regiment of Royal Americans] & Abercrombys [44th Regiment of Foot] with two Companys of Rangers in their front and Lymans Regt [1st Regiment of Connecticut Provincials] in their rear proceeded down the S [south] Shore in the same manner as I did down the North having two Row Galleys in their Front to protect their batteaus. These were under the command of Colonel Haldimand."[115] This brigade landed at what was then known by the French as Pointe de Ganataragoin, which in 1760 had no British name. It is now known as Chimney

Point and is located southwest of the French fort. The topography of the Chimney Point peninsula protected the British landing from any artillery fire from Fort Lévis. The British firing batteries were established on the northeastern shore of Chimney Point, on a slight escarpment five to ten feet above the river's shoreline. The range from these batteries to the center of the French fort was 3,000 feet (1,000 yards), well within the capabilities of the British cannon, but at such a distance that the cannon would have to be carefully aimed to strike the French works. The slight elevation provided by this terrain facilitated an extremely favorable grazing fire by the British cannon against the French forts. To the rear of the firing batteries a low ridge rose less than ten feet, not enough to appear on a modern topographical map, but sufficient to place the British encampments in dead ground, thus protecting them from French gunfire. Chimney Point provided an extremely fine tactical position. Batteries located on Île à la Magdelaine and Île à la Cuisse were for all practical purposes next door to Fort Lévis and, when combined with other British batteries established at Chimney Point, placed the French fort into a devastating enfilading fire.[116]

The provincial regiments that remained in garrison at Fort de La Présentation established a supply base there. Gage brought up the rear guard with the heavy baggage and stockpiles of provisions and matériel. Since Amherst had swept the French navy from the Saint Lawrence River, he was not concerned about a French sortie from Fort Lévis. Accordingly, there was no advantage to be derived from the establishment of the traditional line of countervallation to defend Amherst's siege positions.

To cover Amherst's movements, Williamson maneuvered his naval vessels to engage the attention of the French: "We rowed down One by One at about 50 yards asunder not mind their Fire within reach & took possession of all the other Islands round hemming the Enemy in on every side."[117] Amherst noted that he had ordered the captured *Williamson* "to sail directly down the Center & to anchor within Random shot of the Fort, was perfectly well executed. He took the Fire from the Fort & returned their Shot."[118] Pouchot in Fort Lévis remembered that the British officers, many of whom he had met following his surrender of Fort Niagara the previous summer, "wished him good day as they passed, while others shouted out to him to let them through, as they were his friends."[119] With these maneuvers completed by nightfall on August 18, the

Site of Fort Lévis (Île Oraquointon, modern Chimney Island), from the position of British artillery batteries on Pointe de Ganataragoin (modern Chimney Point), grounds of St. Lawrence Psychiatric Center, Ogdensburg, New York. Photograph by the author.

next morning Amherst gave orders to move his artillery forward and began the difficult and dangerous work of constructing the siege batteries necessary to reduce the French island fortress.

Amherst assigned a working party of five hundred men to the two islands closest to the French fort. The men worked three eight-hour shifts, beginning at noon, at eight in the evening, and at four in the morning, which was close to daybreak in August. The construction on the two islands was directed by Colonel Williamson and Lieutenant Colonel William Eyre of Abercromby's 44th Foot. Another working party of one hundred men was assigned to the southern shore of the river to make fascines for the siege works.

Although he now held a commission in Abercromby's Regiment, Eyre was an efficient and capable engineer. As a captain in 1755, he had been dispatched by the late Major General Edward Braddock to assist William Johnson in his campaign against Crown Point. He had fought with Johnson at the Battle of Lake George, and designed Fort William Henry after Johnson's advance had ground to a halt in the fall of that year. Since then Eyre had been on campaign every year of the long war in North America. Promoted to major in the 44th Regiment of Foot, he had commanded Fort William Henry during the winter of 1756–1757 and repulsed an audacious French winter raid on the fort on Saint Patrick's Day in 1757. Eyre had fought in the assault on Fort Carillon at Ticonderoga in 1758. He had accompanied Amherst in his 1759 campaign against Fort Carillon and Saint Frederick and designed fortifications on the southern end of Lake George during the early stages of that campaign. He had concluded his role in the campaign by designing Fort Crown Point, the largest fortress ever constructed in North America. He had then been dispatched to serve as garrison commander of Fort Niagara for that winter. He was one of the most accomplished British engineers and line officers in the colonies, and Amherst was entirely confident in his skills and abilities.

Colonel Whiting's three provincial regiments moved up the heavy artillery on the night of August 19. Amherst planned to put three 24-pounder cannon, three 12-pounder cannon, one ten-inch mortar, an eight-inch mortar, and two four-and-two-fifth-inch Coehorn mortars at the one battery on the island commanded by his brother. Three 24-pounder and three 12-pounder cannon, one ten-inch mortar, and one eight-inch howitzer were emplaced on the island commanded by Captain Dalyell. He put two 12-pounders on the south shore of the river at Chimney Point. The French artillery fire was extremely light. Amherst noted, "The Fort fired but little," though a single shot at a battery under construction managed to kill three men. Amherst mused: "Mons. Pouchot thinks it necessary I believe not to throw away Powder till our batteries are up."[120]

Construction of the batteries was as much a nautical exercise as an engineering problem. Three times a day the large working parties were moved from Îsle aux Galots to the two smaller islands by bateaux, as the two islands with the batteries were too exposed for the workers to camp on them and hope to get any rest. All munitions and provisions had to be transported from the army's logistical rear around the French fortification by boat, exposing them to the cannon fire that had already proved effective. On August 21, orders were issued concerning the gauntlet that the fragile wooden vessels had to run: "Boats going to and coming from Amherst's and Dalyel's islands are always to keep the passage by the shore, where the Line is encamped, as going between the islands may expose them either to the fire of the enemy or that of our battery on the opposite shore."[121]

To protect the guards and piquets who covered the engineering workers in the unlikely event of a French sortie from the fort, Amherst ordered a fleche constructed on each island. A fleche was a small arrowhead- or V-shaped breastwork with the point facing toward the enemy. It was usually constructed of heavy timber and earth, though given the scarcity of lumber on the islands, the fleche was probably made of fascines, gabions, and earth.

The weather was wet with frequent squalls, typical for the Adirondacks and Saint Lawrence River valley in the heart of summer. The poor weather conditions notwithstanding, Amherst's officers and men performed prodigious feats of labor, and, as early as August 23, Amherst could report: "Col Williamson sent me a note that he would like to begin Fire with the Battery on the right that was completed—that of two 12-Pounders on the opposite Shore."[122] With a single thundering roar that echoed down the river, the batteries opened up at eight in the morning.[123] From this moment, the Saint Lawrence valley was never quiet, as the British gunners poured a torrent of shells into the French fort. Their fire was devastating.

Pouchot himself was wounded, recording: "At the first volleys, M. Bertrand, the artillery officer, was killed instantaneously by a cannonball which struck him in the back. . . . M. Pouchot received a very bad cut from a piece of wood 10 feet long & 14 inches square which was flung in the air by the explosion of a 12-inch bomb and hit him in the back. The injury did not prevent him from doing his duty." This was almost certainly one of the explosive shells fired by the large mortars. Pouchot clearly did not relish being on the receiving end of the bombardment, writing, "All these batteries fired with the utmost vigor and without interruption until noon, which sent debris & splinters flying around the fort."[124]

At the three batteries, the next few days would be monotonous hard work, interspersed with the occasional moment of utter terror as the French responded with counterbattery fire. The British artillerymen were experienced and well drilled, and simply firing the guns would not have been particularly demanding. Maintaining such a bombardment, however, was backbreaking labor. The most demanding task was manhandling the massive quantity of ammunition to the guns. The working parties, composed primarily of New

York and Connecticut provincials, performed most of this labor under the supervision of the gunners. The rounds and powder cartridges were heavy and awkward, as well as highly flammable. And the appetites of the cannon were voracious and incessant.

Late on this day, contrary to his reputation for calm deliberation and cautious temperament, Jeffery Amherst determined to launch an amphibious assault on the French fort. Wanting the French out of the way so that he could continue his movement on Montreal without further interruption, he determined to storm the island. He was deceived by the weak and ineffective response to the British bombardment.

The attack would be directly supported by the three naval vessels, the *Mohawk*, the *Onondaga*, and the newly christened *Williamson*. Amherst: "ordered the Vesels to fall down close to the Fort, and the Grenadiers with a thousand fascines to be ready to assault the Fort, sending with them two Howitzers in the Row Galleys and 300 men of the Light Infantry & Gages to row in the fascines & secure the batteaus & I put as many marksmen on board each ship as the commanding officer chose to have to fire from the Tops. Everything was ready at the Island on the Right & the men in their batteaus."[125]

Lieutenant Colonel William Amherst of the light infantry battalion recorded: "Orders for landing to storm the fort. The three vessels to fall down as close to the Fort as they can, to man their tops and keep the enemy from their guns. The Grenadiers to row in with fascines & scaling ladders, in their shirts, taking only their broad-swords and tomahawks."[126] Captain Hervey, in his role as brigade major, similarly documented the orders: "at 11 a.m. an assault resolved; the 3 vessels ordered to go down immediately as near to the fort as possible, in order to drive the enemy from the works by the small arms from the tops; their stations taken the Grenadiers to row off and assault, officers and serjeants only to have fire arms, the men swords, axes and tomohawks, and in their waistcoats and forage caps."[127]

In retrospect, this seems to have been a desperate maneuver. The small fleet would sail directly up to the French fort and keep the defenders pinned down with their musketry and cannons. Then several score bateaux, packed to the gunwales with grenadiers, would beach and disgorge the soldiers. They carried fascines to fill in the ditch and any craters or breaches that obstructed their advance. They would then storm the fort, capturing it through a *coup de main*.

The naval attack ended up being dreadfully bungled. In the first place, Pouchot had laid a clever trap for the British, as he subsequently described: "Each man remained under cover at his post; only the sentries kept the movements of the enemy under observation. Judging from our silence that we were perhaps in disarray, they brought their ships up to within the distance of a pistol shot of the fort. They were filled with troops, even the crows nest. . . .Fortunately, they could only take up station one after the other around the fort, so that the first ship that arrived had in its sight the gate of the fort. M. Pouchot had had it concealed in advance by large pieces of blindages with just an opening at the side to let a man through."[128] This account, although somewhat garbled, suggests that Pouchot placed either blinds (wooden frames intended to shore up a wall) or paunch mats (mats woven from heavy ropes, primarily used onboard naval vessels) across the embrasures of his guns to conceal them. When the British ships approached he unmasked his guns and unleashed his cannons against them at devastatingly close range. Pouchot's response proved frighteningly effective.

For whatever reason, the three sailing ships separated in their movement toward the fort, and the *Mohawk* got ahead of the other two vessels. This was in violation of Amherst's specific orders, which mandated a concentrated attack by his naval vessels: "My Intentions were and are that the two Snows Should Approach towards the Fort, putting themselves in a Line with the Williamson."[129] Loring's inability to coordinate and control his three vessels broke up the British naval attack, and exposed each ship individually to the French fire. This proved to be a crucial error that doomed Amherst's audacious naval assault, and it must be laid entirely at the feet of Commodore Loring. As the senior Royal Navy officer present, Loring was specifically charged with coordinating the movement of his small flotilla. One observer, Captain John Knox, recorded: "Whether the vessels were confused with the weight of the enemy's fire, or that the miscarriage may be imputed to the navigation, or the wind, is difficult to determine."[130] For forty-five minutes, the *Mohawk* lay off the northern shore of the island, trading blows with the French fort. It was a one-sided exchange, with the British ship getting the worse of it. With a hole blasted through her side, and river water pouring in, the *Mohawk* drifted downstream with the current. She eventually ran aground on the Île des Galots, and was out of the fight.[131] Her crew was hard pressed simply to keep her from foundering.

Belatedly, the other two vessels finally approached Pouchot's alert and active gunners. With the original plan in shambles, Commodore Loring still determined to press the assault with the two other ships, which he again committed piecemeal. This would prove to be a poor decision. The *Williamson* attempted to anchor on a cable to deliver more effective fire, but in short order her cable was shot away, and she was carried away with the current and ran aground near the *Mohawk*. Of the three ships engaged, the *Mohawk* suffered the least but was still severely battered.

The *Onondaga* continued the struggle alone, and her guns and the French guns pounded away. Finally, as Amherst watched aghast, "The Onandaga very unwisely tried to get farther off & the Stream drove her on nearer & aground instead of getting through as the others had done. In this situation she lay much exposed, but nothing could be done immediately to help her." Dead and wounded aboard, shattered and riddled with shot, and now hopelessly aground, the *Onondaga* was crippled. Pouchot exulted at the view from the galleries of his fort: "It was so badly mauled that it struck its colors. There were 350 men on board. The side of the ship facing the fort suffered particularly badly. Its gun decks were touching the water & the gun ports were just one gaping hole. The water which entered the ship made it lean over in the direction of the fort. M. Pouchot ordered the firing to cease in order to save powder. The second captain & the sailors came to offer surrender."[132] Loring, aboard the *Onondaga*, was shot through his right calf and lost considerable muscle.[133]

Commodore Loring's crew struck the *Onondaga's* colors, and at least some of them abandoned her and surrendered. Amherst ordered a boatload of grenadiers, who had volunteered for the service, to go to her assistance. They raised the King's colors again. Her top quarters were ablaze, her sides were stove in and filling with water, and her guns were disabled. The *Onondaga's* crew was demoralized and knocked out of the fight. "Lt Sinclair & Lt Pennington accordingly sent the men off & came last off & reportd to me they had taken the whole away." The shattered timbers and beams of the *Onondaga* were strewn about the north shore of the island, and the ship was subsequently struck from the British rolls.[134]

The three vessels were riddled and their pieces scattered about the Saint Lawrence River. Without the necessary covering gunfire from the ships, the grenadiers' assault never came off. Amherst's amphibious *coup de main* had been repulsed through a

combination of bad seamanship on the British part and hard fighting by the French.

Loring came in for great censure on the manner in which he had
fought his three ships. He had earlier been criticized for his poor
performance at the beginning of the campaign, when he had let
the French vessels escape on Lake Ontario. Later, it was the Royal
Artillery gunboats that fought the action that cleared the French
ships from the Saint Lawrence, while Loring's craft were bumbling
their way through the Thousand Islands. Later in August, Amherst
would write Pitt in disgust regarding Loring's previous actions on
the Saint Lawrence River: "On the 15ᵗʰ, I passed our two Vessels,
that were got out of the right Channel, and could not get down, notwithstanding I had given the best Pilots I could procure."[135]

Loring tried to justify his actions during the attack of August 23,
and his report placed the naval engagement in a much better light:

> Eleven O'Clock, when we received Orders to . . . haul close in
> with the Fort . . . came to an Anchor within Pistol Shot, and after
> the Vessell was properly moored began firing. The Mohawk and
> Williamson . . . came to an Anchor a little below us. The Mohawk
> after laying three Quarters of an Hour cut her Cable and fell down
> the River out of reach of the Enemy's Fire, having received Damage.
> The Williamson in Half an Hour afterwards did the same, having
> three feet Water in her Hold. We were then left alone exposed to
> the whole Fire of the Garrison; in this situation we lay till a Half
> Hour after Three, our Ammunition being then all expended, hav-
> ing fired eight hundred and ninety two shot, Our Vessell allmost
> totally destroyed, eight of our Guns dismounted, and in short every
> thing tore to pieces. I then sent the Boat on Shore to Know if the
> Grenadiers and Light Infantry, who were ready in their Boats, and
> whose Landing the Vessels were to cover were to land, when I was
> informed they would not be landed that Day.[136]

Colonel Williamson left a particularly detailed account of the
engagement, which he observed from the artillery batteries on one
of the islands. He understood that not only were the *Williamson*,
the *Onondaga*, and the *Mohawk* to cover the landing, but they were
to be joined by the four row galleys that had previously rendered
such good service. However, he was stunned to see the *Mohawk*
come downstream first, "without the other 2 who seemed inclin-
eable to follow." He complimented the fight that the *Mohawk* put

up by itself: "fired briskly when very near the Fort for a considerable time, but was so roughly handled she was obliged to cut her Cable away for fear of sinking." As the battered *Mohawk* drifted away, "the Williamson frigate came in play but she receiving a Shot in an unlucky place started a Plank which hurried her away to an Island [the ship had started to sink and had to be run aground]." Finally and belatedly, the *Onondaga* attacked the island, with results most unfortunate: "stop'd in shallow Water pretty near the Enemy who fired every time into her when She could not help herself, tho within 400 Yards of my Battery she struck to the Enemy." Colonel Williamson, aghast the Onondaga had actually surrendered, "sent an Officers party on Board who hoisted the Colours again & saved her for our selves." Williamson was utterly disgusted with Loring's poor leadership and lack of resolution, lambasting him for his timid actions under fire: "Thornton says Loring ordered him to strike &c. tis said he acknowledged he did & can answer it—I am not conversant in Sea Rules, but if he & crew could not stand it out they ought not to strike so near our Batteries under our Noses [underlined for emphasis in original letter] but come over to us leaving every thing standing, waiting for an happier issue. " Finally, Williamson blamed the failure of the amphibious attack entirely on Loring's inability to coordinate the movement of his three ships: "These Vessels coming down separately & not altogether stop'd the Grenadiers from going on."[137]

Loring's excuses notwithstanding, the responsibility for the failed amphibious assault must be laid entirely at his feet. As commodore of the small British flotilla, it was his responsibility to properly plan the attack, to convey his orders to the masters of the three vessels, and then to coordinate and synchronize their movements during the attack. Amherst's orders to Loring were perfectly understandable, and his brother's journal documents that Amherst clearly transmitted these orders. Although Captain Knox gave Loring the benefit of the doubt, musing that there were challenges caused by the currents and winds of the Saint Lawrence River, Loring had spent the entire month of August on the river. He had had every opportunity to become familiar with the nautical conditions by the time Amherst ordered the amphibious attack. Although current and wind conditions on the river can be highly variable on any summer afternoon, Loring should have anticipated such problems and taken measures to ameliorate them. Amherst's and Pouchot's accounts, supported by that of other observers, show that Loring permitted his three vessels to attack Fort Lévis individually. Such an approach violated the "mass" principle of war, and permitted the French fortress to concentrate its superior shore-based firepower on each individual British ship in turn. The success of any British amphibious assault depended on the presence of supporting gunfire from Loring's flotilla, and without adequate fire support the assault simply could not be launched. Loring's leadership on the afternoon of August 23 was badly flawed, and he served General Amherst and the British cause very poorly.

Lieutenant Colonel William Amherst simply recorded in his daily journal: "The manuever of the ships did not answer the end proposed, so the landing was countermanded." The maneuver of the ships had certainly not answered the end proposed. One vessel had had its entire side smashed in, was hopelessly grounded and surrendered. The second ship had a hole battered through its side and was sinking and driven aground. The third was leaking and battered, with three feet of water in her hold, and also aground. General Amherst, probably in embarrassment, succinctly wrote Lord Ligonier in England: "I intended to Assault the Place, but Every thing not being as I Wished I did not Attempt it."[138]

The Indians with Amherst enjoyed the spectacle a great deal. Pouchot recorded: "One thing that amused the garrison at such a serious time was that the Indians had climbed up onto the [British] trenches & batteries to view those ships in battle. They considered them as their own, because of the names they had been given [*Onondaga* and *Mohawk*] & because they had an Indian painted on their flags. They uttered the most frightful shrieks when they saw the ships so badly mauled."[139]

Although Amherst's audacious gambit had failed, the British artillery continued to pound the French island with what the general tersely called "good success" throughout the day and far into the night. The French response was weak and ineffective at suppressing the British land batteries. At first, the guns of the fort had been focused on destroying the British fleet attacking them. When they later shifted their fire to reply to the British land batteries, they were quickly overwhelmed by the accurate and intense British firepower. Had Amherst only been a bit more patient, his amphibious assault would likely have succeeded.

Pouchot recorded the devastation on the island: "This action reduced to rubble all the top parts of the parapets of half the fort and

blasted away all the fascines or shattered all those facing Isle à la
Cuise. . . . That night [August 23] M. Pouchot endeavored to repair
with earth sacks the batteries of the bastion facing the islands in
order to make them serviceable. This bastion was on the point of
collapsing. A man could have climbed up the ramp formed by the
earth that had caved in." Captain Hervey observed "a breach made
in the [northeastern] bastion nearest to the batteries."[140]

On August 24, the British bombardment continued unabated,
and Pouchot's journal showed evidence of its effectiveness: "The
enemy continued their bombardment throughout that night & at
intervals fired from their batteries shots loaded with ball and grapeshot in order to inhibit our repair work. We had 2 men killed & a
number wounded. . . .Fire broke out in the ruins of the storehouse
in the commandant's apartment. . . . The enemy batteries put out of
action all the cannon of the bastion facing the island[s]. The frames
of the parapets were razed to within two feet of the terre-plein thus
leaving the powder magazine, which was only constructed of large
wooden beams, extremely exposed."[141]

Finally, on August 25 Pouchot was able to respond with more
aggressive counterbattery fire, but he sadly noted: "We were simply unable to destroy or even to damage their batteries to any great
extent."[142] Pouchot's efforts at defense failed to improve his situation. Rather, he observed: "Our firing put the English in a bad mood.
In the afternoon they redoubled the bombardment from all their batteries & fired red-hot shot, *pots à feu* & carcasses [flammable shots].
The red-hot shot set fire to the long fascines of the interior revet-
ment wall of the bastion, right down at the very bottom, where we
were able to extinguish it. That made us realize how badly damaged
the rampart was. *Pots à feu* twice more set the debris of the fort
ablaze. Once again we managed to put out the fires with water from
the shell craters."[143]

Colonel Whiting at Oswegatchie, occupied with urgently forwarding supplies to the front, reported: "25th August 10 oclock A.M.
our batterys kept a continual firing of Shells last night & fire Briskly
this morning they fire very Little from the Fort."[144] Still, the French
fire was not entirely ineffective. Lieutenant Alexander Farqharson of
the Royal Highlanders wrote home during the siege: "I was at dinner
with your old friend Alan Campbell (who is now Major of Grenadiers
during the campaign) about half an hour before the fort surrendered,
we had a bottle of Madeira betwixt us on a board—Thump came a

twelve pounder and drove the bottle in a thousand pieces and deprived us of our drink, yet gave me very great uneasiness." Unfortunately for posterity, the battle-hardened Highlander lieutenant failed to clarify whether the unwelcome arrival of the artillery shell or the loss of his wine had been the source of his "very great uneasiness."[145]

Fort Lévis was a smoldering, shattered, cratered wreck. Pouchot reported that he only had two cannon still serviceable; the rest were shattered or collapsed under the ruins of the fortification. In any event, they could no longer be manned, much less fired. Pouchot had repulsed one British assault, he had delayed the British advance until the middle of August simply through his presence, and his small garrison had withstood a week's siege from August 18 through 25. There was no possibility of any relief arriving from Montreal. With no remaining artillery and a substantial breach in his northeastern bastion, Pouchot and his small garrison held no real hope of repulsing the inevitable British amphibious assault to come. Pouchot recalled that by this point in the siege, sixty men were wounded or killed, a full twenty percent of his garrison, and "all the officers had been more or less seriously wounded." Pouchot had only three courses of action available to him. First, he could huddle behind the remnants of his battered parapets until the powder magazine was detonated, killing or wounding the entirety of his garrison. Second, he could wait for the British grenadiers to return, swarm through the breach in his bastion, and storm the works. In this case, contemporary conventions of warfare stated that the entire garrison could be put to the sword. Finally, with no hope of relief, with his artillery disabled, with the garrison incapable of further resistance, and with his works breached, by European standards Pouchot could now surrender honorably.

The opportunity came to Pouchot on August 25. The barrage of combustible bombs and red-hot shot was devastating and unbearable to the French garrison. "This prompted M. Pouchot, with the endorsement of all the officers of the garrison, to write to General Amherst to complain about this manner of making war, which was only used against rebels and not against a brave garrison that did not deserve such treatment. In reply, he sent his aide-de-camp with a kind of surrender document making us prisoners of war together with a threat that, if we did not accept within half an hour, he would continue as before." Pouchot, probably with a sigh of relief, sounded out his garrison: "The latter urged him very strongly to accept the

demands, in view of the impossibility of preventing fire breaking out everywhere & of being able to avoid the flames because of
the small extent of the fort & the obstacles created by the debris."
Pouchot accepted Amherst's terms.[146] A young Connecticut soldier,
Asa Waterman, succinctly recorded in his small diary: "the fort Was
given up About 8 at Night."[147]

Pouchot surrendered the fort, and the garrison became prisoners of war. The fort and all munitions and arms became the property of the British. Any British deserters and Indians in the fort were
exempted from the terms of the surrender. The fact that Pouchot
did not contest this last item suggests that it did not apply to any-
one then counted as a member of the garrison. The French prisoners would eventually be sent under guard down the Mohawk River,
more for protection from the Indians than because of any real fear
that they would escape, and they would eventually be repatriated
from New York City. Amherst gave the assignment of seizing the
fort to Lieutenant Colonel Massey and his Grenadiers Battalion,
who honored the French defenders by entering Fort Lévis through
the breach in the fort. Colonel Williamson, who accompanied them,
recalled: "The morning after the Surrender I went in at the Breach
my hands in my bosom & hoisted the Union on the Top of it."[148] By
doing so, he demonstrated that the fort's defenses had been compro-
mised and were no longer tenable, thus confiming that Pouchot's
surrender had been done under honorable conditions.

Amherst refused to let Johnson's Indians enter the fort, for fear
that they would slaughter the French garrison. Amherst earned the
enmity of the Indians by keeping them under a tight rein and preventing them from committing any possible atrocities (by European
standards) or traditional victory celebrations (by Indian standards).[149]
There was some minor looting by members of the army, but Amherst
put an end to it in short order. In Captain Hervey's orderly book for
August 27, it was published: "Christian Parkey, sutler, Abraham
Willey and Jacob Miller, spruce brewers, tried by a Court-martial
for taking eleven fire-locks and some goods out of Fort Levi, are
found guilty and sentenced to receive 300 lashes each. The General
approves of the sentence, and it is to be put into execution at retreat
beating in the front of the Line between the 2nd Highland battalion
and Montgomery's by the drummers of those regiments."[150]

Beginning the next morning Amherst had his siege works leveled, a routine practice to ensure that they could not be used against

the now British fortress. He also began to reconstruct the French fort, which was renamed Fort William Augustus in honor of the Duke of Cumberland, son of King George II and former captain general of the British army. In commemoration of the victory, the parole of the day for Amherst's army for August 26 was "King George."[151]

The siege had cost Amherst twenty-one men killed and twenty-three wounded, nearly all of them during the abortive amphibious assault on August 23. The French had a total of twelve killed and thirty-five wounded.[152] Amherst probably considered this to be a small price to pay, for the path to Montreal now lay wide open before him.

CHAPTER 8

"It Was Impossible to Make Any Further Resistance"

The Final Act Plays Out before Montreal

To traverse the final steps to Montreal and deal a fatal blow to the French in Canada, Amherst had to complete three necessary tasks and overcome one last significant obstacle. First, the newly christened Fort William Augustus had to be garrisoned and the shattered fortification repaired. A small detachment was assigned from the provincials for this purpose.

The second task was the movement of artillery. Amherst's soldiers had to remove the siege artillery from the batteries, break it down, and reload it aboard the bateaux. The same process had been necessary the previous year when the artillery had been moved from Albany to besiege Fort Niagara. After the successful conclusion of that siege, it had been moved back to Fort Oswego in preparation for a movement down the Saint Lawrence. Gage never made this attack. In early August, the artillery had again been loaded aboard ship for travel on Lake Ontario for the attack on Fort Lévis. This effort had required considerable sweat and muscle power, taking no fewer than five days, from August 26 through 30, to complete. Finally, the *Mohawk* and *Williamson* had to be repaired and rendered seaworthy.[1] The *Onandaga* was so badly shattered that it was not salvageable, but her ammunition, cannon, and stores had to be recovered and used for the reconstruction of the fort.[2]

The third challenge facing Amherst before he could depart Fort William Augustus was Indian diplomacy. For the Indians that had accompanied Amherst, the siege of Fort Lévis had no significance. To an Indian warrior, the entire purpose of spending the full summer on the warpath would have been to demonstrate his prowess through performing deeds of valor, taking scalps, seizing prisoners, and acquiring plunder. But not a single Indian warrior had gained any honor, taken a scalp, or garnered any loot. Amherst had prevented the Native warriors from seizing any of the French prisoners, and he had specifically prohibited Indians from going ashore at Fort Lévis. Thus, instead of fishing or hunting for the benefit of their families and clan or going on the warpath against the Southern Indians to prove themselves as warriors, the Indians felt that they had squandered the summer of 1760.

Amherst permitted the Indians to visit Fort Lévis, but he would not permit them to take anything. Instead, he had Sir William Johnson distribute trade goods.[3] Although this was a magnanimous gesture, the quantity of trade goods at hand was distinctly limited, and what was available did not go far among nearly 700 Indians. Most likely, such a trifling distribution was probably perceived more as an insult than a gift.

Sir William was a master of the art, but even his efforts to keep the disgruntled Indians pacified proved to be in vain. He recorded that shortly after the surrender of the French fort, 506 Indians had departed in disgust with their twenty whaleboats.[4] The Indians who left composed the overwhelming majority of those who had departed Oswego with the British, and the 185 Indians who remained were principally members of the Iroquois Confederation. They stayed because of personal loyalty to Sir William Johnson, who was a senior leader of the Mohawk nation. Johnson attested that: "After taking Fort Lévis many of our Indians, thro some disgust left us, but there still remained a sufficient number to answer our purpose and bring us constant Intelligence, having none [i.e., French-supporting Indians] against us."[5]

The remaining Indians continued to play an important role in the campaign. Of greatest import, they regularly carried messages and news between Amherst's various columns. On August 28, three Indians came up from Montreal and informed Sir William Johnson that "the vessels with Governor Murray's Army was arrived at Montreal."[6] Johnson promptly passed the information on to Amherst. On August 30, Captain Hervey recorded that: "Jacobs the Indian comes in from Cocknawage [Caughnawaga, across the Saint Lawrence River from Montreal] in Montreal."[7] Amherst clarified that this referred to "Capt. Jacobs who was taken with Capt. Kennedy came to me," that is, Captain Jacob Nawnawapeteoonks, who had previously commanded a company of Stockbridge Mohicans with Rogers' Rangers.[8] Although this was a strictly informal means of gaining intelligence, and the accuracy of the information varied widely, this remained one of the few means by which the three British columns could communicate with each other.

The Stockbridge Mohican Captain Jacobs had been specifically released by his French captors. The Indian nations of the Saint Lawrence River valley used him as an emissary to Amherst, in effect suing for peace. Amherst recorded on August 29: "At night Capt Jacobs . . . arrived with Indians from the French & brought me a letter from a Priest to offer peace on the Indian side."[9] As a result, Amherst reported on August 30: "Sr Wm Johnson all day in conference with the Indians."[10] Amherst had written to Johnson with instructions before the Indian Conference: "With . . . the talk you will have from their Sachems, You will be best able to Judge what will be the most likely means to hinder the Indians from joining the Enemy, in which Case, they may be Assured of being permitted to live in Peace and Quiet, and of receiving all the protection they can desire."[11] Sir William Johnson wrote to Pitt several months following the campaign, describing this effort: "As there were nine Severall Nations & Tribes of Indians inhabiting the Country about Montreal consisting of about 800 fighting men, previous to our departure [from Fort Lévis] I judged it highly necessary to gain them if possible, at least to bring them to a Neutrality." Johnson initiated a conference with these Indians: "I therefore proposed to General Amherst the sending them offers of peace & protection, which he agreed to." Johnson's efforts bore fruit, for he noted that the representatives of the Saint Lawrence Indians "ratified a Treaty with us, whereby they agreed to remain neuter on condition that we for the future treated them as friends & forgot all former enmity." Sir William was quite pleased with the results:

> The Peace which I settled with the 9 Nations before mentioned, was productive of such good consequence that some of these Indians joined us & went upon Partys for Prisoners whilst the rest preserved so strict a neutrality that we passed all the dangerous Rapids, and the whole way without the least opposition, & by that means came so near to the other two Armies, that the Enemy could attempt nothing further without an imminent risque of the City & inhabitants. . . . Thus we became Masters of the last place in the Enemy's possession on these parts and made those Indians our friends by a peace, who might otherwise have given us much trouble.[12]

With Indian diplomacy in the able hands of Sir William Johnson, Amherst's fears were focused on the last obstacle—one of nature, and not of man. It was the Saint Lawrence River itself. Although the various rapids of the Saint Lawrence were well known to be treacherous and deadly, Amherst possessed little actual knowledge of them. As required by military tradition to honor a respected opponent, General Amherst hosted Captain Pouchot for dinner on the evening of August 26. At the dinner, Pouchot recalled: "General Amherst had an hour-long conversation alone with M. Pouchot. He endeavored to extract details about what remained to be done in this campaign. It may well be imagined that M. Pouchot did not portray his task as an easy one. He [Amherst] seemed, just like the rest of the army, to dread going down the rapids."[13]

As early as August 20, while the siege was still in progress, Amherst had begun patrolling down the river. On this date, Sir William Johnson dispatched a scouting party with "10 Indians"; and also sent his agent Fonda "with 2 whale Bots & 20 Indians Down the Reaver to see How the pasedge was By water—I found it Verry passabile and Returned the Same Day."[14]

Since he possessed no suitable guides for the voyage down the Saint Lawrence River, Amherst recruited among the crew of the captured French ship *Outaouaise*, and the crew of the *Iroquoise*, who had been marooned on Fort Lévis when their vessel had run aground. Amherst offered these prisoners their release upon his flotilla's arrival at Montreal in exchange for their services as guides during the transit down the river. This must have seemed like an extraordinarily good offer to these men, and Pouchot reported: "From among the Canadians, they took 36 guides for their bateaux."[15] Amherst recorded on August 19 that from the crew of the *Outaouaise*, he "took 19 of the best I could pick out to serve as Pilots down the River, gave one to the care of each Corps & put one Pilot on board the Williamson."[16] Amherst recruited from the crew of the *Iroquoise*, thus accounting for the larger number than Pouchot recalled.

With Johnson reaching an accord with the various Indian nations, and with all necessary repairs and preparations accomplished, Colonel Haldimand's advance guard departed for Montreal on August 31. Lieutenant Colonel William Amherst recorded in his journal: "Rangers, Gage's, Light Infantry of Regts, Grandiers with three Provincial Regiments & row galleys set out this forenoon. We passed the rapids of Galot & Plat & encamped on the Isle au Chat."[17]

The soldiers referred to Île au Chat as Cat Island. This was a good day's journey, as this island was about twenty-four miles east of Fort William Augustus. As with many islands in the Saint Lawrence River, the Île au Chat was a victim of the construction of the Saint Lawrence Seaway. Only a tiny remnant of land exists today, surrounded by shoals southwest of Ingleside, Ontario.

Later in the day Amherst's two brigades followed. In 1760, the Saint Lawrence River was marked by a series of rapids and minor falls. These varied in difficulty of passage from inconvenient to frighteningly perilous. When the Saint Lawrence Seaway was constructed in the 1950s, seven locks and three dams were required to make the river navigable for oceangoing vessels. Every day of their advance from the Oswegatchie River to Montreal, Amherst's army would face rapids with their attendant dangers. Amherst's recruitment of Canadian prisoners to pilot his vessels was an attempt to reduce the risks. The army, however, would still have to run the rapids, as in 1760, the river was the only route that led to the capital city of Canada. The two most dangerous rapids were the Long Sault (Long Rapids), located just north of the modern community of Massena, New York, and the Cedars Rapids, located closer to Montreal at the eastern end of Lac Saint-Francois. Of these two rapids, the Cedars in particular had a dreaded reputation.

On September 1, the main body of the army continued to make good progress, rowing to "Point de Maline about 14 miles from Isle au Chat." The next day the army ran the Long Sault Rapids. Amherst noted: "The Current of the River was very strong & the Rapids frightful in appearance but not dangerous. I took water several times into the whale boat."[18] The army passed this first great obstacle with few problems; Amherst reported only one loss: "A Batteau of the 1st Batt of R Highlanders in coming down the Long Seau this morning & keeping too near the shore was staved & a Corporal & three men drowned." This day the army "rowed in four columns 24 miles to La Pointe a Boudet."[19] No longer known by this name, Pointe à Boudet was in the vicinity of modern Farlingers Point, or Flanigans Point, on the northern shore of the river across from the Saint Regis Mohawk Reservation.[20]

By nightfall on September 2, the advance guard and main body of the army had joined together "on the North side near the entrance of Lake St. Francis."[21] Amherst intended to maintain his pace the next day, but "very violent rain & wind came on in the night; luckily our

Batteaus were in safe Places." Amherst was informed by his guides that "Lake St. Francis is very full of Islands, the depth of water not great, so that when there is high wind the Lake is much agitated & my Pilot tells me they sometimes wait five or six days before they can pass it." Despite his haste to reach Montreal, Amherst had no option but to lose another day to the vagaries of the weather. He grumbled, "It rained and blew hard all morning so that I could not proceed."[22]

For Amherst's soldiers, the most difficult challenge of the day was simply trying to keep warm and dry as a summer cold front passed through the Saint Lawrence valley. This type of weather system generates ice-cold torrential rains that can make life miserable for soldiers huddled under canvas and around fires.[23] The only news of the day was that a scouting party of Indians, dispatched earlier by Sir William Johnson toward Montreal, had met the British flotilla. General Amherst recalled: "A Scout of Indians that went to the Cedars returned with a Prisoner . . . who acquainted me the isle aux noix was taken. . . . He said Br. [Brigadier] Murray was at some distance from the Town."[24] This information was not entirely accurate, as Murray was by now within a few miles of Montreal, not "some distance from the Town." The report of this prisoner demonstrated the unreliable and impromptu methods by which Amherst had to obtain intelligence about the movements of the separate columns of his own army.

Still, this information was important, as it indicated to Amherst that at least one of the two other columns was closing rapidly on Montreal, if it was not already there. Amherst, who wanted to garner the glory of Canada's surrender for himself, was in a hurry to reach Montreal. He had lost a full week in the siege of Fort Lévis, and the urgency that he felt there had been responsible for his failed amphibious attack on the island. Amherst had fallen behind his timetable, and he would accept no further delay. The next day he continued his advance, even though the drenching rains of the day before had swollen the river and turned it to furious whitewater. Amherst was willing to take risks to maintain his momentum.

On September 4, Amherst's army tackled the last great obstacle before Montreal, the Cedars Rapids. Captain Knox recalled: "The rapids are frightful, and full of broken waves."[25] Amherst took every possible precaution and issued clear instructions to his army. He ensured that pilots led every column of boats. The boats advanced

Thomas Davies, "A View of Passage of the Army under the Command of his Excellency Major General Amherst down the Rapids of St. Lawrence River for the Reduction of Canada in the Year 1760" (1760). Courtesy of Library and Archives Canada.

in a double column, and sufficient space between them was maintained to allow them to maneuver around obstacles and dangers. He disembarked most of the men to march on land around the rapids. Despite Amherst's careful preparations, however, the day turned into a disaster.

Lieutenant Colonel William Amherst led the way with the light infantry of the advance guard, a position in the column that he would soon come to regret: "We passed Le Cote du Lac, Les battures des Ceders, Le Buisson, Le Trou & Les Cascades—all rapids, and Le Trou the worst of them, where I lost 2 Sergts, 1 Drummer and 22 men, drowned of my Corps. I had 9 boats lost and staved. . . . Most of the Regts lost men, but not so many as we did, as they used more precautions after our loss."[26] Lieutenant John Grant, an officer with the 2nd Battalion of the Royal Highlanders, described the horrific encounter with the swirling, foaming white water:

> In order to avoid confusion, the boats should go two abreast, and such regts keep together, It was said we had no rapids to fear, in this order we set out and had proceeded some hours along the

majestic river in full security—On a sudden I saw the boat ahead
of me suddenly disappear, and felt the diversion of the water and
immediately divined the cause, I jumped up and called 'a rapid'
and to keep to the right & to pass the word. Caught by the suc-
tion our boat was whirled about and filled with water—the casks
floated and one struck me a blow on the side, that almost stunned
me. Saw several boats upset, and poor fellows struggling in the
eddies below the falls and calling piteously for help."[27]

Private Robert Kirk, a fellow highlander with Lieutenant Grant,
similarly recalled:

We lost an hundred men on our passage down this river, which was
occasioned, by their not being careful to keep their boats in the
right channel, which can only be distinguished by the smoothness
of the surface, and it is always fatal to any who deviate from this
rule. Here you will run 15 miles in 15 minutes, and if you offer to
turn out of this current, which you would imagine would precipi-
tate you in ruin, nothing but being dash'd to pieces, and unavoid-
ably lost will be the consequence. We were forced to run all
hazards, and had certainly been swallowed up in those mountains
of water, if we had not obliged several canoes to shoot the cataracts
at the head of our boats, in order to shew us the way; at the same
time we had prepared ourselves for rowing, and shieving [sheav-
ing] upon occasion [in other words they tied down their cargo]. The
current run as fast as a cannon-ball; and one false stroke of the oar,
would have run us upon the rocks; for we were oblig'd to steer a
zig-zag course pursuant to the thread of the stream, which has fifty
windings. But after all, tho' the risque we run be very great, yet by
way of compensation, one has the satisfaction of running a great
way in a short time. . . .We got at last into still water.[28]

Lieutenant Grant would recall, in horror, "50 or 60 [soldiers]
found a water grave, bonnets, casks, baggage, all floating about in
the eddies." Captain Thomas Stirling of the same regiment observed
that "fellow creatures floating on the wrecks and you passing them
not being able to assist . . . would pierce the most obdurate heart."[29]
Boats would straggle in, battered and leaking, through all hours of
the night.

It would be the next morning before the day's toll could be accu-
rately assessed. Amherst lamented of the fatal passage: "The Pilots
assured me it was very unusual to find so much water in the River

24-pounder cannon lost by Amherst at Cedar Rapids, St. Lawrence River, September 4, 1760. Photograph by the author.

[doubtless due to the heavy rains a day earlier] yet we found it very bad & difficult to pass." Amherst was stunned that "the Rapids cost us dear, notwithstanding every Corps had a Pilot. Several had two & the Pilots sent back as fast as the batteaus passed. We lost 84 men, 20 batteaus of Regts, 17 of Artillery, 17 whaleboats, one Row Galley, a quantity of Artillery Stores & some Guns that I hope may be recovered."[30] Among the guns lost were a 24-pounder cannon, a ten-inch mortar, and a five-and-a-half-inch Royal bronze mortar, along with nearly one hundred mortar shells.[31] These guns were eventually recovered from the bottom of the river in the latter part of the twentieth century. Amherst had sustained greater casualties in a single day's travel on the Saint Lawrence River than he had lost in two pitched naval battles and the entire siege of Fort Lévis.

September 5 was a loss, as the damage the army sustained the day before had, in Amherst's words, "put it out of my Power to proceed this day."[32] Shattered, water-logged boats were still straggling in. Efforts to recover the lost cannon were ultimately unsuccessful. Nearly every bateau and whaleboat had been damaged to some extent and had to be repaired. Personnel and matériel losses had to be tallied, and units had to be reorganized. It appears that the light infantry and the Highlanders had suffered the most. Both battalions needed command attention, rest, and recuperation before they could continue their advance.

Still, on this day one event of monumental significance occurred: for the first time in the campaign, regular communications were established between the three columns. Two days before, Murray and Haviland had established contact when "late last night, an Officer of the Royal Americans, in disguise, with four rangers, arrived from Brigadier Haviland's corps, who they say will actually be at la Prairie in two or three days at the farthest."[33] This officer was Lieutenant John Montresor, who had been dispatched up the Saint Lawrence River specifically to locate Amherst. As Murray's chief engineer, Montresor was in Amherst's confidence, so he could report Murray's progress and future intentions without having to entrust such a critical message to writing.[34] La Prairie was located on the south shore of the Saint Lawrence River, just a few miles upstream from Murray's column, and directly across the river from Montreal.

In less than forty-eight hours, all three columns would be in communication. Lieutenant Colonel William Amherst recorded in his journal: "Lt. Elliott, with a party, came with a letter to the General this afternoon. He left Col. Haviland's army at St. John's last Sun."[35] The party included several rangers that had been detailed by Major Rogers to escort Elliot.[36] Two hours later, Lieutenant Crofton arrived from General Murray's column.[37] From this moment Amherst regained tactical command and control of all three of his columns, and regular communication could now be maintained between himself, Haviland, and Murray. Amherst reported in his journal that he wrote to Murray on September 7 and 8 and that he exchanged liaison officers with both Murray and Haviland on September 8. Amherst was able to meet personally with both of his brigadiers the same evening.[38] For the first time in this campaign Amherst was a true army commander, rather than simply the commander of one of three separate columns.

Having passed the Cedars, Amherst's army encountered the first Canadian settlements. Amherst, well aware that Britain would shortly be in possession of Canada and that the Canadian citizens would soon be British subjects, was concerned that the Canadians be well treated. He respected their persons and property so long as they swore an oath of good behavior and loyalty to King George II. He issued strict injunctions to his soldiers: "The rolls to be frequently called to prevent soldiers from maroding" and "All the prisoners, men women and children, taken upon this island or elsewhere, are to be sent to headquarters this afternoon at 4 o'clock. They are to bring all the arms they have, and to take an oath of fidelity to the king of G.B. [Great Britain], after which they will be allowed to return to their habitations and live under his Majesty's protection."[39] Highlander Thompson recalled that Murray's army was ordered upon landing "to curb their firelocks, that is, to carry the Butts upwards, in token of friendship."[40] Lieutenant Colonel William Amherst recalled: "Several inhabitants of this Island who had fled with their effects to the woods came in this afternoon and took the oaths, upon hearing of the good usage the others had met with."[41] General Amherst reported to Pitt: "[September] 5th the Inhabitants of the Island had all run into the woods and abandoned their houses, some were taken, and some came in, I had the Oath of Allegiance tendered to them, and I put them in quiet possession of their houses and they seemed as much surprised with their treatment as they were happy with it."[42]

Amherst's had not been the first column to arrive in front of Montreal. Rather, that distinction belonged to Murray's Saint Lawrence River column that had arrived at Saint Thérèse Island (Île Sainte-Thérèse) on August 31. With the three columns of the British army now joined, one veteran of Amherst's column recorded: "At Eleven o'Clock we landed on the Island of Montreal (nine miles from Town), fixed our Bayonets, and formed. We marched directly for the Town."[43] Colonel Whiting wrote his wife with the news that "I'm now to come to the Last act of my Drama, which Opens the Whole Scene."[44] Montreal was facing a unified British army with powerful columns operating on both flanks and to the front of the city. The French were all too well aware that "a dark crisis was now at hand for the fate of Canada."[45]

On September 3, Murray's army landed at the northeastern end of Island of Montreal, at "Point de Tremble" (Pointe-aux-Trembles). The log of the *Porcupine* laconically recorded the moment: "Light breezes, with some rain. General Murry with his army land[d] on the Island of Montreal at Point de Tremble."[46] Almost as soon as Murray stepped ashore on the island, he was greeted by a formal communication from the governor of Canada, the Marquis de Vaudrieul, offering to capitulate. Murray formally received this offer and courteously suggested to the governor that he might wish to resubmit it to the commander in chief of British forces in North America, Major General Jefferey Amherst, who was expected at any moment from points west.[47]

Amherst's army moved down the Saint Lawrence River, continuing its final movement in four columns. They rowed their bateaux and whaleboats down the beautiful river under clear skies. The advance guard was in the van, the two regular brigades were massed in the center, and the powerful train of Royal Artillery was in the rear waiting to be called forward. On September 4, Captain Knox with Murray was "assured by some [French] deserters today, that the Commander in Chief's army were arrived at Perrot island, within less than four leagues of the city of Montreal."[48] The Frenchmen had related the truth, for Amherst was on the Île Perrot, just southwest of Montreal Island. Murray was now to the east of Montreal, Haviland to the south, and Amherst closing in from the west. Captain Knox remarked, "In this case his most Christian Majesty [French King Louis] is in a fair way of being speedily *checkmated* in Canada [Knox's emphasis].[49] The jaws of Amherst's trap were closing on the French. On September 6, Amherst's army landed at Lachine, about eight miles southwest of Montreal.

Encircling the city were a number of small forts located on the island of Montreal. These were more properly fortified farms or compounds, resembling La Haye Sainte or Hougoumont Farm on the Waterloo battlefield. They were entirely capable of resisting an Indian raid or a small infantry incursion but had no defensive value against artillery. At Amherst's approach, all of these smaller outlying forts were abandoned and their tiny garrisons consolidated in Montreal.

A small detachment of French cavalry was dispatched to observe the landing, and a brief skirmish of "a very few shots" quickly sent the French scouts galloping in disarray back to the city. Before 1759, the French had no cavalry in Canada. Most of the fighting was either done in the wilderness or in formal sieges, and cavalry would have had little opportunity to make much of a contribution. It had become apparent by June 1759 that the battle for Canada would be fought in the long-cleared farm fields of the Saint Lawrence and Richelieu River valleys. Accordingly, Montcalm determined on the "formation of a mounted troop." Although the French army in

Canada was in desperate straits by the summer of 1759, and the army's magazines and war chest were sorely depleted, priority was given to organizing this troop of cavalry. The Marquis de Montcalm recommended that they be equipped with bearskin caps "to give them a martial look" and armed with sabers and muskets (probably carbines). The resulting troop proved adept at patrolling and reconnaissance, for on November 12, 1759, they engaged in a skirmish in which one unfortunate British soldier was "set upon by ten of the light cavalry, who beat and abused him inhumanly, by wounding him with their sabres, and scarifying his wrists and arms with their knives." By August 1760 they were well appointed, appearing in blue uniforms faced with scarlet, "mounted on neat light horses of difference colors." Their officers wore white uniforms, presumably their original uniforms, which they were loath to discard. Their brief appearance outside of Montreal on September 6 was their solitary contribution to the defense of the city in 1760, and the French had derived little benefit from the resources expended to outfit this Canadian corps of cavalry.[50]

With all other manmade or natural obstacles overcome, Amherst's final impediment to completing the conquest of Canada was the fortifications that surrounded the city. Montreal's defenses now challenging Amherst were, in a word, laughable. The city was surrounded by a stone wall with an exterior dry ditch, counterscarp, and glacis that had been constructed between 1717 and 1744.[51] The ramparts extended 10,800 feet in length, with numerous bastions and a single strong citadel to the northeast. The bastions had been designed to support Canadian militia not used to maneuvering in close lineal tactics, and their gorges and angles were correspondingly large and wide. This made the bastions flatter than was typically seen in a classic Vauban-era fortification. This design increased the bastions' effectiveness against an infantry assault, but meant that artillery mounted within the walls would have a limited capacity to control the ground to the front of the city. Although the walls were an imposing eighteen feet high, they were only four feet thick at the base, and less than three feet thick at the top. The parapets were pieced with musket loopholes every six feet, further weakening their ability to resist artillery. The city's walls had been optimized to resist a strong Indian attack or a powerful infantry raid, and they were entirely adequate for those purposes. A modern chemical engineering study of the mortar used in the fortification's walls

Foundations of Montreal city walls. Photograph by the author.

determined that it was well-mixed, strong, possessed "long-term durability," and reflected the use of "advanced construction practices."[52] Yet even va 6-pounder, more properly considered a field cannon accompanying an infantry battalion rather than a siege gun, could easily penetrate such a thin wall pierced with loopholes, no matter how well constructed it was. This parapet was not intended to resist artillery fire, and Montreal's defenses were simply not configured to oppose a formal European siege. In fact, the ramparts behind the protective parapets were only seven feet deep, far too narrow to accommodate the heavy cannon that would be necessary to resist a British siege, even if such guns had been available. Finally, Montreal's fortifications had no outerworks whatsoever, further reducing their capacity to resist a deliberate siege. The Chevalier Johnstone, who had reached the city with the retreating garrison from Île aux Noix, observed: "Montreal was nowise susceptible of defense. It was surrounded with stone walls, built in the beginning of that colony, merely to preserve the inhabitants from the incursions of the Indians, few imagining at that time it would become the theater of a regular war, and that one day they would see formidable armies of regular, well-disciplined troops before its walls."[53]

The powerful trains of heavy siege guns that Amherst, Murray, and Haviland had brought before Montreal would be fully capable of transforming the fortifications of the city into a mound of expensive rubble in relatively short order.[54] A devastating infantry assault through the breach made by the British cannon would be certain to follow. Montreal was, for all practical purposes, defenseless against any one of Amherst's columns, much less all three combined.[55]

Amherst moved his army to the northwest of the city: "I made the most of the day I could, to get into the open Ground in view of the Town where I formed the Troops & lay on our Arms all night." He also brought up "five 3-pounders, five 6-pounders, two 12-pounders and two Howitzers." The troops lay on their arms that night, the twinkling lights of the city to their front. Amherst stayed up the entire night, surveying the ground under cover of darkness with his engineers, as he planned to begin his siege approaches to the city the next evening. Murray moved his army to the northeast of the city, close by the promontory of Mount Royal. On this date, Robert Rogers with his rangers and the advance guard of Haviland's column reached Longueuil, opposite the river from the city, effectively closing the ring on its defenders.[57]

On September 5, Murray had been approached by eight Sachems of various Indian tribes, including the Hurons and Iroquois, who desired to establish peace with the armies of Great Britain. Murray, as a subordinate to Amherst, was not empowered to enter into a formal treaty with the Natives. That would be left to Amherst and Sir William Johnson following the final defeat of Canada. Murray met at length with them, however, and issued a pass or legal certificate to protect their rights and guarantee their freedom of movement.[58] Personally signed by Murray and issued by his adjutant general on this date, this document stated: "These are to certify that the chief of the Huron Tribe of Indians, having come to me in the name of his Nation to submit to His Brittanick Majesty and make Peace, has been received under my protection with his whole Tribe, and henceforth no English officer or party is to molest or interrupt them in returning to their settlement at Lorette and they are received upon the same terms with the Canadians, being allowed the free Exercise of their Religion, their Customs and liberty of trading with the English Garrisons recommending it to the Officers commanding the posts to treat them kindly."[59]

At daybreak on August 7, both Murray's and Amherst's regiments stood to arms. As Amherst rode about the front, making preparations for the opening of the trenches once the sun set that evening, he "had a Report from the advanced Guard that two Officers were sent from Mons. De Vaudreuil to speak to me." One of the officers was Bougainville, recently returned from his stalwart but doomed defense of Île aux Noix. He was accompanied by Captain Dominique Nicolas de Laas de Gustede of the Regiment de la Reine. He was an officer long in service to the King of France, and he proudly wore about his neck the Cross of the Order of Saint Louis, the mark of a hero of France.[60] These two distinguished officers, the youngest and the oldest heroes of Canada, had been entrusted with the grave responsibility of transmitting a letter from the governor to the commanding general of His Britannic Majesty's forces gathered before Canada's leading city. The letter proposed a cessation of arms until the governor received a long-anticipated courier from France, who was expected to arrive bearing news of a permanent peace reached in Europe. Of course, no such courier could possibly hope to pass through the Royal Navy, and Amherst recognized the ploy as a clever ruse to delay the inevitable. Having paid a terrible price in running the rapids of the St. Lawrence River just two days previously so that he could arrive before the gates of Montreal, Amherst was in no mood to dally. Bluntly, he informed the young and courtly Bougainville and the grey-haired Captain de Gustede that "I was come to take Canada and I did not intend to take anything less."[61] With this brusque response, Amherst showed his will and determination.

In accordance with the established customs of warfare as it was practiced in the middle of the eighteenth century, the surrendering party had the privilege of first proposing the terms under which he would yield. Amherst informed the two officers: "If Mons Vaudreuil had any proposals to make, desired he would write them down." A cease-fire was agreed to until noon, although Amherst wrung a concession out of Bougainville and Captain de Gustede that Murray's and Haviland's armies could continue their advances. This was somewhat unusual for such an armistice, but the French officers had nothing to bargain with and were forced to cede the point.

Amherst, in the field at the head of his powerful army, sent a series of letters threatening the French trapped in the city. Presumably, the slow matches of the artillery pieces were smoldering ominously, with thin trails of smoke rising up from the British batteries. Governor de Vaudrieul and General de Lévis both attempted to soften the terms that Amherst demanded. Amherst was relentless and merciless:

"I have already had the honour to inform your Excellency, that I should not make any alteration in them; I cannot deviate from this resolution."[62] Amherst's concept of negotiations was an ultimatum delivered from the mouth of a cannon.

The French no longer possessed the resolve for a stalwart final defense of Canada, and Governor de Vaudrieul understood his plight from the inside of the fragile city walls of Montreal quite as well as Amherst did from the outside. As the Chevalier Johnstone lamented: "We were all pent up in that miserable, bad place—without provisions, a thousand times worse off than an advantageous position in open fields—whose pitiful walls could not resist two hours' cannonades without being level with the ground, and where we would have been forced to surrender at discretion, if the English had insisted upon it."[63] Amherst would insist on it. He was particularly vindictive toward the French army, which he believed had acted dishonorably in massacres throughout the entire war. He particularly resented the infamous broken truce at Fort William Henry in 1757.

When de Lévis pleaded his case with Amherst through his intermediaries, he was met with a reply that brooked no misunderstanding. Amherst replied that "he was fully resolved, for the infamous part the troops of France had acted in exciting the savages to perpetuate the most horrid and unheard of barbarities in the whole progress of the war, and for other open treacheries, as well as flagrant breaches of faith, to manifest to all the world, by this capitulation, his detestation of such ungenerous practices, and disapprobation of their conduct."[64]

Beginning on September 5, Amherst had granted extremely benevolent terms to the French civilians and the citizens of Canada. But he made French soldiers prisoners of war, with the additional stipulation that they were not to serve "during the present war." This effectively meant that they could no longer be paid in the King's service until a formal treaty of peace was signed. This denied the soldiers, and particularly the officers, their livelihoods, and further denied them the honors of war. It was a bitter pill for the French regulars to swallow.

General de Lévis at first urged, and then implored, the Marquis de Vaudrieul not to surrender the army, but to permit them one final chance for glory from their island garrison of the Île Sainte-Hélène (Saint Helen's Island), located in the Saint Lawrence directly south of Montreal. Negotiations continued through the night, and the

British army outside the city again rested on their arms, ready for immediate action. Their presence constituted an unmistakable and impending threat to the French citizens and their leaders.[65] The governor denied de Lévis's request, and accepted Amherst's otherwise lenient terms, at the expense of the French regular battalions who had so valiantly struggled to defend Canada for six arduous years. On the afternoon of September 8, the Marquis de Vaudrieul signed the terms of capitulation precisely as Amherst had proposed them, and Montreal and all of Canada was in the hands of the British.[66]

New York Colonel Woodhull succinctly assessed Amherst's terms: "The articles of capitulation were signed; which provided that all the soldiers were to be transported to France, and not to take up arms during the continuance of the war, and the inhabitants to enjoy every thing that belonged to them, and to be governed by the Laws of England."[67] The British Navy provided vessels to return the French government officials and administrators, their families, and the army to France.

Colonel Haldimand, Lieutenant Colonel Amherst, two companies of grenadiers, and three companies of light infantry were accorded the honor of entering the city. Colonel Williamson viewed the spectacle: "The 9th on Tuesday a Light 12 Pdr with an Officers party (Davies) of Artillery Union Flag flying, Band of Musick 300 Grenadiers Drums & Fifes entered the Town [underlined and bolded in original letter]. The Flag was taken to the most conspicuous part of the Cittadel escorted by Grenadiers with fixed Bayonets many Drums & Fifes a large Band of Musick and when hoisted three Cheers were given answered by our Parade & so Finis."[68]

All of the other soldiers were prohibited from following the grenadiers and light infantry into the city. Amherst believed that Montreal would now become the capital of British Canada. Always keen to maintain good order and discipline, he had absolutely no intention of releasing hundreds of bored, curious, mischievous, and exclusively Protestant soldiers loose in the city to wreak God only knew what havoc. Amherst was concerned not only with the citizens and their property but also with the political impact of any acts of violence by undisciplined troops. Connecticut provincial Asa Waterman lamented: "the Camp was to ignore their Inhabitants & We Were Not alawed to go in the Sitty Neither Officers Nor Soldiers."[69]

The French army returned two colors from the regular regiments raised by Governor William Shirley and Sir William Pepperell in the colonies in 1755 and captured at the Siege of Oswego in 1756. In an impressive ceremony, they were escorted by a detachment of grenadiers and band of music and paraded down the entire line of Amherst's army.[70] There was, however, no similar ceremony for the captured French regimental colors, for they did not yield their own sacred flags. The French regiments had privately destroyed them on the Île Sainte-Hélène in a secret ceremony the night before. When Amherst demanded compliance with the terms of surrender, de Lévis and the regimental commanders "gave their word of Honour the Troops had none [i.e., no regimental colors] when they capitulated; that they had brought Colours here six years ago, found them troublesome in this Country, that they were quite torn and they had destroyed them." This was technically correct, but the French senior officers adroitly failed to note that the colors had been destroyed *after* the terms of capitulation had been accepted, less than twelve hours before the surrender ceremony. Amherst concluded: "I made all the enquiry I could about this. It would be so scandalous for them to hide them after what they have said that I must believe them."[71]

Sir William Johnson was dispatched with his Indians across the river to the Iroquois community of Caughnawaga to extend the terms to the Indians that Amherst had first formulated that April, and then formalized at Oswegatchie less than two weeks before. The ensuing conference, conducted on September 15 and 16, confirmed Amherst's April 1760 memorandum and the earlier Treaty of Oswegatchie.[72] This was a major conference, and established, at least for the time being, a framework of peace between Great Britain and the Indian nations of the former New France.[73]

Amherst had been delighted with Sir William Johnson's service throughout the campaign. Amherst sang Sir William's praises to Pitt: "Sir William Johnson has taken unwearied Pains in keeping the Indians in humane bounds, and I have the Pleasure to assure you, that not a Peasant, Woman or child has been hurt by them, or a house burnt, since I entered what was the Enemy's Country."[74] Connecticut Colonel Nathan Whiting proudly informed his wife: "Never an Army, I believe did less damage in marching through a Country of their friends, even the Savages were in a great measure restrained."[75]

Those warriors of the First Nations that had accompanied Amherst all the way to Montreal were released to their home villages, with Amherst's thanks and his generous acknowledgement of their good service. Amherst reported to Pitt on September 22:

"I gave our Indians, as a Reward for their behaviour, as many necessarys and trinkets out of the stores, as Sir Wm Johnson though
necessary, and ordered them home."[76] Although Amherst called
these "trinkets," a partial list of the presents supplied to Johnson's
Native American allies suggests that they were liberally rewarded:
"sixty-four necklaces for women, four lace hats for Indian chiefs,
two hundred forty-two pounds of silver trinkets, one hundred nine-
teen pounds of wampum in belts, six thousand cord of bark for
canoes and forty-four anchors [ankers] of brandy."[77] This was certainly not an inconsiderable amount of "trinkets" or "necessarys"
by any measure. So pleased was Amherst with the performance of
his Indian Department that "I have therefore Sent to Sir William
Johnson for an Exact List of those that have remained attached to
Us till the Last, whom I intend to Decorate with Some distinguish-
ing Mark."[78] Amherst eventually decided to present silver medals to
the 182 Indians that had followed him to Montreal, and bestowed
an individual gold medal on Sir William Johnson, for "no one has so
good a right to it as yourself."[79]

Lieutenant Colonel Amherst would write of the successful ter-
mination of the campaign: "It is worthy of observation that the
principal Army under General Amherst with the two inferior ones,
under Murray and Haviland, should set out from places so distant
as Oswego, Quebec, and Crown Point, each meeting with obstruction from the enemy, and from the natural difficulties of a country
unknown to them, especially, the principal Army, from the pecu-
liar and formidable passage of the Rapids. I say, it is very remarkable that these Armies should all meet within the space of 48 hours
at the destined point—Montreal, so as to hem the enemy in on all
sides, and leave them no choice (except a very desperate one, indeed)
but to surrender." His brother, the general, echoed: "I believe never
three Armys, setting out from different & very distant Parts from
each other joyned in the Center, as was intended, better than we did,
and it could not fail of having the effect of which I have just now
seen the consequences."[80]

On September 9, 1760, General Jeffery Amherst sat down at his
headquarters marquee to dictate a letter through his military secretary to Governor Benning Wentworth of New Hampshire. It was
nearly identical to a bevy of similar letters that Amherst transmitted on this date to prominent political leaders throughout North
American and Britain. It was a dispatch of monumental import:

The Troops being formed, and the Light Artillery brought up, the Army lay on their Arms the Night of the 6th. On the 7th in the Morning, two Officers came to an advanced Post, with a Letter from the Marquis de Vaudreuil, referring me to what one of them, Colonel Bouguinville, had to say. The Conversation ended with a Cessation of Arms till twelve o'Clock, when the Proposals were brought in: Soon after I returned them with the Terms I was willing to grant, which both the Marquis de Vaudreuil, and Monsier de Lévis the French General, were very strenuous to have softened; this occasioned sundry Letters to pass between us, during the Day as well as the Night (when the Army again lay on their Arms) but as I would not on any Account relent in the least from my original Conditions, and insisted on an immediate and categorical Answer, Monsieur de Vaudreuil soon after Daybreak, Notified to me, that he had determined to accept of them, and two Setts of them were accordingly signed by him and me, and exchanged Yesterday, when Colonel Haldimand, with the Grenadiers and Light Infantry of the Army took Possession of one of the Gates of the Town, and is this Day to proceed in fulfilling the Articles of the Capitulation, by which the French Troops are all to lay down their Arms; are not to serve during the Continuance of the present War, and are to be sent back to Old France, as are also the Governors, and principal Officers of the Legislature of the whole Country, which I have now the Satisfaction to inform you, is entirely yielded to the Dominion of his Majesty, on which interesting and happy Event, I most sincerely congratulate you.[81]

CHAPTER 9

"ENTIRELY YIELDED TO THE
DOMINION OF HIS MAJESTY"

Conclusions

When Amherst's communiqués were received, celebrations erupted throughout the United Kingdom and the colonies in North America. Finally, after years of strife and far too many reverses, all of Canada was in the hands of the British. The soldiers were too fatigued, and kept too busy by Amherst and his subordinate commanders, to celebrate the capture of Montreal. Lieutenant Bradbury with the hardworking Massachusetts provincials of Haviland's column recorded on September 8: "But through Divine Goodness, at 1 o'clock we arrived oppose the famous city of Montreal—a very beautiful place—so much fatigued with my march that I am scarce able to stand."[1] The provincials were soon returned to their homes to be discharged, and the various regular formations were distributed for the permanent occupation of Canada. A few select units were dispatched to complete the reduction of the far western posts of New France.

Amherst, a strict disciplinarian at the best of times, kept his soldiers under a tight rein. The only actual celebration that can be verified was a sermon of thanksgiving preached to the combined armies outside the city by Chaplain Henry Munro of Montgomery's Highlanders.[2] This was appropriate, as many of the soldiers firmly believed that "we shall plainly See the Over ruling hand of providence conspicuously displayed in the Event before us."[3] Yet if the campaign had been won by the divine hand of providence, that hand had guided Jeffery Amherst as its instrument.

The 1760 campaign has received scant interest from historians. This is surprising, as this critical campaign resulted in the final reduction of Canada. A careful examination of this campaign has much to reveal: how Amherst's three columns independently accomplished their missions and fulfilled their objectives, how Amherst performed command and control to coordinate the movements of these three separated columns, and finally, how General James Murray successfully reached Montreal without having to fight a single pitched battle while simultaneously undermining the support of the Canadian population for the French.

The two columns of Amherst and Haviland faced conventional eighteenth-century military challenges of reducing strong Vauban-model fortifications that obstructed their movement forward and had to be eliminated before Montreal could be reached. When de Lévis failed to employ his interior lines of communication by massing a large relief column to assist either Île aux Noix or Fort Lévis, both fortifications were doomed, and would eventually fall to the long-proven, well-established siegecraft of the eighteenth century.

Amherst and Haviland had to conduct challenging sieges, as the French forts' locations in the middle of impassible rivers simultaneously prevented infantry attacks and precluded artillery batteries from being closely emplaced to breach the walls of the French fortifications. Both of these sieges were carefully and meticulously performed, and both commanders positioned their batteries and maneuvered their forces (Amherst by water and Haviland by land) to enhance their firing positions, enfilade the French works, and interdict the French lines of supply and withdrawal. Both officers conducted these sieges to perfection.

The British armies moving against Montreal in the summer of 1760 faced a formidable strategic reality. The French army that occupied Montreal had the ability to maneuver rapidly on interior lines of communication, using relatively swift and versatile nautical transportation on the Saint Lawrence River or the Richelieu River. The fortified posts of Île aux Noix and Fort Lévis permitted de Lévis to secure these two avenues of maneuver with an economy of force, which should have afforded him with the capacity to mass his remaining units into an offensive striking force. Theoretically, de Lévis had the capability to halt, if not destroy, each British column individually.

In April 1760 the fall of Canada was in no way preordained. In fact, that very month de Lévis launched a vigorous counterattack aimed at Quebec. This attack failed, largely because Brigadier General James Murray had established an effective intelligence service that successfully infiltrated the French intentions and command and provided him with sufficient warning to negate de Lévis's spring assault on Quebec.

Amherst addressed the French advantage by coordinating the movement of all three of his columns simultaneously, thus denying de Lévis the flexibility of facing a single British wing. Amherst did this by fixing August 10 as a common date for both his force and Haviland's to initiate their movement. Amherst did not provide Murray with such a set timetable in writing, although when Lieutenant Montresor personally carried written dispatches to Murray he conveyed verbal instructions that informed Murray of Amherst's schedule.

At the beginning of the campaign, Amherst performed effective command and control. Once the invasion of Canada was launched, however, because of the constraints imposed by distances and obstacles through the wilderness, he could only exercise command over the St. Lawrence column under his personal supervision.

Amherst's preparations for the army's movement from Fort Ontario were particularly superb. He issued comprehensive, clear written orders throughout his movement to Montreal. Once the three columns reached Montreal and re-established communications, Amherst immediately became the commander of the full army again, exchanged liaison officers between the three columns, and initiated written communications with his two subordinate commanders. Amherst's approach to command and control was perfectly adapted to conditions in North America.

The arrival of the three armies in front of Montreal within days of each other was due more to luck and circumstances rather than deliberate coordination. Each column faced a unique opposition. The challenges of eighteenth-century communications, particularly with the French occupying the ground between the various columns, rendered impossible a sophisticated level of communication and unity of effort. Still, although the nearly simultaneous arrival of the three armies before Montreal could be accounted to good fortune, it was good fortune that had been generated by meticulous planning, careful coordination, and good generalship. Successful military leadership creates its own luck.

Amherst's strategic approach was quite well considered. When Amherst and Haviland initiated their joint movements on the same date in early August, the cooperation of these columns maneuvering in conjunction with Murray's actions on the St. Lawrence River effectively paralyzed the political leadership of Governor de Vaudrieul and the military leadership of de Lévis, and with them the heart of the French will to resist. And by ensuring that the movements and actions of his three columns occurred simultaneously, Amherst robbed the ability of de Lévis to mass his forces at any single point. Amherst's aggressive and relatively rapid movements down the St. Lawrence River also denied de Lévis the ability to regain the initiative by maneuvering his force from Montreal.

Because the French civil and military leadership remained indecisive and unwilling to strip the defenses of Montreal to mass their forces against any one of Amherst's three columns, Amherst's victory was assured. Thus, Amherst's strategy of coordinating the initial movements of his three columns to ensure that they moved on Montreal simultaneously, particularly when combined with Murray's integrated political-military operations, proved successful.

Once Amherst's three columns were united with three large and powerful trains of siege artillery in front of Montreal, French surrender was inevitable. By the time the three British columns arrived together before Montreal, the French had lost the capacity to effectively resist. Governor de Vaudreiul realized this, and possessed the personal courage to spare Montreal the horrors of a devastating and entirely unnecessary artillery bombardment and storming by infantry columns. Amherst, with his adroit maneuvering of his own column and synchronization of the other two columns had ensured that the governor's ability to resist had been eliminated.

In the summer and early fall of 1760, Amherst's three columns had been scarcely delayed by the French in tactical terms. They spent only a comparatively few days reducing the two river fortresses. The delay of the British columns could be attributed more to bad weather and poor knowledge of the Saint Lawrence River than any French action. Amherst's offensive had also been set back by the tardy provincials, who were absolutely critical to Amherst's operations. The delay in their recruitment, organization, and arrival was caused by provincial political factors over which Amherst had no influence. Once the provincials arrived in sufficient strength for Amherst to launch his columns, it was all over within a month of campaigning. Amherst's strategy successfully denied the French freedom of action and maneuver, and ensured that by the fall of 1760 "all Canada would be in the hands of the English."

General James Murray on the Saint Lawrence River was presented with a considerably different challenge from the conventional Vauban-era fortifications that were faced by Amherst and Haviland. He was not opposed by any significant fortified position. There were several well-entrenched garrisons on the Saint Lawrence River west of Quebec, but none of these remotely approached the strength of Île aux Noix and Fort Lévis. The river corridor between Quebec and Montreal was the most densely settled portion of Canada and contained the majority of New France's population. Large Indian populations at Caughanwaga and Saint Francis were readily available to reinforce the conventional French army strength. If the Canadian militia and Indians had supported the French garrisons along the Saint Lawrence River, Murray would have faced a daunting scenario. Because of the scurvy that his army had experienced over the winter, his available infantry was distinctly limited. If the militia and Indians had cooperated with the French garrisons, they could have prevented Murray from controlling any landings up the river. The French lacked the defenses and naval vessels to prevent Murray from maneuvering on the river at will. Murray, however, would not have been able to sustain a force ashore at any given location, simply because his army would have been outnumbered and could have been picked apart by adept irregular forces. The small French garrisons on the St. Lawrence could have served as foundations for the militia and Indians to rally around, forming a formidable opposition to Murray's comparatively small army. Yet if Murray could separate the Canadian militia and the Indian warriors from the French army and its leadership, he could isolate the French garrisons, who would then lack the combat power to defy him. Murray could then bypass them at will, isolating and trapping them between the strong fortifications of Quebec and his own maneuver force astride the French lines of communications to Montreal.

Thus, Murray had to employ what is today known as population-centric counterinsurgency warfare. It must be stressed that neither the term nor the doctrine would have been known to Murray because they did not exist in 1760 and would not be developed for another two centuries. Still, Murray well understood the concept. His proclamations and policy of a gentle approach toward the French habitants, augmented by the liberal disbursement of gold and silver, proved to be extremely succesful. Murray's engineer, Lieutenant John Montresor, would write his father at the end of the campaign:

"One must answer (as a reflection) that we might thank our humanity more than our arms for so great an acquisition; in allusion to Mr. Murray's expedition up the river, where above seven thousand men deserted to him and several [French] regulars (on accounts of his placarts and manifestos), the whole brought in their arms, took the oaths of fidelity and were well treated which prevented any of the Canadians appearing in arms when we were before the town [Montreal]."[4] The French militia and population in short order abandoned the French army and government of Canada to its fate. Murray faced determined opposition on only one occasion, at Sorel. His brutal response in devastating an entire district, leaving only a few homes standing with his proclamations nailed to their doors, terrified the French colonists and eroded their will to resist. Without the support of the population of the Saint Lawrence River valley, the French garrison commanders were impotent. This approach by Murray, which set aside 150 years of conflict and five years of recent violence for humanity and forgiveness, entirely succeeded. It was counterinsurgency eighteenth-century style, and by employing it Murray was able to reach Montreal with his army intact. He removed all French opposition from the Saint Lawrence River valley without having had to fight a single pitched battle.

General Jeffery Amherst has long been characterized as being a cautious leader, averse to risk, inflexible and unimaginative, haughty and aloof. A number of historians have embraced this interpretation. Typical is the judgment offered by Howard H. Peckman in 1947: "[Amherst] was detailed in his orders to the point of 'fussiness' and he kept a finger on every department and almost every company. His lack of imagination was no handicap in fighting this war, although it became a fatal weakness in the task of pacifying the French-allied Indians. He never learned to understand them and he would not listen to the advice of his able subordinates."[5] Kevin Sweeney of Amherst University reinforced this assessment of Amherst as recently as 2008: "'Caution' was the fundamental quality of Gen. Amherst, his great strength and his most obvious limitation. A former officer who knew him recounted that 'Amherst's advice to his officers at Table, and upon all occasions was never to lose an inch of ground gained. . . . He moved so slow and cautiously, that he never lost an Inch, or met with a check, by which he acquired the name of snail.'"[6] Sweeney cited the assessment of William Eccles, another modern Canadian historian, who described Amherst as "moving with the speed of a glacier."[7]

Detail of portrait of Lord Jeffery Amherst, "The Cautious Commander" (1778), by T. Walker, London. Courtesy of Jeffery Amherst Collection, Amherst College Archives and Special Collections, Amherst College, Massachusetts.

Amherst's conduct in the 1760 campaign, however, does little to support this interpretation. When French naval vessels appeared before Oswego in July, he immediately sent his Lake Ontario fleet to engage them. In early August, Amherst similarly dispatched Loring's fleet when he heard a rumor that the two French vessels were located where the British fleet could reach them. As soon as Amherst could fix the location of the French ship near Fort de La Présentation on August 16, he aggressively sent his Royal Artillery row galleys to launch an attack without the support of his larger, more capable ships, which were delayed up the river. Days later, Amherst dispatched his ships, carrying his grenadiers ready for service, in an amphibious attack to seize Fort Lévis in an audacious *coup de main*. Because of Commodore Loring's inability to coordinate the movements of his three vessels, this amphibious assault was broken up and was defeated in detail by the French garrison. And as he passed the various rapids of the Saint Lawrence River, Amherst pushed his advance rapidly forward. He was willing to sustain losses in men, matériel, and transport to sustain the momentum of his movement on Montreal. None of Amherst's decisions between July and September 1760 were those of a tentative, hesitant leader. Rather, throughout the campaign, Amherst's maneuvers were conducted as expeditiously and swiftly as the constraints of eighteenth-century transportation capabilities permitted. Amherst's actions were those of a bold, aggressive military officer entirely willing to accept risks to seize the initiative for a sweeping advance, and to maintain it once gained.

It is also frequently asserted by historians that Amherst had detested and hated Indians. This reputation has been fostered largely by an unfortunate suggestion that he included in a set of instructions to a British garrison in 1763. This was at the height of Pontiac's Rebellion, when the British army had suffered grievous and horrific losses at the hands of Indian warriors.[8] During the 1760 campaign, however, he held conferences with Indians on no fewer than three separate occasions. In April he met with various nations at Albany, specifically visiting an Oneida Indian village. In August, following his initial success at overcoming the French defenses at Fort Lévis, he instructed Sir William Johnson to hold discussions with the Oswegatchie Indians at the site of the abandoned French Fort de La Présentation. In September he held a formal council with the Indian tribes at Canauwagha. Amherst regularly and frequently corresponded with Sir William Johnson regarding Indian affairs, as Sir William's papers and accompanying calendars reveal. Throughout the campaign, Amherst made effective use of the Indians accompanying his column, regularly dispatching them on scouting missions and patrols down the Saint Lawrence River. He used them frequently to carry messages to the other two columns. He also was careful to reward those Indians who served him with liberal quantities of gifts. During the 1760 campaign, Amherst clearly made a considerable effort toward gaining the active support of the Iroquois Confederation for the campaign, simultaneously separating Canada from its Indian allies. He proved successful at each endeavor. Contrary to the widely accepted assessment that Amherst failed to appreciate the services of Indians as allies, and that he held the various Indian nations in ill regard, his actions in the 1760 campaign rather demonstrated a spirit of respect and cooperation with the Indians of New York Colony and Canada. Murray effectively stripped support of the Canadian militia and Indians from Montreal through successfully implementing a similar counterinsurgency strategy. Amherst, Murray, and Sir William Johnson worked together to eliminate Indian support from New France.

Entirely discounted and ignored by historians today, Amherst had planned a brilliant and innovative campaign for 1760. The "cautious" Amherst is rather revealed to be a bold, aggressive general in the 1760 campaign, which was entirely of his own design. It was a masterpiece, successfully negating every conceivable French advantage while optimizing British advantages and capabilities. Amherst had to overcome the great obstacles imposed by an inefficient, unreliable, and painfully slow communication system. He overcame this potential roadblock to his operations by dispatching clearly written communications, supplemented by oral messages, which established a simple timetable and concept of operations. He reinforced this by dispatching multiple messages by different means and routes. Thus, Amherst successfully overcame the communications obstacles to effective command and control imposed by the wilderness conditions and distances of the North American theater of operations. In doing so, General Jefferey Amherst won the campaign in convincing fashion.

In 1760, General Jefferey Amherst's objective had been the total subjugation of Canada. He planned for nothing less, and he would accept nothing less. Within four weeks of initiating his movement aimed at Canada's heart of Montreal, all of Canada was in the hands of the British.

COMMAND AND CONTROL, COMMUNICATIONS, AND INTELLIGENCE IN THE BRITISH ARMY, 1760

An understanding of what command and control actually means is necessary. It must be stressed that the formal military term "command and control" was not in use by Amherst or any other professional military officer during the eighteenth century. Rather, command and control is a relatively modern definition, developed in the United States by the military education and doctrine system that Secretary of War Elihu Root established beginning in 1900 and subsequently institutionalized at the Command and General Staff College at Fort Leavenworth, Kansas, and the Army War College at Carlisle Barracks, Pennsylvania.

The concept was not unfamiliar to Julius Caesar during the Gallic Wars, fought between 58 and 52 B.C. His famous treatise on the Gallic War may be considered an account of how Caesar performed command and control during these campaigns.[1] The concept was well known by the middle of the eighteenth century, as both the French general Count Lancelot Turpin de Crissé and the Prussian King Frederick the Great addressed these military leadership fundamentals in their studies of military art and strategy.[2]

Today, the U.S. Army defines command and control as "the exercise of authority and direction by a properly designated commanding officer over assigned and attached forces in the accomplishment of the mission."[3] Command and control is the art of interpreting a mission or objective into a plan, and it is performed by a military leader at every level from squad leader to Army Group commander.

Command is at first an intellectual activity. It is the art of creating the commander's intent to perform the mission and achieve an objective, and then turning the commander's intent into a realistic and achievable plan. Command then becomes a physical process as it consists of motivating, inspiring, and leading subordinates, and allocating and managing resources in the conduct of that plan. Finally, command becomes a contest of will and resolution, directing the implementation of that plan under adverse circumstances, whether they be weather, terrain, enemy opposition, or the normal friction of war.[4] Command and control must be considered to be a continuously evolving process throughout a campaign, rather than an event on a single field of battle.

Communications is the art of disseminating this plan to the full range of subordinates that have to actually implement it on the ground. These subordinates may employ men, machines, or animals. Communications are performed through two media, written and oral. The art of communications is the ability to compose understandable, clear and comprehensive instructions, and being able to adjust these instructions to accommodate the realities of delays in transmission. In the case of Amherst, as throughout the eighteenth century, all communications had to be performed by foot messengers, aides mounted on horses, or by written messages dispatched through the vagaries of nautical or ground transportation. Thus, Amherst had to prepare his instructions reflecting the realities of consistent and significant delays between transmission, receipt, and execution.

One of the challenges that any commander faces in communications is that a wide and diverse range of subordinates must be issued with instructions, ranging from government civilians, teamsters, citizens, and both trained professional and inexperienced amateur soldiers. Communications is the art of transmitting a commander's intent and plan to these subordinates, so that these various individuals with a breadth of different training, experience, education, and interests can fully comprehend and then implement the plan. Beginning less than a century after Amherst's campaign, a wide and diverse range of highly capable inventions such as telegraph and telephone, then radio, and eventually digital internet greatly facilitated communications. It must be understood, however, that communications consists of issuing effective verbal and written instructions and transmitting information, regardless of the device that is used to transmit these messages. Communications is not technology, and it must not be confused with technology, for the range of various fancy and complex modern machines merely expedites and facilitates communications. Technology cannot compensate for the absence of effectively formulated instructions.

Intelligence is the art of seeing and comprehending an ever-changing and extremely complex battlefield and theater of operations. Thus, Julius Caesar began his study of the Gallic Wars with the sentence: "Gaul is a whole divided into three parts," and he then proceeded in the first chapter of his history to describe the topography, logistics, and inhabitants of Gaul.[5] Like command and control, intelligence is also an intellectual process that entails the meticulous study of a range of factors that compose the battlefield and theater of war. These factors include topography, geology, key terrain, weather, soil conditions, lines of communication, transportation infrastructure, enemy capabilities, friendly capabilities, and the human terrain across which the plan must be executed. Certainly Caesar's *Gallic Wars* was readily available to Amherst.

All of this, in fact, is quite simple and elementary. But as General von Clausewitz, the great Prussian military philosopher, warned: "Knowledge in war is very simple, being concerned with so few subjects, and only with their final results at that. But this does not make its application easy."[6]

Numerous military treatises existed in 1760, and were readily available and frequently consulted by British officers. Unfortunately, no primary source documents have been located that address which of these early military manuals influenced or guided Amherst or his principal subordinates. It is known that Brigadier General John Forbes, a close personal friend of Amherst for fifteen years who had served with him throughout the War of the Austrian Succession, relied on a French military treatise prepared by the Count Lancelot Turpin de Crissé, *An Essay on the Art of War*, during his 1758 campaign against Fort Duquesne in western Pennsylvania.[7] Turpin, an experienced French general highly respected by the famed Prussian King Frederick the Great, had written this essay in 1754, and it was one of the more widely read studies of warfare in the middle of the eighteenth century.[8] It was translated into English in 1761. General James Wolfe also kept a copy of Turpin in his professional library.[9] It is likely that Amherst was as familiar with Turpin as were both his friend Forbes and his subordinate Wolfe.

As Caesar had done centuries before, Count Turpin began his lengthy two-volume treatise on the military art with a first chapter that addressed the requirement for an effective commander to acquire "the knowledge of a Country."[10] Turpin also addressed all of the functional elements of command and control, summarizing: "The success of the general's designs is ascertained by his own forecast, and the dispatch with which his orders are executed, negligence and sloth are always productive of miscarriages."[11]

Amherst would have been intimately familiar with Lieutenant General Humphrey Bland's *Treatise of Military Discipline*, which was the British army's standard drill and tactical manual of the century. It was so widely used that it went through numerous editions, and was consulted by every officer in the British army. Bland's *Treatise* contained detailed and useful instructions on military drill, tactical evolutions, maneuvers on the battlefield, measures to conduct a march, procedures to be followed in an encampment, and directions to be followed by infantry either conducting or sustaining a siege. It contained, however, no real guidance for either military tactics or leadership, much less command and control. Furthermore, it entirely failed to address the principles of strategy, a concept not then formally recognized.[12]

Frederick the Great had prepared various instructions for his generals in 1747 that had been disseminated throughout the Prussian Army. It is conceivable that copies of Frederick's works were available to British officers including Amherst, as Prussia was allied with Great Britain, and Amherst had previously served alongside Prussian officers. The Prussian king and highly accomplished general specifically stated of intelligence: "One should know one's enemies, their alliances, their resources, and the nature of their country in order to plan a campaign. One should know what to expect of one's friends, what resources one has oneself, and see the future effects to determine what one has to fear or hope from political maneuvers.[13] Frederick the Great also addressed command and control as he practiced it: "Well-thought-out instructions should be prepared, but they should not be delivered to the officers who are charged with the duty until the moment of execution. The general can discuss the war with some of his corps commanders who are most intelligent and permit them to express their sentiments freely in conversation. The principal task of the general is mental, large projects and major arrangements. But since the best dispositions become useless if they are not executed, it is essential that the general should be industrious to see whether his orders are executed or not."[14] Frederick the Great, who had experienced firsthand the

vagaries of the friction of war both to his advantage and to his det-
riment, observed:

> When a general conducts himself with all prudence, he can still
> suffer ill fortune, for how many things do not cooperate at all with
> his labors! Weather, harvest, the officers, the health or sickness of
> his troops, blunders, the death of an officer on whom he counts,
> discouragement of the troops, exposure of your spies, negligence of
> the officers who should reconnoiter the enemy, and finally betrayal.
> These are the things that should be kept continually before your
> eyes so as to be prepared for them and so that good fortune will not
> blind us."[15]

Another contemporary study was prepared by Lieutenant Thomas
Webb of then Colonel Thomas Dunbar's Regiment of Foot (numbered the 48th), who had arrived in Virginia with General Edward
Braddock early in 1755. Webb had survived the Fort Duquesne campaign, and had subsequently fought his way through North America
to the Plains of Abraham with Wolfe, where he had been desperately wounded in September 1759. While he convalesced from his
wounds, Webb wrote a study on military art and theory specifically
focused on service in North America. Webb devoted a full chapter
to "The Necessity of understanding the Geography of that Country
which is the Seat of War."[16] Whether or not Amherst saw or utilized
Webb's study is unknown.

Among the greatest command and control challenges that
Amherst faced was to maintain communications between his three
widely separated columns. To do this, Amherst had three alternatives. First, he could dispatch small parties of rangers to penetrate
the wilderness, avoid French and Indian scouts, and reach the other
British columns. This was a relatively secure approach, as their
dispatches could be written in code or cipher, and could be readily destroyed if they were intercepted. They could, for example, be
dropped into a river tied in a weighted bag, or burned. This was also
a high risk approach, however, as the survival of these ranger parties
was uncertain under the best of circumstances. Alternately, he could
use loyal and trustworthy Indians to carry messages. The Indians
had a much higher likelihood of making their way through enemy
lines, but they could only be entrusted with the most simple of messages. This could not be considered to be a secure means of communications. That this method was certainly employed is confirmed

by a letter sent on September 3, 1760 from Colonel Henry Bouquet to Brigadier General Robert Monckton at Fort Pitt during this campaign. Monckton's brigade major acknowledged: "In Obedience to the Generals Commands I have the pleasure to Acknowledge the receipt of Your letter to Him by Hickman the [Delaware] Indian, who got here at five Yesterday evening with all the Letters."[17] Finally, Amherst and his subordinates could transmit written or verbal messages through the long line of communications, transiting oceans, lakes, and rivers. Unlike entrusting letters to parties of rangers, such communications were almost certain to reach their destination, and unlike entrusting letters to Native Americans this was a quite secure solution. It was also a painfully slow solution, and timeliness was often a key factor.

To coordinate their movements, communications between Amherst and Murray at Quebec, or between Amherst and Pitt in London, had to be carried by a lengthy and circuitous route. First, a letter from Amherst or Murray had to be carried by bateau, whaleboat, or sloop from their headquarters to a port, typically Quebec or New York City. From the port, the correspondence would be carried by sailing vessel across the North Atlantic. On May 19, 1760, Amherst recorded in his journal, written from Albany: "I received an Express from Boston sent by Gov Pownall with a Letter from Gen Murray that on the 28 April he had marched out to attack the Enemy."[18] Thus, a letter between Murray and Amherst could easily require three weeks to be delivered. Murray had written to Pitt from Quebec on May 25 with news of his successful defense of that city. This letter was received by Pitt in London on June 27.[19] This confirms a minimum of four weeks transit time in a single direction from Quebec to New York City or London, a period that was often doubled in the event of severe North Atlantic storms. During the American Revolution, a letter from Lord George Germain in London to Governor General Guy Carleton in Quebec, written and dispatched in late August 1776, was not delivered until May 1777.[20]

Amherst's communications with Colonel William Haviland were every bit as lengthy and circuitous. Haviland, Amherst's subordinate at Fort Crown Point during the winter of 1759–1760, would command one column of Amherst's army on Lake Champlain in 1760. Whaleboats, bateaux, or sailing vessels would carry messages between Amherst and Haviland on the Hudson River, Mohawk River, and Lake Champlain. The various portages on the corridor also had to be negotiated. To facilitate this, Amherst directed that whaleboats, faster than the flat-bottomed bateaux, be specifically dedicated to carrying express messages. Amherst instructed Colonel Haviland on June 18: "You'll settle Whaleboats for Correspondence between us on Lake George."[21] Even in good weather and with no obstructions, a letter could require no fewer than seven days to be transmitted from New York City to Albany by water-borne messenger. Once the campaign proceeded and Amherst penetrated into the interior of Canada, communications could only become even more complex.

Thus, the time required for communications was extremely variable and quite vulnerable to bad weather. Adverse winds or storms could considerably lengthen transit times, while favorable winds could considerably expedite the arrival of a message. Typical transit times were four to six weeks for a letter dispatched from Halifax or New York to reach London. A message sent from Quebec could easily take one to two weeks longer. Because of the prevailing winds in the North Atlantic, a letter written from London to the North American colonies normally required five to twelve weeks. In exceptional circumstances, communications across the North Atlantic could actually become nearly impossible. Dispatching instructions and information between garrisons and headquarters across the interior of the continent could be just as problematic. Severe weather such as blizzards, storms, and floods frequently isolated commanders and armies alike.

Highlighting the delays of communications, on August 30 Amherst received "a Letter from Mr. Pitt of 14th & 20th June," a nine-week lag from London to the commander in America, or between four or five months for round-trip communications.[22] Because of these delays, the British commander in North America, or the British ministry in London, had the opportunity to communicate the objectives of the campaign only once in the spring. Amherst or Pitt could expect to receive one update sometime during the summer. Wisely, neither attempted to issue orders in response to circumstances that would almost certainly have changed in the two to four months that round-trip communications required. They could expect one final set of dispatches in the fall, articulating the results and the costs of the summer's campaign. Thus, the commander of a column performing what would be referred to by the modern military as an operational-level campaign, such as Murray's column moving from Quebec on Montreal, received an absolute minimum of guidance.

These dispatches consisted of little more than the objective and timing of the summer's campaign and a description of the resources provided to execute it. Beyond that, an operational commander such as Murray had to depend on his own judgment, wisdom, experience, and innovation to direct his operations.[23]

Intelligence constituted another challenge to be added to that of lengthy communications. In modern armies, commanders are advised and supported by a dedicated intelligence staff, consisting of numerous highly skilled, trained, and experienced intelligence officers and enlisted personnel. These resources are supplemented by a complex and capable range of intelligence-focused organizations and technologies. In the British army of the mid-eighteenth century, a commanding general was expected to operate his own intelligence network and perform his own intelligence assessment and analysis. Brigadier General Thomas Gage complained to Sir William Johnson on March 26, 1760, regarding the lack of intelligence that he was receiving at Albany: "What Condition the Enemy is in at Present, in general throughout Canada, we are ignorant of, having neither Prisoner or Deserter, since the Close of the Campaign."[24]

However, Brigadier General James Murray had established an extremely efficient intelligence system in Quebec. This system was required because of the proximity of his garrison to the French army, and his necessary interactions with the recently hostile French inhabitants of the Saint Lawrence River valley.[25] Murray particularly relied on the close relationships between British merchants and French customers in Montreal. This relationship had been well established before the outbreak of hostilities and, surprisingly, had continued throughout the war. Trade was routed through the West Indies to avoid the respective French and British armies.[26] On November 25, 1759, Murray had observed that this illicit commerce was continuing, complaining that "the [British] merchants, ever greedy of gain, to purchase furs had transmitted a good deal of cash to Montreal."[27] Still, he took advantage of its existence, and exploited the avarice of the merchants to employ them as intelligence agents who regularly provided him with information from Montreal.

Amherst had operated an intelligence system with some success during the War of the Austrian Succession, in the British army's operations in Flanders a decade before.[28] Amherst had established an effective system between himself, Murray in Quebec, and Haviland at Crown Point. When valuable intelligence was obtained, each officer immediately disseminated the contents. When Amherst issued his command to Colonel Haviland to execute the attack down Lake Champlain against the French fortified position at Îsle aux Noix, he provided Haviland with both "a plan of Isle aux Noix and the French Engineers Letter."[29] When intelligence was obtained, prisoners were kept separate until they could be interrogated, and various reports were carefully compared, contrasted, and evaluated against other reports. Two cases document how these officers performed their intelligence duties. In early June, Haviland reported to Amherst in a fascinating account that addressed not only intelligence but counterintelligence:

> Christopher Broadfoot Draughted out of the 4th Batn Royal Americans at Fort Edward about 16 months ago into the rangers was taken [illegible, one word blotted and too dark] near twelve months at Ticonderoga, & wounded in two places. Sergt [first name illegible blotted and too dark] Chamberlain a ranger taken last Feby on the Ice below Crown Point & Ticonderoga left Montrail on 7th June & Cocknawaga the 10th, Arrived here 19th June 1760. They say the French retired from Quebeck about 24 days ago, with the loss of Most of their troops and in particular all their Grenadiers that the English had but little loss, till they retreated, that the French did not carry on a Siege above three or four Days, and that they left all their heavy Cannon Behind that the French Troops and Canadians are all apart & gone to Quarters. That the Cocknawaga Indians are divided, one half proposed to go to Sir Wm Johnson, the other half to go into the woods.[30]
>
> They report at Montrail that Genl Amherst would go up St. Lawrence that Mr Boulimarche & Mr. Levy were at Montrail, the former wounded. No talk of the french Army Assembling, no provisions from france[.] That Colo Young & Nine Officers were taken at Quebeck and that it was reported he with all the prisoners taken there, would be sent back for want of provisions—
>
> Four English Men of War Arrived at Quebeck & more were near it, about 200 men at Isle aux Noix 30 pieces of cannon & Earthworks.
>
> That a post was made at the three rivers [the city of Trois Rivières], That Soldiers & Indians were with fresh meat, as they had little or no Salt provisions in Canada,
>
> They heard that Major Rogers, when down the Lake had killed Several Indians, and in particular a mowhawk Interpeter, greatly lamented.

About 200 Men at Jock Cartier, About 24 Batteaus with provisions and Eight men in each were sent to Oswegotchy lately.

4 of the Royal Americans were taken prisoners from Oswego, by whom the French were informed, that the English would soon Attack them that way[.][31]

Colonel Haviland had previously provided Amherst with a similar report:

Wm Warring Robt Stowes The first a Boston man, the other from Cranberry in the Jerseys, both Indians, and were taken prisoner at Fort W[m] Henry, left Montrail 18th Inst. Arrived here 26 in the Evening, Say they heard the French was returning from Quebeck, in A great hurry that the women were all in tears, for the loss they had met with there, and that every one said the Country was taken, and that they Expected a great Army down by Oswego.

They crossed the river on A raft, between Chamblee & S[t.] Johns, and came on the East Shore, that some Miles below this fort, they think about a days Journey they came to the Lake Side; where they Saw A Canoe & Eight Indians, and two french men; upon discovering them, they made into the woods, and were pursued by Eight, as they afterwards reckend [reckoned] them, they came to a Lake where they made A raft that would carry but two, so that Another Indian (who had Escaped with them had been in the Jersey Regt & was taken prisoner at Fort W[m] Henry) was taken by the Eight that pursued, they likewise fired several Shots at them—

They further say that some distance from the town of Quebeck, Some of Our troops met the French, Engaged them there for A Small time, and continued retreating, till the Enemy had come near some Cannon we had, Out of the town, which after firing on them the English left, and retreated into the town They likewise he did, that the french had beat the walls so low, that they could reach up to the top of them, and reported for several nights they would Storm the town, so came by letter to Mr. Vaudrieul, but they never heard they had attempted it—

It was but two days before they left Montrail that they heard the french were retreating from Quebeck, as fast as they could both the above Indians are known by [illegible?] who was mentioned in a former letter—[32]

Amherst, Murray, and Haviland operated a sophisticated, relatively modern intelligence system, which provided them with effective and important service throughout the 1760 campaign.

SUPPLEMENTAL INFORMATION ON ARTILLERY BATTERIES

The design and construction of artillery siege batteries is discussed in chapter 6. Two contemporary manuals by military engineers, one English and one French, provide longer and more comprehensive analysis of this topic. Too lengthy to be incorporated into the narrative, these two descriptions are provided in their entirety in this appendix.

The most expansive discussion on the design and construction of artillery batteries was by Guillaume LeBlond, an accomplished French engineer, in his classic *A Treatise on Artillery*. This work was first translated into English in 1746. Because this is one of the most thorough descriptions of mid-eighteenth-century artillery batteries, it is provided in its entirety below.[1]

All places where cannon, mortars &c. are mounted, are called batteries, whether to fire on an enemy, or to attack or destroy a fortification. In an engagement cannon are fired without being covered, that is, without there being any ground thrown up to cover or defend the persons appointed to charge and work them. For as the pieces in these cases have no fixt situation, but are perpetually changing place as the general from time to time sees proper, the difficulty of covering them is evident, and the haste, in which these kinds of actions are performed, does not permit the use of that precaution which would render the service much less dangerous. But in the attack of a place it is otherwise, the cannon are then fixt firmly each in its proper place, and it is absolutely necessary to their being made use of, that they should be placed behind a parapet, thick enough to resist the cannon shot of the besieged. The construction of a parapet is what is properly called the construction of a battery, we shall give the particulars of it, as they stand in *M. de Vauban's* memoirs. The bed of the cannon, that is, the spot of ground on which it is placed, should, if possible, be raised some feet above the level of the field. The parapet should be three fathoms [eighteen feet] thick, and seven foot and half high. These parapets are constructed of earth, and fascines, which are a kind of faggots. The situation and extent of these batteries are first marked out by laying down a line . . . this done, the ground before the battery is broke, and a small trench opened; a bed of the earth that is dug out is first laid, and well beaten down; then a layer of fascines is placed transversely upon the earth, or so that their length shall reach from side to side of the parapet, crossing it at right angles, and so alternately a bed of earth and a layer of fascines, the fascines well fastened together, and stakes driven through them, so as to make the several layers of fascines and earth, as it were, one body; both sides of the parapet are also faced or lined with fascines, laid lengthways, or parallel to the parapet, and well fasten'd with stakes to the inside of it. This parapet being raised two feet and a half, or three feet, the embrasures must be marked out on the outside. Embrasures are well known to be openings in parapets to receive the cannon, and the part between two embrasures is called the merlon; from the middle of one embrasure to another there ought to be 18 feet, the embrasure ought to be three feet wide on the battery side, and 9 feet on the outside of the parapet. The embrasures being well marked out, the rest of the parapet, called the epaulment of the battery, must be raised, leaving the space marked for the embrasures open; that part of the parapet above the embrasures must have a proper slope, or shelving, that the materials of the parapet or the merlons may not be beat down into the embrasures. That part of the parapet, which reaches from the ground to the bottom of the embrasures, is called the knee of the battery. The parapet being finished, platforms must be prepared against the embrasures, to place the cannon upon. These platforms are a kind of strong floors, made to prevent the cannon from sinking into the ground, and to render the working of them more easy. They are composed of joists, or pieces of wood laid lengthways, the whole length of the intended platform; and to keep them firm in the places they are laid in, stakes must be driven into the ground close to them on each side; these joists must then be covered with very thick planks, laid parallel to the parapet; and over that part of the last, which touches the inside of the parapet, a kind of thick girder, or rafter, must be placed . . . because when the cannon is fired, the wheels of its carriage first knock or strike against it, and afterwards recede from it, by the effort of the powder made against the breech of the piece, which is the cause of what is called its recoil, as we have said before. As a check to this recoil, and to render it as little as possible, the ground, on which that part of the platform is laid, which is farthest from the parapet, should be raised, as much as circumstances will permit, higher than the part nearest the parapet. Platforms ought to be about 18 or 20 feet long, 7 and a half wide near the parapet at their narrowest part, and 13 at the widest. When the platforms are finished, the cannon must be brought to the batteries, and placed with their carriages on the several platforms allotted them. It is usual to make little cells or cavities near to the batteries, at a convenient distance, in which to keep the gunpowder. These cells are covered with clay, or something of the like kind, to preserve them from being fired, and are called little magazines of the battery.[2]

Professor John Muller of the Royal Military Academy at Woolwich also provided detailed guidance for the construction of an artillery battery in his 1757 *Treatise on Artillery* and his 1757 *The Attack and Defence of Fortified Places*. Muller's instructions from his *Treatise on Artillery* run to several printed pages, and go into great details regarding the selection and use of materials. Relevant passages of his battery design are abridged below:

To make a battery before the face of a vigilant enemy strong and durable, and to use no more materials and workmen than are necessary, is perhaps the most important work in a siege. From the known dimensions of a battery, the quantity of the materials may be determined and their kind from their situation. For the parapet or breast-work is 18 or 20 feet thick, and 7.5 or 8 feet high; each gun takes up 18 feet parapet, and each end about 10, the embrasures are 3 feet from the ground, 2 feet wide within, and 15 or 16 without; so that the merlons or parts between the embrasures are 16 feet long on the inside, and 4.5 or 5 feet high. When a battery is enfiladed by some of the outerworks, they must have flanks from 10 to 12 feet thick, and 18 long. The length of platforms are commonly 18 feet, 8 feet broad before, 15 or 16 behind, the planks a foot broad, and from 2 to 2.5 thick. The hurter to stop the wheels from damaging the fascines is 5 by 6 inches square, and 8 feet long. There are five sleepers to each platform to lay the planks upon, 3 by 4 inches square, and 18 feet long, each sleeper is fastened by pickets drove fast in the ground, two at each end, and two in the middle, and the last plank by 4 to keep them close together.[3]

The distance from the center of one embrasure to that of the next, is generally three fathoms of 18 feet . . . the embrasures are two feet wide within, and about nine without, slanting outwards about a foot and a half. Whilst the earth is throwing up for the parapet, the gunners should lay the platforms . . . beginning to lay five joists or sleepers longways from the parapet, securing them on both sides with stakes; then the Hurter is laid next to the parapet, which is a piece of timber about Six inches one way, and five the other; and after that the planks of about three inches thick. . . . The platforms are 15 feet broad behind, 9 before, and 18 long, with a lope upwards, of about nine or ten inches.[4] In the case of the mortar batteries they were considerably simpler, as they could fire over the parapets and did not recoil, thus a simple square timber platform and a solid parapet sufficed.

Notes

Preface

1. J. Clarence Webster, ed. *Journal of Jeffery Amherst, Recording the Military Career of General Amherst in America from 1758 to 1763.* (Toronto: Ryerson, 1931), 246.

Chapter 1. "The Entire Reduction of Canada"

1. Gertrude Selwyn Kimball, ed., *Correspondence of William Pitt, When Secretary of State, With Colonial Governors and Military and Naval Commissioners in America* (London: Macmillan, 1906; repr., New York: Kraus Reprint, 1969), 2:238.
2. Richard Middleton, ed., *Amherst and the Conquest of Canada,* vol. 20 (UK: Publications of the Army Records Society, 2003), 151.
3. "Jeffery Amherst, 1st Baron Amherst" in *Dictionary of Canadian Biography,* http://www.biographi.ca/009004-119.01-e.php?id_nbr=1732 (accessed March 5, 2010). Amherst's two biographers claim that he received his first commission as an ensign with the First Regiment of Foot Guards. Lawrence Shaw Mayo, *Jeffery Amherst: A Biography* (New York: Longmans, Green & Company, 1916), 8, and J. C. Long, *Lord Jeffery Amherst: A Soldier of the King* (New York: MacMillan, 1933), 16. Middleton subscribes to the same belief, Middleton, *Amherst and the Conquest of Canada,* xv.
4. Mayo, *Jeffery Amherst,* 18-19, 20, Long, *Lord Jeffery Amherst,* 20.
5. For Amherst's leadership at Louisbourg, the author highly recommends Hugh Boscawen, *The Capture of Louisbourg, 1758* (Norman: University of Oklahoma Press, 2011).
6. For Ligonier, see Rex Whitworth, *Field Marshal Lord Ligonier: A Story of the British Army, 1702–1770* (London: Oxford University Press: 1958), and Brenda J. Buchanan, *Sir John Ligonier: Military Commander and Member of Parliament for Bath* (Bath, U.K.: Bath Archaeological Trust and Millstream Books, 2000).
7. Sir William Johnson has been the subject of numerous biographies and studies. The most enjoyable book-length biography remains James Thomas Flexner, *Mohawk Baronet: A Biography of Sir William Johnson* (Syracuse, N.Y.: Syracuse University Press, 1959; reprint 1979). An older biography that remains valid is Arthur Pound, *Johnson of the Mohawks* (New York: Macmillan, 1930). The most authoritative biography of Johnson is by the editor of his papers, Milton W. Hamilton, *Sir William Johnson: Colonial American, 1715–1763* (Port Washington, N.Y.: Kennikat Press, 1976). Regrettably, Hamilton succeeds in treating one of the most vibrant, exciting, and intriguing colonial American

personalities in a dull, plodding, monotonous narrative that fails to capture the ebullience of Johnson and scarcely does credit to the subject.

8. Middleton, *Amherst and the Conquest of Canada*, 173.

9. Ibid., 195.

10. Formally referred to today by the U.S. Armed Forces as Command, Control, Communications, and Intelligence, or C3I. I have identified only two previous efforts by a single author to evaluate command and control as it was practiced by military leaders during the mid-eighteenth century: Herman O. Benninghoff II, *Valley Forge: A Genesis for Command and Control, Continental Army Style* (Gettysburg, Pa.: Thomas Books, 2001), and Herman O. Benninghoff II, *The Brilliance of Yorktown, A March of History: 1781 Command and Control, Allied Style* (Gettysburg, Pa.: Thomas Publications, 2006). These two studies are badly flawed, however, and fundamentally misunderstand C3I.

11. Letter in author's collection.

12. Jean Elizabeth Lunn, "Agriculture and War in Canada, 1740–1760," *Canadian Historical Review* 16, no. 2 (June 1935): 123, 128, 129, 130, 135–36. The only historian to address agriculture in Canada, Ms. Lunn assessed the situation as so serious that "agriculture had reached a state that was little short of prostration."

13. George M. Wrong, *The Fall of Canada—A Chapter in the History of the Seven Years' War* (Oxford: Clarendon Press, 1914), 81, Francois Micheloud, "Canada's Playing Card Money," www.micheloud.com/ FXM/MH/canada.htm (accessed January 5, 2004), and P. N. Breton, *Illustrated History of Coins and Tokens Relating to Canada* (Montreal: P. N. Breton & Company, 1894), 10–20.

14. Edward P. Hamilton, ed., *Adventures in the Wilderness: The American Journals of Louis Antoine de Bougainville, 1756-1760*. (Norman: University of Oklahoma Press, 1964; paperback edition 1990), 124–25, 252, 254.

15. Francois Gaston, Chevalier de Lévis, "Journal of the Battle of Sillery and Siege of Quebec." In E.B. O'Callaghan, ed., *Documents Relative to the Colonial History of the State of New York* (Albany: Weed, Parsons and Company, 1858), 10:1070, 1084-1086.

16. Information on this fort was derived from Douglas R. Cubbison, *National Register of Historic Places Nomination, Fort de La Presentation/ Fort Oswegatchie/Fort Ogdensburg Archaeological Site, Ogdensburg, St. Lawrence County, New York* (Ogdensburg, New York: Fort La Presentation Association, June 2009).

17. O'Callaghan, *Documents*, 10:203.

18. Ibid., 10:205.

19. Ibid., 10:204-205.

20. Ibid., 10:204.

21. Ibid., 10:197.

22. Pierre Pouchot, *Memoirs on The Late War in North America Between France and England*, Brian Leigh Dunnigan, ed. (1781; rev. ed. Youngstown, New York: Old Fort Niagara Association, 1994), 376-377.

Dunnigan's superbly edited version remains the authoritative work on Pouchot.

23. Paul Fortier, "La Galette versus Cataraqui—The Forgotten Rivalry for Dominance on the Upper St. Lawrence, 1673–1796" (unpublished manuscript, 1979), 10.

24. Hamilton, *Adventures in the Wilderness*, 17.

25. O'Callaghan, *Documents*, 10:239.

26. Ibid., 10:349.

27. James Sullivan, ed., *The Papers of Sir William Johnson*, (Albany: University of the State of New York, 1921–1962) 3:133–35.

28. Ibid., 2:655.

29. Pouchot, *Memoirs*, 322–324.

30. Hamilton, *Adventures in the Wilderness*, 16–17.

31. O'Callaghan, *Documents*, 10:350–51.

32. Gilbert Hagerty, *Massacre at Fort Bull, the deLery expedition against Oneida Carry, 1756* (Providence, Rhode Island: Mowbray, 1971), 43.

33. Sullivan, *The Papers of Sir William Johnson*, 9:861.

34. Pouchot, *Memoirs*, 155, and O'Callaghan, *Documents*, 10:824.

35. Pouchot, *Memoirs*, 234-235.

36. Pouchot, *Memoirs*, 238.

37. Ibid., 289.

38. O'Callaghan, *Documents*, 10:1090.

Chapter 2. "Worthy antagonists!"

1. James Thompson, *A Short Authentic Account of the Expedition Against Quebec in the Year 1759 under Command of Major General James Wolfe* (Quebec: Middleton & Dawson, 1872), www.transactions. morrin.org/docsfromclient/books/328/328.html (accessed July 21, 2010).

2. Estelle Quick, *James Thompson: A Highlander in Quebec* (Tain, Rosshire, Scotland: Tain & District Museum Trust, 2009), 35.

3. Unfortunately, this accomplished officer has been the subject of only a single biographical study, R. H. Mahon, *The Life of General the Honorable James Murray, A Builder of Canada* (London: John Murray, 1921), Although a superlative effort, this biography is now badly outdated.

4. In 1760, the British Regiments of Foot were known by their colonel's names. The regiments were not generally referred to by their numbered assignments until later in the 1760s. However, because most readers are familiar with the regiment's numerical designations, these have been utilized in the narrative in addition to their colonel's designations.

5. Mahon, *James Murray*, 19, 42–43, 51, 69.

6. Chevalier Johnstone, *The Campaign of 1760 in Canada* (1887; repr. Philadelphia: D. N. Goodchild, 2007), 14.

7. James Murray, *Journal of the Siege of Quebec, 1760* (Quebec: Middleton & Dawson, 1871), 8.

8. Quoted in Mahon, *James Murray*, 249.

9. John Johnson, "Memoirs of the Quartermaster Sergeant," in *The Siege of Quebec and the Battle of the Plains of Abraham*, A. G. Doughty and G. W. Parmalee, eds. (Quebec: Dussault & Proulx, 1901), 115-116.

10. Johnson, "Memoirs," 118.

11. Murray, *Journal*, 8.

12. Murray, *Journal*, 8.

13. Middleton, *Amherst and the Conquest of Canada*, 133–34. It should be noted that the microfilm copies of the Amherst papers were predominantly relied on for this study. However, Middleton's published transcription of selected documents from Amherst's papers was relied on when the microfilm quality was particularly poor and portions of the manuscripts were questionable.

14. Murray, *Journal*, 10.

15. Murray, *Journal*, 22–23, and Wrong, *The Fall of Canada*, 120–21.

16. Johnson, "Memoirs," 119–20.

17. Murray, *Journal*, 15.

18. Malcolm Fraser, "The Capture of Quebec: A Manuscript Journal Relating to the Operations Before Quebec From 8th May 1759 to 17th May 1760." *Journal of the Society for Army Historical Research* no. 18 (1939): 161.

19. Quick, *James Thompson*, 35, and Earl John Chapman and Ian Macpherson McCulloch, eds., *A Bard of Wolfe's Army: James Thompson, Gentleman Volunteer 1733–1830* (Montreal: Robin Brass Studio, 2010), 191–92.

20. "Hospitals in North America, 25 December 1759–24 June 1760, Report by James Napier, Director of Hospitals," Amherst Papers, David Library of the American Revolution, Washington Crossing, Pennsylvania.

21. Stephen R. Brown, *Scurvy, How a Surgeon, a Mariner, and a Gentleman Solved the Greatest Medical Mystery of the Age of Sail* (New York: St. Martin's Press, 2003), and William R. McBride, " 'Normal' Medical Science and British Treatment of the Sea Scurvy, 1753–1775." *Journal of the History of Medicine and Allied Sciences* 46, no. 2 (1991): 158–77.

22. Murray, *Journal*, 23, 24, 30.

23. Erica M. Charters, "Disease, Wilderness Warfare, and Imperial Relations: The Battle for Quebec, 1759–1760." *War in History* 16, no. 1 (2009), 1. This recent and superlative study is highly recommended for comprehensive details on the health challenges faced by the Quebec garrison in the spring of 1760.

24. Quoted in Charters, "Disease, Wilderness Warfare, and Imperial Relations," 15.

25. James Miller, "Memoirs of an Invalid," Amherst Papers, Centre for Kentish Studies, Maidstone, United Kingdom.

26. Johnson, "Memoirs," 119.

27. Ibid., 119.

28. Mahon, *Life of General James Murray*, 209–212.

29. John Montresor to Jefferey Amherst, Boston, February 26th, 1760" in G. D. Scull, ed., *Collections of the New York Historical Society for the Year 1881* (New York: New York Historical Society, 1982), 525.

30. As discussed by Wrong, *The Fall of Canada*, 113, 127.

31. Jean-Daniel Dumas, "Treatise On the Defense Of the Colonies" ca. 1775. French manuscript, Collection of Braddock's Battlefield Association, Braddock, Pennsylvania, 162, 169. Translation by Bob Messner.

32. Middleton, *Amherst and the Conquest of Canada*, 144.

33. Fraser, "The Capture of Quebec," 162.

34. Ibid., 162.

35. Murray, *Journal*, 28.

36. Kimball, *Correspondence of William Pitt*, 2:292.

37. Murray, *Journal*, 29.

38. Fraser, "The Capture of Quebec," 162.

39. Ibid., 162.

40. Wrong, *The Fall of Canada*, 134–35.

41. D. Peter MacLeod, "Microbes and Muskets: Smallpox and the Participation of the Amerindian Allies of New France in the Seven Years' War." *Ethnohistory* 39 no. 1 (Winter 1992), 52.

42. Knox, *Campaigns in North America*, 385–88.

43. Lévis, "Journal," 1080.

44. John Knox, *An Historical Journal of the Campaigns in North America For The Years 1757, 1758, 1759 and 1760* (1799; repr. Toronto: Champlain Society, 1914), 391–92. All references to volume 2 unless otherwise indicated.

45. Fraser, "The Capture of Quebec," 163.

46. Murray, *Journal*, 31.

47. Mahon, *Life of Murray*, p. 228.

48. Murray, *Journal*, 31.

49. Knox, *Campaigns in North America*, 389.

50. Johnson, "Memoirs," 120.

51. Mahon, *Life of Murray*, 229, and Murray, *Journal*, 31–32.

52. Knox, *Campaigns in North America*, 390.

53. The best order of battle for this engagement is provided by Ian McCulloch, "From April Battles & Murray Generals, Good Lord Deliver Me: The Battle of Sillery, 1760," in *More Fighting for Canada: Five Battles*, Donald Graves, ed. (Toronto: Robin Brass, 2004), 313-317, and this source should be consulted for specifics regarding this fight.

54. It should be noted that two similar military terms were distinctive, and are easily confused. "Pickets" were wooden stakes or logs, sharpened at one or both ends, that were used in military earthworks and fortifications. "Piquets" were a body of soldiers, typically from a dozen to several score in number who were deployed as sentries around an army, or as reinforcements in case of enemy attack. Soldiers typically spelled "piquets" phonetically as "pickets" and their original spelling will be retained in all direct quotes.

55. Mahon, *Life of Murray*, 236.
56. Fraser, "The Capture of Quebec," 166.
57. Johnson, "Memoirs," 122–23.
58. Middleton, *Amherst and the Conquest of Canada*, 178. Murray used nearly identical language in a letter to William Pitt written on May 25th. Kimball, *Correspondence of William Pitt*, 2:294.
59. Knox, *Campaigns in North America*, 389.
60. Knox, *Campaigns in North America*, 394.
61. Johnson, "Memoirs," 121.
62. Johnstone, *Campaign of 1760*, 15–16.
63. Chapman and McCulloch, eds., *A Bard of Wolfe's Army*, 199.
64. Miller, "Memoirs of an Invalid."
65. Quoted in Knox, *Campaigns in North America*, 393.
66. Johnstone, *Campaign of 1760*, 16–18.
67. Quick, *James Thompson*, 26.
68. Miller, "Memoirs of an Invalid."
69. Fraser, "The Capture of Quebec," 165.
70. Knox, *Campaigns in North America*, 394.
71. Chevalier de Lévis, "Journal of the Battle of Sillery and Siege of Quebec," In *Documents Relative to the Colonial History of the State of New York*, E. B. O'Callaghan, ed. (Albany: Weed, Parsons and Company, 1858), 10:1083.
72. Lévis, "Journal," 1084–86.
73. Mahon, *Life of Murray*, 221, 235.
74. Quoted in Mahon, *Life of Murray*, 236, and McCulloch, "'From April Battles,'" 59.
75. Wrong, *The Fall of Canada*, 132.
76. Knox, *Campaigns in North America*, 395.
77. Miller, "Memoirs of an Invalid."

Chapter 3. "The whole garrison were alert, the General was indefatigable"

1. Bougainville, *Adventures in the Wilderness*, 186.
2. The only modern assessment of these fortifications is provided by Matthew J. Wayman, "Fortifications at Quebec, 1759–1760: Their Condition and Impact on the Sieges and Battles," *Journal of America's Military Past* 30, no. 1 (Winter 2004): 5–25.
3. Knox, *Campaigns in North America*, 393n.
4. Lévis, "Journal," 1087.
5. Thompson, *The Expedition Against Quebec*. This account is valuable, as Sergeant Thompson later became an engineer responsible for the fortifications of Quebec, and he wrote this account after serving nearly fifty years in this service. He became intimately familiar with military engineering and fortifications, and particularly the defensive works of Quebec.
6. Middleton, *Amherst and the Conquest of Canada*, 177, and Quick, *James Thompson*, 35.

7. Chapman and McCulloch, *A Bard of Wolfe's Army*, 21, 329.
8. Middleton, *Amherst and the Conquest of Canada*, 176.
9. Mahon, *James Murray*, 223.
10. Mackellar, Quoted in Knox, *Campaigns in North America*, 393.
11. Quoted in Mahon, *James Murray*, 249.
12. Middleton, *Amherst and the Conquest of Canada*, 177.
13. For examples of this, refer to James Young, *An Essay on the Command of Small Detachments* (London: J. Millan, 1766), 9, 21–24, and Lewis Lochee, *Elements of Field Fortifications* (London: T. Cadell and T. Egerton, 1783), 71, 90, 97–100, 105–106.
14. The only architectural historian who has comprehensively assessed this phenomenon is Horst De La Croix, in *Military Considerations in City Planning: Fortifications* (New York: George Braziller, 1972), 54.
15. Murray, *Journal*, 32.
16. Knox, *Campaigns in North America*, 398.
17. Murray, *Journal*, 32.
18. Murray, *Journal*, 34.
19. Knox, *Campaigns in North America*, 401. *In terrorem* is Latin for "in [order to] frighten," a legal term used to describe a warning.
20. Knox, *Campaigns in North America*, 405.
21. Miller, "Memoirs of an Invalid."
22. Murray, *Journal*, 33.
23. Murray, *Journal*, 33. *Hors d'insulte*: safe from surprise attack.
24. Murray, *Journal*, 33.
25. Murray, *Journal*, 34–35.
26. Knox, *Campaigns in North America*, 411.
27. John Muller, *The Attac and Defense of Fortified Places, The 1757 Second Edition*, Notes by David Manthey (London: J. Millan, 1757; repr. Arlington, Virginia: Flower-de-Luce Books, 2004), 47–50, 148–49.
28. Muller, *Attac and Defense*, 145.
29. Knox, *Campaigns in North America*, 400–401.
30. Muller, *Attac and Defense*, 18.
31. Lévis, "Journal," 1080, and Wrong, *The Fall of Canada*, 171–72.
32. Ibid., 1087.
33. Muller, *Attac and Defense*, 46–47.
34. Lévis, "Journal," 1087.
35. Muller, *Attac and Defense*, 35.
36. Knox, *Campaigns in North America*, 409.
37. Lunn, "Agriculture and War in Canada, 1740–1760," 123–36.
38. The logistics of Canada during the Seven Years' War has received almost no attention from historians (and essentially none since 1935), and is fully deserving of comprehensive study and evaluation.
39. Lévis, "Journal," 1089.
40. Murray, *Journal*, 35.
41. Murray, *Journal*, 34
42. Murray, *Journal*, 35–37.
43. Knox, *Campaigns in North America*, 412.

44. John Muller, *A Treatise Containing the Elementary Part of Fortification, Regular and Irregular* (London: J. Nourse, 1746; repr., Ottawa, Canada: Museum Restoration Service, 1968), 213–14.
45. Ian K. Steele, *Betrayals: Fort William Henry & The "Massacre"* (New York: Oxford University Press, 1990), 100, 102, 104, 105, 109.
46. Knox, *Campaigns in North America*, 413–14.
47. Murray, *Journal*, 35, 37–39.
48. Knox, *Campaigns in North America*, 414.
49. Johnson, "Memoirs," 125.
50. Miller, "Memoirs of an Invalid."
51. Knox, *Campaigns in North America*, 419.
52. Lévis, "Journal," 1087, and Murray, *Journal*, 40.
53. Muller, *Attac and Defense*, 36–37.
54. Murray, *Journal*, 40–41.
55. Fraser, "The Capture of Quebec," 167.
56. Murray, *Journal*, 41.
57. Lévis, "Journal," 1087, and Murray, *Journal*, 41.
58. Fraser, "The Capture of Quebec," 167.
59. Johnson, "Memoirs," 124.
60. Knox, *Campaigns in North America*, 405.
61. James Miller, "Memoirs of an Invalid."
62. Murray, *Journal*, 40–41.
63. Murray, *Journal*, 42.
64. Knox, *Campaigns in North America*, 410–11.
65. Murray, *Journal*, 36, 39, 40, 42, 43.
66. Knox, *Campaigns in North America*, 431.
67. Murray, *Journal*, 44.
68. Johnstone, *Campaign of 1760*, 21–22.
69. Lévis, "Journal," 1088–89.
70. Murray, *Journal*, 44–45.
71. Quick, *James Thompson*, 37.
72. Murray to Amherst, 23 May 1760, Amherst Papers.
73. Knox, *Campaigns in North America*, 430.
74. Lévis, "Journal," 1087, 1089.
75. Knox, *Campaigns in North America*, 397n.
76. Knox, *Campaigns in North America*, 433.
77. Lévis, "Journal," 1087–88.
78. Catherine Sullivan, *Legacy of the Machault: A Collection of 18th-century Artifacts* (Ottawa: Parks Canada: 1986), 7.
79. Quoted in Wrong, *The Fall of Canada*, 21.
80. Mahon, *The Life of General Murray*, 244.
82. Ian McCulloch, "'From April Battles,'" 20, 68.
83. Quoted in Wrong, *The Fall of Canada*, 180.
84. Knox, *Campaigns in North America*, 413.

Chapter 4. "We might thank our humanity more than our arms"

1. Middleton, *Amherst and the Conquest of Canada*, 169–71.

2. Ibid., 185.
3. Amherst intimates as much in his letter dated May 19th to Murray. Middleton, *Amherst and the Conquest of Canada*, 182.
4. Middleton, *Amherst and the Conquest of Canada*, 186.
5. Ibid., 185.
6. Mahon, *James Murray*, 252, 254.
7. Because of the comparatively small number of soldiers in Murray's St. Lawrence River column, primary source accounts are extremely scarce. I have been forced to rely for the most part on Captain Knox and Engineer Montresor. Probably because water transport was limited, Murray wrote few letters during his operations this summer.
8. Knox, *Campaigns in North America*, 463–64.
9. Because of the habitual shortage of qualified officers to serve as detachment commanders, British Army senior officers in North America were given the authority to elevate selected officers to higher rank for service in-theater only. This promotion was not permanent, and upon return to England the officers would revert to their permanent (and lower) rank in the British Army.
10. Ian M. McCulloch and Tim J. Todish, *British Light Infantrymen of the Seven Years' War, North America, 1757–1763* (Oxford: Osprey Publishing, 2004), 11, 13, 14, 15, 21, 38, 62–63, and Boscawen, *The Capture of Louisbourg*, 129, 141–42, 324.
11. Knox, *Campaigns in North America*, 503, and John Montresor, "Expedition to Les Prairies De La Magdalene" in G. D. Scull, ed. *Collections of the New York Historical Society for the Year 1881* (New York: New York Historical Society, 1882), 249.
12. *Bateaux* is French for "boats." *Batteau* is singular, and *bateaux* is plural.
13. Knox, *Campaigns in North America*, 468, and William Wood, ed., *The Logs of the Conquest of Canada* (Toronto: The Champlain Society, 1909), 163.
14. For this, refer to Henry Forbush Howe, "Malachi James at the Fall of Montreal, 1760," *Proceedings of the Massachusetts Historical Society* 70 (1950–1953), 33–49.
15. Montresor, "Expedition to Les Prairies," 241.
16. "Letters of Vaudreuil, Lévis and Dumas in 1760," Library and Archives, Canada, *Sessional Papers No. 18* (Ottawa: S. E. Dawson, 1906), 32.
17. "Letters of Vaudreuil, Lévis and Dumas in 1760," 37.
18. "Letters of Vaudreuil, Lévis and Dumas in 1760," 38.
19. "Letters of Vaudreuil, Lévis and Dumas in 1760," 34.
20. "Letters of Vaudreuil, Lévis and Dumas in 1760," 35.
21. Johnson, "Memoirs," 137.
22. Ibid., 137–38.
23. Knox, *Campaigns in North America*, 467.
24. Ibid., 480–81.
25. Wood, *Logs of the Conquest*, xx–xxiv.

26. Mahon, *Life of James Murray*, 258.
27. Knox, *Campaigns in North America*, 468.
28. Montresor, "Expedition to Les Prairies," 237.
29. Knox, *Campaigns in North America*, 468.
30. Ibid., 469–70.
31. Montresor, "Expedition to Les Prairies," 238.
32. Knox, *Campaigns in North America*, 469.
33. Montresor, "Expedition to Les Prairies," 238–39.
34. Knox, *Campaigns in North America*, 471.
35. Ibid., 473.
36. Ibid., 473.
37. Ibid., 475.
38. Ibid., 474.
39. Dino Lemonofides, "Standing Orders at Quebec, 1759," *Journal of the Society for Army Historical Research* 78 (2000), 302.
40. Wrong, *The Fall of Canada*, 82.
41. Wrong, *The Fall of Canada*, 132–33.
42. Knox, *Campaigns in North America*, 477.
43. Montresor, "Expedition to Les Prairies," 243.
44. Knox, *Campaigns in North America*, 477–78.
45. Quoted in Mahon, *Life of General James Murray*, 257.
46. Montresor, "Expedition to Les Prairies," 244.
47. Knox, *Campaigns in North America*, 488.
48. Montresor, "Expedition to Les Prairies," 246.
49. Montresor, "Expedition to Les Prairies," 246.
50. Knox, *Campaigns in North America*, 494.
51. Montresor, "Expedition to Les Prairies," 247–48.
52. Montresor, "Expedition to Les Prairies," 249, and Knox, *Campaigns in North America*, 500.
53. Montresor, "Expedition to Les Prairies," 250.
54. Ibid., 251.
55. Montresor, "Expedition to Les Prairies," 251.
56. Knox, *Campaigns in North America*, 506.
57. Ibid., 511.
58. Montresor, "Expedition to Les Prairies," 242.
59. "Letter to Lieutenant Colonel James Montresor, Quebec, December 16, 1760" in G.D. Scull, ed., *Collections of the New York Historical Society for the Year 1881* (New York: New York Historical Society, 1882), 235.
60. Montresor, "Expedition to Les Prairies," 243.
61. Knox, *Campaigns in North America*, 494.
62. Montresor, "Expedition to Les Prairies," 246, and Knox, *Campaigns in North America*, 495.
63. Montresor, "Expedition to Les Prairies," 250.
64. Quoted in Mahon, *Life of General James Murray*, 260, and Knox, *Campaigns in North America*, 504.
65. Ibid.

66. Knox, *Campaigns in North America*, 496.
67. Ibid., 483–84.
68. Ibid., 505.
69. Knox, *Campaigns in North America*, 506–507.
70. Ibid., 508–509.
71. Ibid., 512–14.
72. Johnstone, *Campaign of 1760*, 31.
73. The author concurs with the assessment of renowned Canadian historian George M. Wrong, formerly of the University of Toronto: " The oath was mild enough and Murray insisted that it should be scrupulously observed. From time to time he himself went ashore. Since he knew French well he could speak to the people in their own tongue. He told them that, while the cause of France was hopeless, the might of Britain as shown in her ships, artillery, and other equipment was resistless. He added that he would in no way molest the persons and property of the men who were attending to their duties, but that he would burn all the houses from which the men were absent. This resolution caused extensive desertions from the French army. Many of the militia returned to their parishes in order to avert the destruction by the British of their houses, should they not be there. In village after village the whole male population took the oath, saying, in some cases, that they were glad to have the excuse of Murray's demand for so doing." Wrong, *The Fall of Canada*, 199.

Chapter 5. "The Attack on the Île au Noix will be Your Care"

1. "Municipality of Sainte-Paul-de-l'Île-aux-Noix,"www.ile-aux-noix.qc.ca/ eng/tourisme/histoire.html (accessed 9 February 2010).
2. Russell P. Bellico, *Sails and Steam in the Mountains: A Maritime and Military History of Lake George and Lake Champlain* (Fleischmanns, New York: Purple Mountain Press, 1992), 86.
3. Joseph Bayley, "Part of the Journal of Capt. Jacob Bayley in the Old French War." in Frederick P. Wells, *History of Newbury, Vermont* (St. Johnsbury, Vt.: Caledonian Company, 1902), 379, and Russell P. Bellico, *Chronicles of Lake Champlain, Journeys in War and Peace* (Fleischmanns, New York: Purple Mountain Press, 1999), 155.
4. Johnstone, *Campaign of 1760*, 11.
5. Andre Charbonneau, *The Fortifications of Isle Aux Noix* (Ottawa: Parks Canada, 1994), 26, 27, 28, 30, and 32.
6. Map No. 256, Peter Force Map Collection, Geography and Map Collection, Library of Congress. http://memory.loc.gov/cgi-bin/query/ D?gmd:3:./temp/~ammem_Ji1h (accessed December 10, 2004).
7. Discussion of the history of river defenses in the eighteenth century is derived from Douglas R. Cubbison, *Historic Structures Report: The Hudson River Defenses at Fortress West Point, 1778–1783.* USMA, West Point, New York (January 2005), www.stonefortconsulting.com/ analysis.html (accessed April 1, 2011).

8. A typical example is Charles E. Miller, Jr., Donald V. Lockey and Joseph Visconti, Jr., *Highland Fortress: The Fortification of West Point During the American Revolution, 1775–1783* (West Point, New York: Department of History, U.S. Military Academy, 1979).

9. Roger, Earl of Orrery, *A Treatise on the Art of War* (Savoy: Henry Herringman, 1677), 121–23.

10. J. T. DeSauguliens, trans., *A Treatise of Fortifications Containing the Ancient and Modern Method of the Construction and Defense of Places and the Manner of Carrying Sieges, Written Originally in French by Monsieur Ozanam, Professor of Mathematics at Paris* (London: J. Jackson & J. Worrall, 1727), 148.

11. Muller, *Elementary Part of Fortification*, 171–72.

12. John Muller, *Attac and Defense*, 107–108.

13. "History of Girne (Kyrenia) Castle and Harbor, Cyprus," www.allcrusades.com/CASTLES/CYPRUS/KYRENIA/KYRENIA_TOWN/kyrenia_town_txt_1.htm (accessed December 8, 2004), www.allcrusades.com/CASTLES_COUNTRIES/castles_cyprus_overview-3.html (accessed December 8, 2004), and William Dreghorn, "A Guide to the Antiquities of Kyrenia," www.stwing.upenn.edu/%7Edurduran/drky1.html#town (accessed December 8, 2004).

14. Walled Towns Friendship Circle, "Padua's Medieval Walls," www.walledtowns.com/wtfc/towninfo/italy/padua.html (accessed December 8, 2004).

15. David Mallia, "Malta: A Case Study in the Development of Fortifications," www.icomos-ciic.org/CIIC/pamplona/PROYECTOS_David_Mallia.htm (accessed December 8, 2004), and "The Chain at Malta," www.simonhedges.com/photos/malta/birgu/stangelo/chain.htm (accessed December 8, 2004).

16. Ernle Bradford, *The Great Siege* (New York: Harcourt, Brace & World, 1961), 50, 135, 142–43, 194.

17. "History of The Harbor of Famagusta," www.allcrusades.com/CASTLES/CYPRUS/FAMAGUSTA/PHO_PIC_WEB/citadel-or-othellos-tower/pictures/s3500179.html (accessed December 8, 2004) and www.allcrusades.com/CASTLES/CYPRUS/FAMAGUSTA/MAPS/famagusta_town_map_1.html (accessed December 8, 2004), Stefano Gibelliino, "The Siege of the Turks (1571)," www.allcrusades.com/CASTLES/CYPRUS/FAMAGUSTA/MAPS/cyp-famagusta-Gibellino-1571/Cyp-FamagustaGibellino1571.html, (accessed December 8, 2004), and William Dreghorn, "Famagusta and Salamis, A Guide Book" accessed on-line at www.stwing.upenn.edu/~durduran/drfm1.html, (accessed December 8, 2004).

18. Charles Wintersmith, "Plan of Ticonderoga and Mount Hope, 1777" (reprint; Ticonderoga, New York: Fort Ticonderoga Museum, n.d.).

19. Edward P. Hamilton, *Fort Ticonderoga, Key to a Continent* (1964; second ed., Ticonderoga, New York: Fort Ticonderoga Museum, 1995), 96.

20. Bellico, *Sails and Steam in the Mountains*, 105, 107.

21. Amherst, *Journal of Jeffery Amherst*, 146.

22. Nigel Bly, "The Fall of Quebec" www.geocities.com/Athens/Academy/3967/quebec.html (accessed December 10, 2004).

23. Quoted in Jacques Lacoursiere, *The Battlefield: The Plains of Abraham, 1759–1760* (Sillery, Quebec, Canada: Septentrion, 2001), 6–7, 10.

24. Charbonneau, *The Fortifications of Isle Aux Noix*, 52.

25. Bayley, "Journal," 380.

26. David Holden, "Journal kept by Sergeant David Holden of Groton, Massachusetts During the Latter Part of the French and Indian War, February 20–November 29, 1760." *Proceedings of the Massachusetts Historical Society* (June 1889), 399.

27. Hamilton, *Adventure in the Wilderness*, 326.

28. Johnstone, *Campaign of 1760*, 23.

29. Amherst, *Journal of Jeffery Amherst*, 203.

30. Middleton, *Amherst and the Conquest of Canada*, 189–90.

31. W. Thomas, "Stations of Troops in North America, 1757–1760," *Journal of the Society for Army Historical Research* 14 (1935), 236.

32. Middleton, *Amherst and the Conquest of Canada*, 139.

33. Timothy J. Todish, ed., *The Annotated and Illustrated Journals of Major Robert Rogers* (Fleischmans, New York: Purple Mountain Press, 2002), 44, 155, 194–95.

34. John R. Cuneo, *Robert Rogers of the Rangers* (New York: Richardson & Steirman, 1987), 121.

35. Rogers' June raid is covered by Cuneo, *Robert Rogers of the Rangers*, 120–24; Todish, *Journals of Major Robert Rogers*, 198–204; and Patrick Frazier, *The Mohicans of Stockbridge* (Lincoln and London: University of Nebraska Press, 1975), 140–41.

36. *Orderly Book of Captain Barron's Company, June 4, 1760–February 6, 1764, and Orders at Fort Crown Point, July 27, 1761* (Early American Orderly Books, Jefferson Hall, U.S. Military Academy, West Point, New York).

37. Holden, "Journal," 400.

38. Todish, *Journals of Major Robert Rogers*, 202, and Rogers to Amherst, 21 June 21 1760, Amherst Papers.

39. Sullivan, *The Papers of Sir William Johnson*, 3:260.

40. Quoted in Alan J. Guy, *Oeconomy and Discipline: Officership and Administration in the British Army, 1714–1763* (Manchester: University Press, 1985), 157.

41. Middleton, *Amherst and the Conquest of Canada*, 195.

42. Amherst, *Journal of Jeffery Amherst*, 218.

43. Ibid., 200.

44. Amherst, *Journal of Jeffery Amherst*, 208.

45. Amherst to Haviland, n.d., Amherst Papers.

46. Amherst, Orders to Haviland, 12 June 1760, Amherst Papers.

47. Ibid.

48. Amherst to Haviland, 14 May 1760, and Haviland to Amherst, 17 April 1760 and 10 May 1760, Amherst Papers.
49. Haviland to Amherst, 13 June 1760, Amherst Papers.
50. Hugh Hastings, ed., *Orderly Book and Journal of Major John Hawks on the Ticonderoga–Crown Point Campaign Under General Jefferey Amherst, 1759–1760* (New York: Society of Colonial Wars in the State of New York, 1911), 73–92.
51. Peter Kimball, *Diary, March 4, 1760–October 29, 1760* (New Hampshire Historical Society).
52. Haviland to Amherst, 6 July 1760, Amherst Papers.
54. Frazier, *The Mohicans of Stockbridge*, 139–41.
55. Ian Glenn MacDonald, "Whaleboats, Row-Galleys and Floating Batteries: British Gunboats in the 1760 Canada Campaign" (master's thesis, Queen's University, 1999), 59.
56. Winthrop Sargent, *The History of An Expedition Against Fort DuQuesne in 1755* (1855, repr. Lewisburg, Pennsylvania: Wennawoods Publishing, 2005), 364.
57. Gary Paine, "Ord's Arks: Angles, Artillery and Ambush on Lakes George and Champlain," *American Neptune* 58, no. 2 (Spring 1998): 107–108.
58. Paine, "Ord's Arks," 117, and Knox, *Campaigns in North America*, 1:501.
59. Brinnen Stiles Carter, "Armament Remains from His Majesty's Sloop *Boscawen*" (master's thesis, Texas A&M University, 1995), 28.
60. French for "raft." *Radeau* is singular; *radeaux* is plural.
61. Amherst, *Journal of Jeffery Amherst*, 174.
62. MacDonald, "Whaleboats," 43–44.
63. Haviland to Amherst, 23 June 1760, and Amherst to Haviland, Albany, not dated [June 1760], Amherst Papers.
64. Carter, "Armament Remains" 26, 27.
65. Carter, "Armament Remains" 35.
66. Whaleboats differed from bateaux, in that they had a keel and could be more readily sailed and maneuvered than the flat-bottomed bateaux. Whaleboats could also be rowed. They were a more efficient vessel, but were more difficult to operate. The keel made them more complex and slower to build.
67. Middleton, *Amherst and the Conquest of Canada*, 205.
68. Ibid., 210.
69. Sidney Perley, ed., "Diaries Kept by Lemuel Wood of Boxford" *Essex Institute Historical Collections* 20 (1883) 290.
70. Haviland to Amherst, 10 and 11 August 1760, Amherst Papers.
71. *Orderly Book of Captain Silas Brown's Company, Colonel Timothy Ruggle's Regiment of Massachusetts Provincials* (Boston: Massachusetts Historical Society)

Chapter 6. "The English Flag is Flying on the Île aux Noix"

1. Bayley, "Journal," 379.

2. Samuel Jenks, "Journal of Captain Jenks." *Proceedings of the Massachusetts Historical Society* (March 1890), 367., and Perley, "Lemuel Wood Diaries," 290.
3. Holden, "Journal," 396.
4. Jenks, "Journal," 367, Holden, "Journal," 396, and John Frost, Jr., "Military Journal, May to November 1760" *Old Eliot* 8 (1908), 113–14. During the research for this project the author performed a comprehensive three-day nautical survey of Lake Champlain, using primary and secondary sources and historic and modern navigational charts of the lake, to explore the route that Haviland's flotilla took between Fort Crown Point and Isle Aux Noix. The author is deeply appreciative for the considerable assistance that his friend Mr. Bob Frederick provided, as captain of his vessel, "Double Trouble."
5. Frost, "Military Journal," 114, Holden, "Journal," 397, and Perley, "Lemuel Wood Diaries," 290, John Bradbury, "Military Journal, April 1760 to August 1762" in J. M. Bradbury, *Bradbury Memorial* (Portland, Maine: 1890), 275; and Jenks, "Journal," 367.
6. Holden, "Journal," 397.
7. MacDonald, "Whaleboats," 77.
8. Bradbury, "Military Journal,"275.
9. Frost, "Military Journal,"114.
10. Bayley, "Journal," 379.
11. Bradbury, "Military Journal,"275.
12. Jenks, "Journal," 367.
13. Ibid., 367–68, Holden, "Journal," 397, Bayley, "Journal," 379, and Bradbury, "Military Journal,"275.
14. Holden, "Journal," 397
15. Canada Hydrographic Service, *Small-Craft Chart, Richelieu River, Chambly to Lake Champlain* (Ottawa: Minister of Fisheries and Oceans Canada,1984).
16. John Muller, *Attac and Defense,* 10–18.
17. Jenks, "Journal," 368.
18. Bradbury, "Military Journal,"276.
19. Holden, "Journal," 397.
20. *Journal of Major Robert Rogers,* 206.
21. Frost, "Military Journal,"114; Bayley, "Journal," 379; and Perley, "Lemuel Wood Diaries," 291.
22. Jenks, "Journal," 368.
23. Bradbury, "Military Journal,"276.
24. Holden, "Journal," 397.
25. Jenks, "Journal," 368.
26. Bradbury, "Military Journal,"276.
27. Frost, "Military Journal,"114, and MacDonald, "Whaleboats," 86.
28. Jenks, "Journal," 368.
29. Bradbury, "Military Journal,"277.
30. Holden, "Journal," 397.
31. Bayley, "Journal,"379.

32. Perley, "Lemuel Wood Diaries," 291.
33. *Orderly Book, Colonel John Thomas's Regiment of Massachusetts Provincials, 7–29 August 1760* (Massachusetts Historical Society, Boston, Massachusetts).
34. Quoted in MacDonald, "Whaleboats," 80–81.
35. Holden, "Journal," 397.
36. Frost, "Military Journal," 114, Bayley, "Journal,"379, and Perley, "Lemuel Wood Diaries," 291.
37. Jenks, "Journal," 368.
38. Holden, "Journal," 397.
39. Bradbury, "Military Journal," 276–77.
40. MacDonald, "Whaleboats," 80–81.
41. Bellico, *Sails and Steam in the Mountains*, 107.
42. Bradbury, "Military Journal," 276.
43. Jenks, "Journal," 369.
44. Bayley, "Journal,"379.
45. Frost, "Military Journal," 114.
46. Holden, "Journal," 397–98.
47. Bradbury, "Military Journal,"277.
48. Holden, "Journal," 398.
49. Bradbury, "Military Journal,"277.
50. *Orderly Book, Colonel John Thomas's Regiment of Massachusetts Provincials.*
51. Jenks, "Journal," 369.
52. Bradbury, "Military Journal," 277.
53. Ibid., 277–78.
54. *Orderly Book, Colonel John Thomas's Regiment of Massachusetts Provincials.*
55. Discussion of the artillery batteries is derived from Cubbison, *Historic Structures Report.*
56. J. T. DeSauguliens, trans., *A Treatise of Fortifications Containing the Ancient and Modern Method of the Construction and Defense of Places and the Manner of Carrying Sieges, Written Originally in French by Monsieur Ozanam, Professor of Mathematics at Paris* (London: J. Jackson & J. Worrall, 1727), 168–69.
57. J. G. Tielke, *The Field Engineer, or Introduction Upon Every Branch of Field Fortifications*, trans. Edwin Hewgill (1769; rev. ed., London: J. Walter, 1789), 1:301–311.
58. Charles W. Rudyerd, *Course of Artillery at the Royal Military Academy, As Established by His Grace, The Duke of Richmond, Master General of his Majesty's Ordnance* (Woolwich: Royal Military Academy, 1793).
59. Jenks, "Journal," 369.
60. Bradbury, "Military Journal,"278.
61. Perley, "Lemuel Wood Diaries," 292.
62. Jenks, "Journal," 370.
63. Ibid., 370.

64. Ibid., 370.
65. Bradbury, "Military Journal,"278.
66. Holden, "Journal," 398.
67. Bradbury, "Military Journal,"279.
68. Frost, "Military Journal,"114.
69. Bayley, "Journal,"379.
70. Perley, "Lemuel Wood Diaries," 292.
71. Jenks, "Journal," 370.
72. Bradbury, "Military Journal,"278.
73. Johnstone, *Campaign of 1760*, 24.
74. Muller, *Attac and Defense*, 46–47.
75. Jenks, "Journal," 370.
76. Bayley, "Journal," 379.
77. Holden, "Journal," 398.
78. Bayley, "Journal," 379.
79. Jenks, "Journal," 371.
80. Holden, "Journal," 398.
81. Frost, "Military Journal,"115.
82. Bradbury, "Military Journal,"279.
83. Bayley, "Journal," 379.
84. André Lépine, "A Wreck Believed to be a French 'Bateau' Sunk during Action in 1760 off Isle-aux-Noix in the Richelieu River, Quebec, Canada," *International Journal of Nautical Archaeology* 10, no. 1 (1981), 41–50.
85. This operation is described in three secondary sources: Bellico, *Sails and Steam in the Mountains*, 107, MacDonald, "Whaleboats," 89, and Frazier, *The Mohicans of Stockbridge*, 142. A dramatic and exciting rendition, generally accurate but highly romanticized, is found in Harrison Bird, *Navies in the Mountains: The Battles on the Waters of Lake Champlain and Lake George, 1609–1814* (New York: Oxford University Press, 1962), 106-118.
86. *The Journals of Major Robert Rogers*, 206.
87. Jenks, "Journal," 371–72.
88. Bradbury, "Military Journal," 279.
89. Jenks, "Journal," 372.
90. Holden, "Journal," 398.
91. Bradbury, "Military Journal,"280.
92. Johnstone, *Campaign of 1760*, 24.
93. Bradbury, "Military Journal,"280.
94. Bradbury, "Military Journal,"280.
95. Frost, "Military Journal,"115.
96. Holden, "Journal," 399.
97. Jenks, "Journal," 372.
98. Ibid., 372.
99. Bradbury, "Military Journal,"281.
100. Johnstone, *Campaign of 1760*, 25.
101. Ibid., 26.

102. Ibid, 26–29.
103. Jenks, "Journal," 372.
104. Bradbury, "Military Journal," 280.
105. Holden, "Journal," 399.
106. Johnstone, *Campaign of 1760*, 29.
107. Hamilton, *Adventure in the Wilderness*, 326.
108. Johnstone, *Campaign of 1760*, 29.
109. Beattie, *General Jeffery Amherst and the Conquest of Canada*, 215, and Wrong, *The Fall of Canada*, 209–210.
110. Perley, "Lemuel Wood Diaries" 293.
111. Frost, "Military Journal,"115, 116.
112. Perley, "Lemuel Wood Diaries" 293.
113. Holden, "Journal," 399.
114. Bradbury, "Military Journal,"281.
115. Perley, "Lemuel Wood Diaries" 293.
116. Bradbury, "Military Journal,"281.
117. Todish, *Journals of Major Robert Rogers*, 206–207.
118. Cuneo, *Robert Rogers of the Rangers*, 127–28.
119. Bradbury, "Military Journal," 282, and Perley, "Lemuel Wood Diaries," 293–94.
120. Perley, "Lemuel Wood Diaries," 293–94.
121. Bradbury, "Military Journal," 283.
122. Bradbury, "Military Journal," 283.
123. *Orderly Book of Captain Silas Brown's Company*.
124. Perley, "Lemuel Wood Diaries," 294.

Chapter 7. "I have come to take Canada"

1. A 1756 British guardhouse was discovered and investigated by the New York State Museum in 1988. It is the only documented structure surviving from British army's occupation of Albany during the Seven Years' War. Charles L. Fisher, "Soldiers in the City: The Archaeology of the British Guard House" in Charles L. Fisher, ed., *People, Places, and Material Things: Historic Archaeology of Albany, New York* (Albany: New York State Museum Bulletin 499, 2003), 39–46.
2. John F. Luzander, Louis Torres, and Orville W. Carroll, *Fort Stanwix, History: Historic Furnishing, and Historic Structure Reports* (Washington, DC: National Park Service, U.S. Department of the Interior, 1976), 3–6.
3. Thomas, "Stations of Troops in North America, 1757–1760," 236.
4. Middleton, *Amherst and the Conquest of Canada*, 189–90.
5. Kimball, *Correspondence of William Pitt*, 2:231–37.
6. Sullivan, *The Papers of Sir William Johnson*, 3:192–93.
7. Ibid., 3:197.
8. Ibid., 3:199–200.
9. Amherst, *Journal of Jeffery Amherst*, 199.
10. Quoted in Long, *Lord Jeffery Amherst*, 128–29.

11. Francis Parkman, *The Conspiracy of Pontiac and the Indian War after the Conquest of Canada*, introduction by Michael M. McConnell (1851; rev. ed., Lincoln: University of Nebraska Press, 1994), 1:173.

12. Gregory Evans Dowd, *War under Heaven: Pontiac, the Indian Nations and the British Empire* (Baltimore: John Hopkins University Press, 2002), 64.

13. Colin G. Calloway, *The Scratch of a Pen: 1763 and the Transformation of North America* (London: Oxford University Press: 2006), 69.

14. Amherst did note that the Indians were troublesome when inebriated. This observation could have been made in 1760 during any nocturnal inspection of his own barracks, or indeed during any weekend visit to a university fraternity in 2013.

15. Jelles Fonda, "Journal, 1760" (New York Historical Society, New York City).

16. Middleton, *Amherst and the Conquest of Canada*, 207.

17. Quoted in Pound, *Johnson of the Mohawks*, 289.

18. Sullivan, *The Papers of Sir William Johnson*, 3:206.

19. I own a house in Pamelia, Jefferson County, in northern New York, built circa 1810, which is eligible for the National Register of Historic Places. I can personally attest through hard experience to the effects of these heavy rains.

20. Sullivan, *The Papers of Sir William Johnson*, 3:256.

21. Ibid., 3:264.

22. Middleton, *Amherst and the Conquest of Canada*, 192–93.

23. Quoted in John Shy, *Toward Lexington: The Role of the British Army in the Coming of the American Revolution* (Princeton: Princeton University Press, 1965), 100.

24. Sullivan, *The Papers of Sir William Johnson*, 3:260.

25. Amherst to Pitt, 21 June 1760," Amherst Papers.

26. Amherst, *Journal of Jeffery Amherst*, 207–209.

27. Nathaniel Woodhull, "A Journal Kept by General Nathaniel Woodhull, When Colonel of the 3rd Regiment New York Provincials, in the Expedition to Montreal in 1760," *Historical Magazine* 5, no. 9 (September 1861): 257.

28. J. W. Fortescue, *A History of the British Army* (London: Macmillan, 1910), 404; and Wrong, *The Fall of Canada*, 193.

29. Knox, *Campaigns in North America*, 187.

30. Todish, *Journals of Major Robert Rogers*, 185, 187.

31. J. C. Webster, *Journal of William Amherst in America, 1758–1760* (London: Frome and London, 1927), 60, and Jean N. McIlwraith, *Sir Frederick Haldimand* (London: Oxford University Press, 1926), 35.

32. Captain William Hervey, *Journals of the Honorable William Hervey in North America and Europe from 1755 to 1814, With Order Books at Montreal, 1760–1763* (Bury St. Edmunds: Paul & Mathew, 1906), 56.

33. McIlwraith, *Sir Frederick Haldimand*, 3, 5, 6, 8–10, 11, 21, 22, 25, 26, 29, and "Sir Frederic Haldimand" in *Dictionary of Canadian Biography*, www.biographi.ca/009004-119.01-e.php?&id_nbr=2445 (accessed March 2010).

34. Amherst to Pitt, 19 May 1760, Amherst Papers.
35. "Embarkation Return of His Majesty's Forces Under the Command of Major General Amherst from the Camp at Fort Ontario, 9th of August 1760," Amherst Papers.
36. Middleton, *Amherst and the Conquest of Canada*, 17.
37. John R. Cuneo, "Factors Behind the Raising of the 80th Foot in America," *Military Collector & Historian*, 11, no. 4 (Winter 1959), 97–103, and Eric I. Manders, Brian Leigh Dunnigan, John R. Elting, "80th Regiment of Foot, 1757–1764" *Military Collector & Historian*, 39, no. 4 (Winter 1987), 172–73.
38. "George Williamson" in *Dictionary of Canadian Biography*, www.biographi.ca/009004-119.01-e.php?&id_nbr=2215&&PHPSESSID=ychzfqkvzape (accessed 5 March 2010).
39. Hervey, *Journals*, 57.
40. MacDonald, "Whaleboats," 63.
41. Farqharson, 22 August 1760. Letters, Invercauld Estate, Ballater, Aberdeenshire, United Kingdom.
42. Robert Malcomson, "Not Very Much Celebrated: The Evolution and Nature of the Provincial Marine, 1755–1813," *Northern Mariner* 11, no. 1 (January 2001), 28.
43. Williamson to Ligonier, 26 August 1760. George Williamson Papers, National Archives and Library of Canada, Ottawa, Ontario.
44. Amherst, *Journal of Jeffery Amherst*, 223.
45. Wrong, *The Fall of Canada*, 214, and Amherst to Pitt, 26 August 1760, Amherst Papers.
46. Amherst, *Journal of Jeffery Amherst*, 219.
47. W.A. B. Douglas, "Joshua Loring" in *Dictionary of Canadian Biography*, www.biographi.ca/009004-119.01-e.php?&id_nbr=2031 (accessed March 7, 2010), and Eva Phillips Boyd, "Commodore Joshua Loring: Jamaica Plain by Way of London," *Old-Time New England Magazine* (April–June 1959), www.jphs.org/people/2005/4/14/commodore-joshua-loring-jamaica-plain-by-way-of-london.html. (accessed 7 March 2010).
48. Malcomson, "Not Very Much Celebrated," 28.
49. Williamson to Ligonier, George Williamson Papers, and MacDonald, "Whaleboats," 60–61.
50. Farqharson, 22 August 1760, Farqharson Letters.
51. Hervey, *Journals*, 57.
52. Richard E. Day, *Calendar of the Sir William Johnson Manuscripts in the New York State Library* (Albany: University of the State of New York, 1909), 104, and Amherst to Captain Loring, 6 August 1760 in Haldimand Papers, David Library of the American Revolution, Washington Crossing, Pennsylvania.
53. Sullivan, *The Papers of Sir William Johnson*, 3:248.
54. Fonda, "Journal."
55. Amherst, *Journal of Jeffery Amherst*, 207.
56. Webster, *William Amherst's Journal*, 58–60.
57. Hervey, *Journals*, 83.

58. Amherst, *Journal of Jeffery Amherst*, 222.
59. Amherst to Haldimand, 29 July 1760, Haldimand Papers.
60. Undated Instructions, Amherst to Colonel Haldimand, 1760, Haldimand Papers.
61. Hervey, *Journals*, 85, 94.
62. Amherst, *Journal of Jeffery Amherst*, 223.
63. Hervey, *Journals*, 95.
64. Amherst, *Journal of Jeffery Amherst*, 224.
65. Hervey, *Journals*, 88.
66. Joseph Booth, "Military Journal, July to October 1760" in Charles E. Booth, *One Branch of the Booth Family* (New York: 1910), 142.
67. My brother, the Rev. Dr. Robert "Bob" Kaylor of the United Methodist Church, generously assisted with the interpretation of this sermon.
68. Williamson to Ligonier, 26 August 1760, George Williamson Papers.
69. Robert Malcomson, *Warships of the Great Lakes, 1754–1834* (Rochester, Kent, United Kingdom: Chatham Publishing, 2001), 16–19, and Pierre Pouchot, *Memoirs*, 191n, 260–61.
70. Amherst to Loring, 20 July 1760, Amherst Papers.
71. Webster, *William Amherst's Journal*, 59–60.
72. Loring to Amherst, 23 July 1760, Amherst Papers.
73. Amherst, *Journal of Jeffery Amherst*, 217–21.
74. Amherst to Loring, 24 July 1760, Amherst Papers.
75. Middleton, *Amherst and the Conquest of Canada*, 209, and Amherst to Loring, 6 August 1760, Amherst Papers.
76. Malcomson, *Warships of the Great Lakes*, 19, and Robert J. Andrews, "Two Ships, Two Flags: The *Outaouaise/Williamson* and the *Iroquoise/Anson* on Lake Ontario, 1759–1761." *Northern Mariner* 14, no. 3 (July 2004): 44.
77. Amherst, *Journal of Jeffery Amherst*, 225.
78. Webster, *William Amherst's Journal*, 60–64.
79. Webster, *Journal of Jeffery Amherst*, 229.
80. Fonda, "Journal."
81. *Knox, Campaigns in North America*, 538.
82. Amherst, *Journal of Jeffery Amherst*, 227–28.
83. Farqharson, 22 August 1760, Letters.
84. Hervey, *Journals*, 57.
85. Webster, *Journal of Jeffery Amherst*, 228–30. The author acknowledges the generous assistance of his friend Dr. Timothy Abel, former executive director of the Jefferson County Historical Society, for his interpretation of Amherst's route.
86. Webster, *Journal of Jeffery Amherst*, 228.
87. Ibid., 232.
88. Williamson to Ligonier, George Williamson Papers.
89. MacDonald, "Whaleboats," 81, 82–85.
90. Amherst, *Journal of Jeffery Amherst*, 231.
91. Mayo, *Jeffery Amherst*, 177.

92. Lemuel Aiken Welles, "Letters of Colonel Nathan Whiting, Written From Camp During the French and Indian War" *Papers of the New Haven Colony Historical Society* 6 (1900), 146.
93. Hervey, *Journals*, 58.
94. Farqharson, 22 August 1760, Letters.
95. Fonda, "Journal."
96. Webster, ed., *Journal of Jeffery Amherst*, 232, Woodhull, "Journal," 258, and Webster, *William Amherst's Journal*, 64.
97. Amherst to Pitt, 26 August 1760, Amherst Papers, and Knox, *Campaigns in North America*, 542.
98. Pouchot, *Memoirs*, 5–31.
99. Today, this island is known as Chimney Island, and unfortunately the French fortifications that had survived were entirely removed by the construction of the St. Lawrence Seaway in the 1950s and 1960s. This construction, which occurred before the enactment of Federal historic preservation and environmental protection laws, eradicated a significant portion of the military heritage of the St. Lawrence River valley. Chimney Island was reduced in size and dramatically altered in topography, and it is considerably smaller and higher in the St. Lawrence River today than it was in 1760. A professional colleague with the Board of the Fort La Presentation Association, my wife, and I made a comprehensive visit to the island in May 2010.
100. Pouchot, *Memoirs*, 260–62.
101. Williamson to Ligonier, 26 August 1760, George Williamson Papers.
102. Webster, *Journal of Jeffery Amherst*, 239.
103. Pouchot, *Memoirs*, 262, 263n, and Webster, *Journal of Jeffery Amherst*, 239. Lagrange was a bag filled with miscellaneous metal chunks and pieces, intended exclusively for close-range service against attacking infantry.
104. Middleton, *Amherst and the Conquest of Canada*, 211.
105. Welles, "Letters of Colonel Nathan Whiting," 145.
106. Woodhull, "Journal," 258.
107. Amherst, *Journal of Jeffery Amherst*, 232–33.
108. Pouchot, *Memoirs*, 302.
109. Andrew Gallup, ed., "Memoirs of a French and Indian War Soldier" in "Siege of Fort Lévis from Eyewitness Accounts," David Dickinson, ed., *St. Lawrence County Historical Association Quarterly* 46 (2001), 28.
110. Amherst, *Journal of Jeffery Amherst*, 233.
111. Woodhull, "Journal," 258.
112. The author wishes to express his deep appreciation to his friend Jim Regan for providing a boat for a site visit to Chimney Island in May 2010.
113. *The Nautical Seaway Trail: Chartbook and Waterfront Guide to New York State's Great Lakes–St. Lawrence Region* (Hammond, New York: Blue Heron Enterprises, 1991), Chart 45.
114. T. Fortune, *The Artillerist's Companion, Containing the Discipline, Returns, Reports, Pay, Provision, &c. of that Corps, In Field, in Forts,*

at Sea, &c. (London: J. Millan, 1778: repr. ed. Alexandria Bay, New York: Museum Restoration Service, 1992), 11.

115. Amherst, *Journal of Jeffery Amherst*, 233–34.
116. The British Chimney Point positions are today on the grounds of the St. Lawrence Psychiatric Center, Ogdensburg, New York.
117. Williamson to Ligonier, 26 August 1760, George Williamson Papers.
118. Webster, *Journal of Jeffery Amherst*, 234.
119. Pouchot, *Memoirs*, 303.
120. Webster, *Journal of Jeffery Amherst*, 236.
121. Hervey, *Journals*, 113.
122. Webster, *Journal of Jeffery Amherst*, 236.
123. Hervey, *Journals*, 59.
124. Pouchot, *Memoirs*, 306, 311.
125. Webster, *Journal of Jeffery Amherst*, 236–37.
126. Webster, *William Amherst's Journal*, 65.
127. Hervey, *Journals*, 59.
128. Pouchot, *Memoirs*, 306–307.
129. Amherst, Orders to Loring, 22 August 22 1760, Amherst Papers.
130. Knox, *Campaigns in North America*, 544.
131. Other accounts state that the *Mohawk* deliberately cut the cable. The evidence is not conclusive. Whether the cable was severed by a British axe or French cannonball, the results were the same.
132. Pouchot, *Memoirs*, 308.
133. Knox, *Campaigns in North America*, 551.
134. Amherst, *Journal of Jeffery Amherst*, 237–38.
135. Kimball, *Correspondence of William Pitt*, 2:325.
136. Knox, *Campaigns in North America*, 550.
137. "Williamson to Ligonier, 26 August 1760, George Williamson Papers.
138. Middleton, *Amherst and the Conquest of Canada*, 214.
139. Pouchot, *Memoirs*, 306, 311.
140. Hervey, *Journals*, 60.
141. Pouchot, *Memoirs*, 306, 311–12.
142. Ibid., 306, 312. The only other French account of the siege, that of a French Artilleryman named Charles Bonin, also recorded this heavy bombardment, although his short rendition is full of hyperbole. Gallup, "Memoirs of a French and Indian War Soldier: Jolicoeur Charles Bonin," 28.
143. Pouchot, *Memoirs*, 312–13.
144. Welles, "Letters of Colonel Nathan Whiting," 146.
145. Farqharson, 22 August 1760 Letters.
146. Pouchot, *Memoirs*, 313–14, and Webster, *Journal of Jeffery Amherst*, 239.
147. Asa Waterman, "Military Journal, June to September 1760" in W.F. Eddy, *Leaflet* (Brooklyn, New York: 1904), Connecticut State Archives, Hartford, Connecticut.
148. Webster, *Journal of Jeffery Amherst*, 239, Knox, *Campaigns in North America*, 3:257, Hervey, *Journals*, 60, and Williamson to Ligonier, 26 August 1760, George Williamson Papers.

149. Webster, *Journal of Jeffery Amherst*, 239.
150. Hervey, *Journals*, 116.
151. Webster, *Journal of Jeffery Amherst*, 239–40; Pouchot, *Memoirs*, 315; Webster, *William Amherst's Journal*, 65; Hervey, *Journals*, 115–16; and Asa Waterman, "Military Journal."
152. Webster, *Journal of Jeffery Amherst*, 240,

Chapter 8. "It was Impossible to make any further resistance"

Chapter title from Johnstone, *Campaign of 1760*, 31.

1. "Williamson to Ligonier, 26 August 1760, George Williamson Papers.
2. Webster, *Journal of Jeffery Amherst*, 240.
3. The goods issued were 50 Pieces of Red Stroud; 18 Pieces of Brown Stroud; 15 Pieces of Blue Stroud; 29 Coarse Shirts; 16 Small Pieces of Canvas; 7 Small Pieces of Shalloon [a cheap, twilled lightweight woolen cloth used for lining clothes]; a Coat and two Bed Gowns; 161 Pieces of Gartering & Tape; 3 Dozen of Combs; 2 Dozen of Knives; a quantity of Rings and Thimbles; 9 Bear Skins; one Buffalo Skin; and 64 Dressed Deer Skins. Sullivan, *The Papers of Sir William Johnson*, 10:176.
4. Ibid., 10:180–85, Knox, *Campaigns in North America*, 555, and Webster, *Journal of Jeffery Amherst*, 243.
5. Sullivan, *The Papers of Sir William Johnson*, 3:269–75,
6. Webster, *Journal of Jeffery Amherst*, 240.
7. Hervey, *Journals*, 61.
8. Webster, ed., *Journal of Jeffery Amherst*, 241. Captain Quinton Kennedy of the 44th Foot, along with a Lieutenant Hamilton and "several Indians" had been captured carrying dispatches from Amherst at Crown Point to Wolfe at Quebec in 1759. "Captain Jacobs" was almost certainly one of these Indians. Todisch, *Journals of Robert Rogers*, 198, 314.
9. Webster, *Journal of Jeffery Amherst*, 241.
10. Ibid., 241.
11. Quoted in Denis Vaugeois, *The Last French and Indian War, An Inquiry into a Safe-Conduct Issued in 1760 that Acquired the Value of a Treaty in 1990* (Montreal: McGill-Queen's University Press, 2002), 149.
12. Sullivan, *The Papers of Sir William Johnson*, 3:269–75.
13. Webster, *Journal of Jeffery Amherst*, 240, Pouchot, *Memoirs*, 316.
14. Fonda, "Journal."
15. Pouchot, *Memoirs*, 316.
16. Webster, *Journal of Jeffery Amherst*, 235.
17. Ibid., 65.
18. Ibid., 242.
19. Ibid., 242–43.
20. *The Nautical Seaway Trail: Chartbook and Waterfront Guide to New York State's Great Lakes–St. Lawrence Region*, Chart 52.
21. Webster, *William Amherst's Journal*, 65.

22. Webster, *Journal of Jeffery Amherst*, 243.
23. As the author, who has extensively trekked in the Adirondacks using only eighteenth-century clothing, rations, and equipment, can personally attest.
24. Webster, *Journal of Jeffery Amherst*, 243–44.
25. Knox, *Campaigns in North America*, 556.
26. Webster, *William Amherst's Journal*, 66.
27. John Grant, *Journal of John Grant, 1741–1763* (Alexander Turnbull Library, Wellington, New Zealand), and Ian McColloch and Timothy Todish, eds., *Through So Many Dangers, The Memoir and Adventures of Robert Kirk, Late of the Royal Highland Regiment* (Fleischmanns, N.Y.: Purple Mountain Press, 2003), 71.
28. McColloch and Todish, eds., *The Memoir and Adventures of Robert Kirk*, 72–74.
29. Quoted in McCulloch, *Sons of the Mountains*, 1:254.
30. Webster, *Journal of Jeffery Amherst*, 244.
31. The 24-pounder bronze cannon is in the Stewart Museum in Montreal, and the two mortars are in the Musée régional de Vaudreuil-Soulanges, also in Montreal. A photograph of the 24-pounder cannon is in this book. Photographs of the other artifacts are in Denis Vaugeois, *The Last French and Indian War*, 56–57. See Museum Records at the Musée régional de Vaudreuil-Soulanges, Montreal; and Sébastien Daviau, "Mortier de Marine Calibre 10" *Au fil du temps, Publication de la Société d'histoire et de généalogie de Salaberry* 17, no. 1 (March 2008): 19–21.
32. Webster, *Journal of Jeffery Amherst*, 245.
33. Knox, *Campaigns in North America*, 512.
34. Montresor to Murray, 3 September 1760, Montresor Family Papers, David Library of the American Revolution, Washington Crossing, Pennsylvania.
35. Webster, *William Amherst's Journal*, 67.
36. Todisch, *Journals of Robert Rogers*, 207.
37. "Military Journal, August to September 1760" in *All Canada in the Hands of the English* (Boston, 1760; repr., Early American Imprints, Series 1, #8527), 14.
38. Webster, *Journal of Jeffery Amherst*, 245–47.
39. Hervey, *Journals*, 122.
40. Quick, *James Thompson*, 38.
41. Webster, *William Amherst's Journal*, 66.
42. Kimball, *Correspondence of William Pitt*, 2:330.
43. "Military Journal, August to September 1760," 14.
44. Welles, "Letters of Colonel Nathan Whiting," 147.
45. Johnstone, *Campaign of 1760*, 31.
46. Wood, *Logs of the Conquest*, 328.
47. Kimball, *Correspondence of William Pitt*, 2:341.
48. Knox, *Campaigns in North America*, 515.
49. Ibid., 515.

50. Eugene Leliepvre and Rene Chartrand, "Corps of Cavalry, Canada, 1759–1760" *Military Collector & Historian* 27, no. 3 (Fall 1976), 131, and Donald W. Holst, "French Provincial Light Horse, 1759–1760" *Military Collector & Historian* 18, no. 2 (Summer 1966), 60.

51. The best study of the fortifications of Montreal is Phyllis Lambert and Alan Stewart, eds., *Opening the Gates of Eighteenth-Century Montreal* (Montreal: Canadian Center for Architecture, 1992), 20–24.

52. Shondeep L. Sarkar, "Microstructural Investigation of Renaissance Mortar from Montreal, Quebec, Canada." *Cement and Concrete Research* 22, no. 6 (November1992): 1016, 1017.

53. Johnstone, *Campaign of 1760*, 31–32.

54. A section of the historic fortified wall has been excavated at the Place de Mars in Montreal, and is open to visitors to that beautiful city.

55. René Chartrand, *French Fortresses in North America 1535–1763, Québec, Montréal, Louisbourg and New Orleans* (Oxford: Osprey Publishing, 2005), 32–44.

56. Kimball, *Correspondence of William Pitt*, 2:330.

57. Todish, *Journals of Major Robert Rogers*, 207.

58. Vaugeois, *The Last French and Indian War*, 58–60.

59. Vaugeois, *The Last French and Indian War*, 210.

60. Knox, *Campaigns in North America*, 559, and Marin L. Nicolai, "A Different Kind of Courage: The French Military and the Canadian Irregular Solder during the Seven Years' War" *Canadian Historical Review* 70, no. 1 (1989): 74.

61. Webster, *Journal of Jeffery Amherst*, 245–46.

62. Knox, *Campaigns in North America*, 560.

63. Johnstone, *Campaign of 1760*, 32.

64. Knox, *Campaigns in North America*, 561.

65. The complete text of the entire exchange between Amherst and Vaudrieul is re-printed in Knox, *Campaigns in North America*, 559–65.

66. The terms of capitulation are printed in the entirety in Knox, *Campaigns in North America*, 566–89.

67. Woodhull, "Journal," 260.

68. Williamson to Ligonier, Montreal, not dated [ca. September 1760], George Williamson Papers.

69. Waterman, "Military Journal."

70. *All Canada in the Hands of the English*, 15.

71. Knox, *Campaigns in North America*, 590, Webster, *Journal of Jeffery Amherst*, 248, and Kimball, *Correspondence of William Pitt*, 2:335.

72. "Treaty of Oswegatchie, 1760" *The Canadian Encyclopaedia*, www.thecanadianencyclopedia.com/index.cfm?PgNm=TCE&Params=A1ARTA0010705 (accessed 28 March 2010).

73. Vaugeois, *The Last French and Indian War*, 64–65, 214–21.

74. Kimball, *Correspondence of William Pitt*, 2:332.

75. Welles, "Letters of Colonel Nathan Whiting," 147.

76. Kimball, *Correspondence of William Pitt*, 2:338.

77. Quoted in Long, *Lord Jeffery Amherst,* 138. An "anker" is approximately 10.3 modern gallons.
78. Middleton, *Amherst and the Conquest of Canada,* 228.
79. Sullivan, *The Papers of Sir William Johnson,* 3:278–79.
80. Webster, *William Amherst's Journal,* 68, and Webster, *Journal of Jeffery Amherst,* 247.
81. Amherst to Wentworth 9 September 1760." *Early American Imprints,* First Series, No. 41128. Electronic Copy at Jefferson Hall, U.S. Military Academy, West Point, New York.

Chapter 9. "Entirely yielded to the Dominion of his Majesty"

1. Bradbury, "Military Journal,"283.
2. Ian McCulloch, "Highland Chaplaincy in the French & Indian War, 1756–1763" www.electricscotland.com/history/scotreg/mcculloch/story3.htm (accessed 15 September 2009).
3. Johnson, "Memoirs," 139.
4. John Montresor to James Montresor, 16 December 1760, in Montresor Family Papers.
5. Howard H. Peckman, *Pontiac and the Indian Uprising* (1947: repr. Chicago: University of Chicago Press, 1961), 57.
6. Kevin Sweeney, "The Very Model of a Modern Major General" *Amherst Magazine* (Fall 2008), www.amherst.edu/aboutamherst/magazine/issues/2008fall/lordjeff (accessed 12 February 2010).
7. William J. Eccles, *The Canadian Frontier, 1534–1760* (Hinsdale, Illinois: The Dryden Press, 1969), 180.
8. For an analysis of this, refer to Elizabeth A. Fenn, "Biological Warfare in Eighteenth-Century North America: Beyond Jefferey Amherst," *Journal of American History* 86, no. 4 (March 2000), 1552–1580. A careful evaluation of this subject, generally ignored, is by Bernhard Knollenberg, "General Amherst and Germ Warfare," *Mississippi Valley Historical Review* 41 no. 3 (December 1954): 489–94.

Appendix A. Command and Control, Communications, and Intelligence, in the British Army, 1760

1. Julius Caesar, *The Gallic War* trans. H. J. Edwards (1917: repr., Cambridge, Massachusetts: Harvard University Press, 2000).
2. Captain Joseph Otway, *An Essay on the Art of War, Translated from the French of County Turpin, In Two Volumes* (London: A. Hamilton, 1761), i–xvi, and "The Instruction of Frederick the Great for his Generals, 1747" in *Roots of Strategy: The 5 Greatest Military Classics of All Time* T. R. Phillips, ed. (Harrisburg, Pa.: Stackpole Books, 1985), 314.
3. U.S. Army, *Field Manual 3-0, Operations* (Washington, D.C.: Department of the Army, 2001), 5–17.
4. A few short decades after Amherst conducted his campaign in Canada, the great Prussian general Carl von Clausewitz would devote an entire chapter of his treatise *On War* to military friction. Carl von

Clausewitz, *On War*, ed. and tr. Michael Howard and Peter Paret (New York: Knopf, 1973), 138–40.

5. Julius Caesar, *The Gallic War*, 3–11.

6. Clausewitz, *On War*, 169.

7. Count Turpin, *An Essay on the Art of War*, and Douglas R. Cubbison, *The British Defeat of the French in Pennsylvania in 1758: A Military History of the Forbes Campaign against Fort Duquesne* (Jefferson, North Carolina: McFarland Publishers, 2010), 32–40.

8. Robert B. Asprey, *Frederick the Great, The Magnificent Enigma* (New York: History Book Club, 1999), 394.

9. Michel Brisebois, "Books from General Wolfe's Library at the National Library of Canada." *National Library News* 28, no. 2 (February 1996), www.collectionscanada.ca/bulletin/015017-9602-15-e.html.

10. Count Turpin, *An Essay on the Art of War*, 1:1–15.

11. Count Turpin, *An Essay on the Art of War*, 1:17.

12. Lieutenant General Humphrey Bland, *Treatise of Military Discipline* (London: Eighth Edition, 1759). The best secondary source on training and instruction of the British Army between Marlborough and Napoleon is J. A. Houlding, *Fit for Service, The Training of the British Army, 1715–1795* (Oxford: Clarendon Press, 1981). A recently published study that explores which military treatises were actually studied by British Army officers during the period of the American Revolution is Ira D. Gruber, *Books and the British Army in the Age of the American Revolution* (Chapel Hill: University of North Carolina Press, 2010). For the concept of strategy during the 18th Century, refer to Dave R. Palmer, *George Washington's Military Genius* (Washington, D.C.: Regnery History, 2012), 1–8.

13. "The Instructions of Frederick the Great for His Generals, 1747," in Phillips, *Roots of Strategy*, 314.

14. Ibid., 348–49.

15. Ibid., 392.

16. Thomas Webb, *A Military Treatise on the Appointments of the Army, Containing Many Useful Hints, not touched upon before by any Author: And Proposing some New Regulations in the Army, which will be particularly useful in carrying on the War in North-America* (Philadelphia: W. Dunlap, 1759), 21–26.

17. Louis M. Waddell, John L. Tottenham and Donald H. Kent, eds., *The Papers of Henry Bouquet* (Harrisburg, Penn.: The Pennsylvania Historical and Museum Commission, 1984), 5:17, 28.

18. Webster, *Journal of Jeffery Amherst*, 201.

19. Kimball, *Correspondence of William Pitt*, 2: 318.

20. As documented in Douglas R. Cubbison, *Burgoyne and the Saratoga Campaign: His Papers* (Norman: University of Oklahoma Press, 2012), 36–37, 153–54, 188.

21. Amherst to Haviland, 18 June 1760, Amherst Papers.

22. Webster, *Journal of Jeffery Amherst*, 241.

23. As defined by modern military art and science, operational-level military activities are regarded as being an intermediate level, between

tactics (fighting battles) and strategy (fighting wars). Thus, operational-level military activities are conducted across a military theater, and can be considered to fight campaigns.

24. Sullivan, *The Papers of Sir William Johnson*, 3:203.
25. Murray's intelligence efforts are well documented in D. Peter MacLeod, "Treason at Quebec: British Espionage in Canada during the Winter of 1759–1760" *Canadian Military History* 2: no. 1 (1993), 49–62.
26. Thomas M. Truxes, *Defying Empire: Trading with the Enemy in Colonial New York* (New Haven: Yale University Press, 2008), 106.
27. Quoted in MacLeod, "Treason at Quebec," 51.
28. Rex Whitworth, *William Augustus, Duke of Cumberland* (London: Leo Cooper, 1992), 112, 173.
29. Haviland to Amherst, 6 July 1760 Amherst Papers.
30. I interpret this to mean that one half of the Natives were to join Sir William Johnson to support the English, and the other half were to go into the woods and launch raids and fight for the French.
31. Enclosure in Haviland to Amherst, 8 June 1760, Amherst Papers.
32. Enclosure in Haviland to Amherst, 26 May 1760, Amherst Papers.

Appendix B. Supplemental Information on Artillery Batteries

1. Guillaume LeBlond, *A Treatise on Artillery* (London: E. Cave, 1746, repr., Ottawa, Ontario: Museum Restoration Service, 1970), 66–69.
2. LeBlond, *A Treatise on Artillery*, 66–69.
3. John Muller, *A Treatise of Artillery* (London: John Millan, 1780: repr., Bloomfield, Ontario: Museum Restoration Service, 1977), 36–43.
4. Muller, *Attac and Defense*, 40.

Bibliography

Archival Sources

Amherst, General Jeffery, correspondence with Colonel John Bradstreet. Lloyd W. Smith Collection, Morristown National Historical Park, Morristown, New Jersey.

Amherst, Jeffery. "Letter to Governor Wentworth, dated Montreal, September 9, 1760." *Early American Imprints*, First Series, No. 41128. CD-ROM.

Amherst, Jeffery. Papers. Microfilm copy at David Library of the American Revolution, Washington's Crossing, Pennsylvania.

Dumas, Jean-Daniel. *Treatise on the Defense Of the Colonies.* c. 1775; French manuscript in collection of Braddock's Battlefield Association, Braddock, Pa., transcription by Mr. Bob Messner.

Farqharson, Lieutenant Alexander, 42nd Foot (Royal Highlanders). Letters. Invercauld Estate, Ballater, Aberdeenshire, United Kingdom.

Fonda, Jelles. "Journal, 1760." New York Historical Society, New York, New York.

Gordon, Archibald. Archibald Gordon Papers. Library and Archives, Canada.

Grant, John. "Journal of John Grant, 1741–1763." Alexander Turnbull Library, Wellington, New Zealand.

Haldimand, Frederick. Papers. Library and Archives, Canada.

Kimball, Peter. *Diary, March 4, 1760–October 29, 1760.* New Hampshire Historical Society.

Miller, James. "Memoirs of an Invalid," Amherst Papers, Centre for Kentish Studies, Maidstone, United Kingdom.

Montresor Family Papers. David Library of the American Revolution, Washington Crossing, Pa.

Moore, James. "The Journal of John Moore of Carrickfergus, Ireland." Sutler during 1760 campaign up Richelieu River. Public Record Office of Northern Ireland; Microfilm Reel accessed at Library and Archives, Canada. Microfilm Reel A-1724.

Murray, James. James Murray Collection, Library and Archives, Canada.

Orderly Book, Colonel John Thomas's Regiment of Massachusetts Provincials, 7 August–29 August 1760. Boston: Massachusetts Historical Society, Boston, Massachusetts.

Orderly Book of Captain Barron's Company, June 4, 1760–February 6, 1764; and Orders at Fort Crown Point, July 27, 1761. Early American Orderly Books, New York Historical Society. Microfilm Copy at Jefferson Hall, U.S. Military Academy, West Point, New York.

Orderly Book of Captain Silas Brown's Company, Colonel Timothy Ruggle's Regiment of Massachusetts Provincials. French and Indian

War Orderly Books, Massachusetts Historical Society, Boston, Massachusetts.

Orderly Book of 44th Royal Highlanders, May 31–July 16, 1760. Early American Orderly Books, New York Historical Society. Microfilm Copy at Jefferson Hall, U.S. Military Academy, West Point, New York.

Sawtell, Nathaniel. *Orderly Book, Silas Brown's Company, Timothy Ruggle's Regiment of Massachusetts Provincials, 31 August–9 October 1760.* Massachusetts Historical Society, Boston.

Townshend, James. Papers. Library and Archives, Canada.

Turner, John. "Plan of the Battle Fought on the 28th of April 1760 Upon The Height of Abraham, Near Quebec, Between the British Troops Garrison'd in that Place and the French Army That Came to Besiege It." (1760). Ottawa: Canadian National Archives.

Williamson, George. "Journal for 7–31 August 1760, from Oswegatie to Montreal." Library and Archives, Canada.

Printed Primary Sources

Advice to the Officers of the British Army, With the Addition of Some Hints to the Drummer and Private Soldier. London: W. Richardson, 1783.

Amherst, Jeffery. *Journal of Jeffery Amherst, Recording the Military Career of General Amherst in America from 1758 to 1763,* edited by J. Clarence Webster. Toronto: Ryerson, 1931.

Amherst, William. *Journal of William Amherst in America, 1758–1760,* edited by J. C. Webster. London: Frome and London, 1927.

Bayley, Jacob. "Part of the Journal of Capt. Jacob Bayley in the Old French War." In *History of Newbury, Vermont,* by F. P. Wells (1902), 376–80.

Bill, E. G. W. "A Cadet at the Royal Military Academy, 1778–1780." *Journal of the Royal Artillery* 84 (October 1957): 310–12.

Bland, Humphrey, *Treatise of Military Discipline.* Eighth ed. London: R. Baldwin, 1759.

Booth, Joseph. "Military Journal, July to October 1760" in Charles E. Booth, *One Branch of the Booth Family.* New York: 1910, 142–44.

Bradbury, J. M. "Military Journal, April 1760 to August 1762." In *Bradbury Memorial* (Portland, Maine: n.p., 1890), 261–95.

Burrell, John. "Diary of Sergeant John Burrrell, 1759–1760." *New England Historical and Genealogical Register* 59 (October 1905), 352–54.

Caesar, Julius. *The Gallic War.* tr. H. J. Edwards. 1917. Reprint, Cambridge: Harvard University Press, 2000.

Chapman, Earl John and McCulloch, Ian Macpherson, eds. *A Bard of Wolfe's Army; James Thompson, Gentleman Volunteer 1733–1830.* Montreal: Robin Brass Studio, 2010.

A complete history of the present war, from its commencement in 1756, to the end of the campaign, 1760. In which, all the battles, sieges, and sea-engagements; with every other transaction worthy of public attention, are faithfully recorded; with political and military observations. London : printed for W. Owen; L. Davis and C. Reymers; and J. Scott, 1761.

Day, Richard E. *Calendar of the Sir William Johnson Manuscripts in the New York State Library.* Albany: University of the State of New York, 1909.

De Jeney. *The Partisan: or, The Art of Making War in Detachment with Plans proper to facilitate the understanding of the several Dispositions and Movements necessary to Light Troops, in order to accomplish their Marches, Ambuscades, Attacks and Retreats with Success, Translated from the French of Mr. de Jeney by an Officer in the Army.* London, 1760.

De Lévis, Chevalier [François de Gaston]. "Journal of the Battle of Sillery and Siege of Quebec." In vol. 10 of *Documents Relative to the Colonial History of the State of New York,* edited by E. B. O'Callaghan. Albany: Weed, Parsons and Company, 1858.

DeSauguliens, J. T., trans. *A Treatise of Fortifications Containing the Ancient and Modern Method of the Construction and Defense of Places and the Manner of Carrying Sieges, Written Originally in French by Monsieur Ozanam, Professor of Mathematics at Paris.* London: J. Jackson & J. Worrall, 1727.

Fortune, T. *The Artillerist's Companion, Containing the Discipline, Returns, Reports, Pay, Provision, &c. of that Corps, In Field, in Forts, at Sea, &c.* 1778. Reprint. Alexandria Bay, N.Y.: Museum Restoration Service, 1992.

Fraser, Malcolm. "The Capture of Quebec: A Manuscript Journal Relating to the Operations Before Quebec From 8th May 1759 to 17th May 1760." *Journal of the Society for Army Historical Research* no. 18 (1939): 135–68.

Frederick, King of Prussia. "The Instruction of Frederick the Great for His Generals, 1747." In *Roots of Strategy: The 5 Greatest Military Classics of All Times,* edited by Thomas R. Phillips. Harrisburg, Pa.: Stackpole Books, 1985.

Frost, John, Jr. "Military Journal, May to November 1760" *Old Eliot* 8 (1908), 109–117.

Glasier, Benjamin. "French and Indian War Diary of Benjamin Glaiser of Ipswich, 1758–1760." *Essex Institute Historical Collections* 86 (January 1950), 65–92.

Hagerty, Gilbert. *Massacre at Fort Bull, The deLery Expedition against Oneida Carry, 1756.* Providence, Rhode Island: Mowbray, 1971.

Hamilton, Edward P., ed. *Adventures in the Wilderness: The American Journals of Louis Antoine de Bougainville, 1756–1760.* Norman, Okla.: University of Oklahoma Press, 1964; paperback edition 1990.

Hastings, Hugh, ed. *Orderly Book and Journal of Major John Hawks on the Ticonderoga–Crown Point Campaign Under General Jeffrey Amherst, 1759–1760.* New York: Society of Colonial Wars in the State of New York, 1911.

Hervey, William. *Journals of the Honorable William Hervey in North America and Europe from 1755 to 1814, With Order Books at Montreal, 1760–1763.* Bury St. Edmunds, UK: Paul & Mathew, 1906.

Holden, David. "Journal kept by Sergeant David Holden of Groton, Massachusetts During the Latter Part of the French and Indian War, February 20–November 29, 1760." *Proceedings of the Massachusetts Historical Society* (June 1889), 384–407.

Howe, Henry Forbush. "Malachi James at the Fall of Montreal, 1760." *Proceedings of the Massachusetts Historical Society* 70 (1950–1953), 33–49.

Hutchins, Thomas. "Military Journal, July 1760" *Pennsylvania Magazine of History and Biography* II (1878), 149–53.

Jenks, Samuel. "Journal of Captain Jenks." *Proceedings of the Massachusetts Historical Society* (March 1890), 352–91.

Johnson, John. "Memoirs of the Quartermaster Sergeant." In *The Siege of Quebec and the Battle of the Plains of Abraham,* edited by A. G. Doughty and G. W. Parmalee. Quebec: Dussault & Proulx, 1901.

Johnstone, Chevalier. *The Campaign of 1760 in Canada.* 1887; Reprint. Philadelphia: D. N. Goodchild, 2007.

Jones, Barbara Bullock, ed. *Rev. Samuel MacClintock's Journal 1760 and Names of Men in Col. Goffe's Regiment.* rev. ed. 1972. Rutland, Vt.: Academy Books, 2001.

Kent, Jacob. "Military Journals, May to October 1760" in Frederice P. Wells, *History of Newbury, Vermont.* St. Johnsbury, Vt.: Caledonian Co.,1902), 380–82.

Kimball, Gertrude Selwyn, ed. *Correspondence of William Pitt When Secretary of State, With Colonial Governors and Military and Naval Commissioners in America.* 1906. Reprint. New York: Kraus, 1969.

Knox, John. *An Historical Journal of the Campaigns in North America For The Years 1757, 1758, 1759 and 1760.* 1799. Reprint. Toronto: Champlain Society, 1914.

LeBlond, Guillaume. *A Treatise on Artillery.* 1746. Reprint. Ottawa, Ontario: Museum Restoration Service, 1970.

Lemonofides, Dino. "Standing Orders at Quebec, 1759." Orders Captain Bayard, 2nd Battalion, 60th Royal Americans at Quebec, 1759–1760. *Journal of the Society for Army Historical Research* 78 (2000), 300–302.

"Letters of Vaudreuil, Lévis and Dumas in 1760." Library and Archives, Canada. *Sessional Papers No. 18* (Ottawa: S. E. Dawson, 1906).

Lincoln, Charles Henry. *Manuscript Records of the French and Indian War in the Library of the American Antiquarian Society.* Westminster, Md.: Heritage Books, 2007.

Lochee, Lewis. *Elements of Field Fortifications.* London: T. Cadell and T. Egerton, 1783.

McBride, William R. "'Normal' Medical Science and British Treatment of the Sea Scurvy, 1753–1775." *Journal of the History of Medicine and Allied Sciences* 46, no. 2 (April 1991): 158–77.

McColloch, Ian M. and Timothy Todish, eds. *Through So Many Dangers, The Memoir and Adventures of Robert Kirk, Late of the Royal Highland Regiment*. Fleischmanns, N.Y.: Purple Mountain Press, 2003.

Mayer, Josephine, ed. "The Reminiscences of James Gordon." *New York History* 34 (1936), 316-333, and 423-439.

Merriman, Samuel. "Journal, 1760." In *A History of Deerfield, Massachusetts*, edited by George Sheldon. 1895; repr., Greenfield, Mass: E. A. Hall, 2010.

Middleton, Richard, ed. *Amherst and the Conquest of Canada.* Publications of the Army Records Society 20 (2003).

A Military Dictionary Explaining and Describing the Technical Terms, Works and Machines, Used in The Science of War With an Introduction to Fortification. Dublin: C. Jackson, 1780

"Military Journal, August to September 1760" in *All Canada in the Hands of the English*. Boston, 1760. Early American Imprints, Series 1, #8527.

Montresor, Captain John. "Expedition to Les Prairies De La Magdalene." *Collections of the New York Historical Society for the Year 1881,* edited by G. D. Scull. New York: New York Historical Society, 1882, 236-252.

Muller, John. *The Attac and Defense of Fortified Places, the 1757 Second Edition.* Edited by David Manthey. Arlington, Va.: Flower-de-Luce Books, 2004.

———. *A Treatise of Artillery.* 1757; reprint of 1780 rev. ed., Alexandria Bay, N.Y.: Museum Restoration Service, 1977.

———. *A Treatise Containing the Elementary Part of Fortification, Regular and Irregular.* 1746. Reprint. Ottawa: Museum Restoration Service, 1968.

Murray, James. *Journal of the Siege of Quebec, 1760.* Quebec: Middleton & Dawson, 1871.

Otway, Joseph. *An Essay on the Art of War, Translated from the French of County Turpin, In Two Volumes.* London: A. Hamilton, 1761.

Pargellis, Stanley, ed. *Military Affairs in North America, 1748–1765, Selected Documents from the Cumberland Papers in Windsor Castle.* 1936. Reprint, Hamden, Conn., Archon Books, 1969.

Perley, Sidney, ed. "Diaries Kept by Lemuel Wood of Boxford." *Essex Institute Historical Collections* 19 (1882), 61–74, 143–52, 183–92, 20 (1883) 156–60, 198–208, 289–96, 21 (1884), 63–68.

Phillips, T. R., ed. *Roots of Strategy, The 5 Greatest Military Classics of All Time.* Harrisburg, Pa.: Stackpole Books, 1985.

Pouchot, Pierre. *Memoirs on The Late War in North America Between France and England.* Brian Leigh Dunnigan, Editor. 1781. 1st rev. ed. Youngstown, N.Y.: Old Fort Niagara Association, 1994.

Putnam, Rufus. *Journal of General Rufus Putnam Kept in Northern New York During Four Campaigns of the Old French and Indian War, 1757–1760.* Reprint. Albany, N. Y.: Munsell's, 1886.

Rudyerd, Charles W. *Course of Artillery at the Royal Military Academy, As Established by His Grace, The Duke of Richmond, Master General of his Majesty's Ordnance.* Woolwich, UK: Royal Military Academy, 1793.

Simes, Thomas. *A Treatise on Military Science which Comprehends the Grand Operations of War and General Rules for Conducting an Army in the Field.* London: H. Reynell, 1780.

———. *The Military Guide for Young Officers.* London, 3rd edition, 1781.

Smith, George. *An Universal Military Dictionary.* London: J. Millan, 1779.

Stark, Caleb, ed. *Memoirs and Official Correspondence of General John Stark.* Concord, N.H.: G. Lyon and Company, 1860.

Sullivan. James, ed. *The Papers of Sir William Johnson,* vol. 3. Albany, N.Y.: The University of the State of New York, 1921.

Thompson, James. *A Short Authentic Account of the Expedition Against Quebec in the Year 1759 under Command of Major General James Wolfe.* Quebec: Middleton & Dawson, 1872, www.transactions.mor rin.org/docsfromclient/books/328/328.html (accessed July 21, 2010).

Tielke, J. G.. *The Field Engineer, or Introduction Upon Every Branch of Field Fortifications.* Translated by Edwin Hewgill. 2 vol. 1769. Rev. ed. London: J. Walter, 1789.

Todish, Timothy J., Editor. *The Annotated and Illustrated Journals of Major Robert Rogers.* Fleischmans, N.Y.: Purple Mountain Press, 2002.

Von Clausewitz, Carl. *On War.* Edited and translated by Michael Howard and Peter Paret. New York: Knopf, 1973.

Walker, James. "Military Journal, June to September 1760." In *History of Bedford, New Hampshire* (Boston: n.p., 1851), 122–23.

Waddell, Louis M., John L. Tottenham, and Donald H. Kent. *The Papers of Henry Bouquet Volume IV, September 1, 1759–August 31, 1760.* Harrisburg: Pennsylvania Historical and Museum Commission, 1978.

Waterman, Asa. "Military Journal, June to September 1760." In *Leaflet,* edited by W. F. Eddy. Brooklyn, N.Y., 1904; Connecticut State Archives, Hartford.

Webb, Thomas. *A Military Treatise on the Appointments of the Army, Containing Many Useful Hints, not touched upon before by any Author: And Proposing some New Regulations in the Army, which will be particularly useful in carrying on the War in North-America.* Philadelphia: W. Dunlap, 1759.

Welles, Lemuel Aiken. "Letters of Colonel Nathan Whiting, Written From Camp During the French and Indian War" *Papers of the New Haven Colony Historical Society* 6 (1900).

Wintersmith, Charles. "Plan of Ticonderoga and Mount Hope, 1777." Reprint. Ticonderoga, New York: Fort Ticonderoga Museum, n.d.

Wolfe, James. *General Wolfe's Instructions to Young Officers.* London: J. Millan, 1780

Wood, Lemuel. "Diaries Kept by Lemuel Wood of Boxford." *Essex Institute Historical Collections* 19 (1882), 61–74, 143–52, 183–92, 20 (1883), 156–60, 198–208, 289–96, 21 (1884), 63–68.

Wood, William, ed. *The Logs of the Conquest of Canada*. Toronto: The Champlain Society, 1909.

Woodhull, Nathaniel. "A Journal Kept by General Nathaniel Woodhull, When Colonel of the 3rd Regiment New York Provincials, in the Expedition to Montreal in 1760." *Historical Magazine* 5, no. 9 (September 1861): 257–60.

Young, Sir James. *An Essay on the Command of Small Detachments*. London: J. Millan, 1766.

Secondary Sources

Alden, John Richard. *General Gage in America*. 1948; repr., New York: Greenwood Press, 1969.

"Jeffery Amherst, 1st Baron Amherst" in *Dictionary of Canadian Biography*, http://www.biographi.ca/009004-119.01-e.php?id_nbr=1732 (accessed March 5, 2010).

Anderson, Fred. *Crucible of War: The Seven Years' War and the Fate of Empire in British North America, 1754–1766*. New York: Alfred A. Knopf, 2000.

Anderson, W. J. *Military operations at Quebec: from the capitulation by De Ramezay, on the 18th September, 1759 to the raising of the siege by De Lévis, between the night of the 17th and the morning of the 18th May, 1760*. Quebec : Middleton & Dawson: 1870. Microform.

———. "Military Operations at Quebec in 1759–1760." *Transactions of the Literary and Historical Society of Quebec*. Fifth Series, Quebec, Canada: 1877.

Andrews, Robert J. "Two Ships–Two Flags: The *Outaouaise/Williamson* and the *Iroquoise/Anson* on Lake Ontario, 1759–1761." *Northern Mariner* 14, no. 3 (July 2004): 41–55.

Barnsley, R. E. "The Life of an 18th Century Army Surgeon." *Journal of the Society of Army Historical Research* 44, no. 179 (September 1966): 130–34.

Beattie, Daniel J. *General Jeffery Amherst and the Conquest of Canada 1758–1760*. PhD diss., Duke University, 1975.

Bellico, Russell P. *Chronicles of Lake Champlain, Journeys in War and Peace*. Fleischmanns, N.Y.: Purple Mountain Press, 1999.

———. *Sails and Steam in the Mountains, A Maritime and Military History of Lake George and Lake Champlain*. Fleischmanns, N.Y.: Purple Mountain Press, 1992.

Benninghoff, Herman O., II. *The Brilliance of Yorktown, A March of History: 1781 Command and Control, Allied Style*. Gettysburg, Pa.: Thomas Publications, 2006.

———. *Valley Forge, A Genesis for Command and Control, Continental Army Style*. Gettysburg, Pa.: Thomas Publications, 2001.

Bird, Harrison. *Navies in the Mountains: The Battles on the Waters of Lake Champlain and Lake George, 1609–1814*. New York: Oxford University Press, 1962.

Boscawen, Hugh. *The Capture of Louisbourg 1758*. Norman, Okla.: University of Oklahoma Press, 2012.

Boyd, Eva Phillips. "Commodore Joshua Loring, Jamaica Plain by Way of London" *Old-Time New England Magazine* (April–June 1959), /www.jphs.org/people/2005/4/14/commodore-joshua-loring-jamaica -plain-by-way-of-london.html (accessed March 7, 2010).

Breton, P. N. *Illustrated History of Coins and Tokens Relating to Canada.* Montreal: P. N. Breton & Company, 1894.

Brisebois, Michel. "Books from General Wolfe's Library at the National Library of Canada." *National Library News* 28, no. 2 (February 1996), www.collectionscanada.ca/bulletin/015017-9602-15-e.html.

Brumwell, Stephen. *Redcoats: The British Soldier and the War in the Americas, 1755–1763.* New York: Cambridge University Press: 2002.

Buchanan, Brenda J. *Sir John Ligonier, Military Commander and Member of Parliament for Bath.* Bath, U.K.: Bath Archaeological Trust and Millstream Books, 2000.

Calloway, Colin G. *The Scratch of a Pen: 1763 and the Transformation of North America.* New York: Oxford University Press, 2006.

Canada Hydrographic Service, *Small-Craft Chart, Richelieu River, Chambly to Lake Champlain.* Ottawa: Minister of Fisheries and Oceans Canada, 1984.

Carter, Brinnen Stiles. "Armament Remains from His Majesty's Sloop *Boscawen.*" Master's thesis, Texas A&M University, 1995.

Charland, Thomas Marie. "The Lake Champlain Army and the Fall of Montreal," *Vermont History* 28 (1960): 292–301.

Charters, Erica M. "Disease, Wilderness Warfare, and Imperial Relations: The Battle for Quebec, 1759–1760." *War in History* 16, no.1 (2009), 1–24.

Chartrand, René. "42nd and 78th Highlander's Uniforms, 1759–1760." *Military Collector & Historian* 62:2 (Summer 2011), 87.

Chartrand, René. *French Fortresses in North America 1535–1763: Québec, Montréal, Louisbourg and New Orleans.* Oxford: Osprey Publishing, 2005.

Cohn, Arthur B. "The Fort Ticonderoga King's Shipyard Exavation: 1984 Field Season Report." *Bulletin of the Fort Ticonderoga Museum* 14, no. 6 (Fall 1985): 337–56.

Cory, Rory M. *British Light Infantry in the Seven Years' War.* Master's thesis. Simon Fraser University, 1993.

Crisman, Kevin J. "The Construction of the *Boscawen.*" *Bulletin of the Fort Ticonderoga Museum* 14, no. 6 (Fall 1985): 357–70.

———. "The Fort Ticonderoga King's Shipyard Excavation: The Artifacts." *Bulletin of the Fort Ticonderoga Museum* 14, no. 6 (Fall 1985): 375–436.

Cubbison, Douglas R. *Historic Structures Report, The Hudson River Defenses at Fortress West Point, 1778–1783.* USMA, West Point, New York (January 2005).

———. *National Register of Historic Places Nomination, Fort de La Presentation/Fort Oswegatchie/Fort Ogdensburg Archaeological Site, Ogdensburg, St. Lawrence County, New York.* Ogdensburg, N.Y.: Fort La Presentation Association, June 2009.

Cuneo, John R. "Factors behind the Raising of the 80th Foot in America." *Military Collector & Historian* 11, no. 4 (Winter 1959): 97–103.
———. *Robert Rogers of the Rangers*. New York: Richardson & Steirman, 1987.
Curtis, Edward E. *The British Army in the American Revolution*. 1926; repr., Gansevoort, N.Y.: Corner House Historical Publications, 1998.
Daviau, Sébastien. "Mortier de Marine Calibre 10." *Au fil du temps, Publication de la Société d'histoire et de généalogie de Salaberry* 17, no. 1 (March 2008): 19–21.
De La Croix, Horst. *Military Considerations in City Planning: Fortifications*. New York: George Braziller, 1972.
Dickinson, David, ed. "Siege of Fort Lévis from Eyewitness Accounts." *St. Lawrence County Historical Association Quarterly* 46 (2001): 2–34.
Dowd, Gregory Evans. *War under Heaven: Pontiac, the Indian Nations & the British Empire*. Baltimore: John Hopkins University Press, 2002.
Eccles, William J. *The Canadian Frontier, 1534–1760*. Hinsdale, Ill.: Dryden Press, 1969.
Fenn, Elizabeth A. "Biological Warfare in Eighteenth-Century North America: Beyond Jeffrey Amherst." *Journal of American History* 86, no. 4 (March, 2000), 1552–80.
Fisher, Charles L. "Soldiers in the City: The Archaeology of the British Guard House." In *People, Places, and Material Things: Historic Archaeology of Albany, New York*, edited by Charles L. Fisher, 39–46. Albany, N.Y.: New York State Museum Bulletin 499, 2003.
Flanigan, Alan Thomas. "The Rigging Material from *Boscawen*: Setting the Sails of a Mid-Eighteenth Century Warship During the French and Indian War." master's thesis, Texas A&M University, 1999.
Flexner, James Thomas. *Mohawk Baronet: A Biography of Sir William Johnson*. Syracuse, N.Y.: Syracuse University Press, 1959; reprint 1979.
Fortescue, J. W. *A History of the British Army*. London: Macmillan and Company, 1910.
Fortier, Paul. "La Galette versus Cataraqui—The Forgotten Rivalry for Dominance on the Upper St. Lawrence, 1673–1796." Unpublished manuscript, 1979.
Frazier, Patrick. *The Mohicans of Stockbridge*. Lincoln, Neb.: University of Nebraska Press, 1975.
Gruber, Ira D. *Books and the British Army in the Age of the American Revolution*. Chapel Hill, N.C.: The University of North Carolina Press, 2010.
Guy, Alan J. *Oeconomy and Discipline, Officership and Administration in the British Army, 1714–1763*. Manchester, UK: Manchester University Press, 1985.
Hamilton, Milton W. *Sir William Johnson, Colonial American, 1715–1763*. Port Washington, N.Y.: Kennikat Press, 1976.
Holst, Donald W. "French Provincial Light Horse, 1759–1760." *Military Collector & Historian* 18, no. 2 (Summer 1966): 60–61.

Houlding, J. A. *Fit for Service: The Training of the British Army, 1715–1795*. Oxford: Clarendon Press, 1981.

Knoblauch, Edward H. "Mobilizing Provincials for War: The Social Composition of New York Forces in 1760." *New York History* 78, no. 2 (April 1997): 147–72.

Knollenberg, Bernhard. "General Amherst and Germ Warfare." *Mississippi Valley Historical Review* 41, no. 3 (December 1954): 489–94.

Kopperman, Paul E. "Religion and Religious Policy in the British Army, c. 1700–96." The *Journal of Religious History* 15 (1987): 390–405.

Kruger, John W. "The Fort Ticonderoga King's Shipyard Excavation: An Overview" *Bulletin of the Fort Ticonderoga Museum* 14, no. 6 (Fall 1985): 335–36.

"A Lake Champlain Gunboat of 1760," *Magazine of History* 8, no. 7 (July 1882): 498–99.

Lambert, Phyllis and Alan Stewart, eds. *Opening the Gates of Eighteenth-Century Montreal*. Montreal: Canadian Center for Architecture, 1992.

Lee, David. "The Contest for Isle-aux-Noix, 1759–1760: A Case Study in the Fall of New France." *Vermont History* 37, no. 2 (Spring 1969): 96–107.

Lefkowitz, Arthur S. *George Washington's Indispensable Men*. Harrisburg, Pa.: Stackpole Books, 2003.

Leliepvre, Eugene and Rene Chartrand. "Corps of Cavalry, Canada, 1759–1760." *Military Collector & Historians* 27, no. 3 (Fall 1976): 131–32.

Lépine, André. "A Wreck Believed to be a French 'Bateau' Sunk during Action in 1760 off Isle-aux-Noix in the Richelieu River, Quebec, Canada." *International Journal of Nautical Archaeology* 10, no. 1 (1981): 41–50.

Long, J. C. "Amherst in 1759." *New York History* 15 (1934): 50–58.

———. *Lord Jeffery Amherst, A Soldier of the King*. New York: Macmillan Company, 1933.

Lunn, Jean Elizabeth. "Agriculture and War in Canada, 1740–1760." *Canadian Historical Review* 16, no. 2 (June 1935): 123–36.

Luzader, John F., Louis Torres, and Orville W. Carroll. *Fort Stanwix: History, Historic Furnishing, and Historic Structure Reports*. Washington, D.C.: National Park Service, 1976.

MacDonald, Ian Glenn. *Whaleboats, Row-Galleys and Floating Batteries: British Gunboats in the 1760 Canada Campaign*. Master's thesis, Queen's University, 1999. Library and Archives, Canada, Microfiche.

MacLeod, D. Peter. "Microbes and Muskets: Smallpox and the Participation of the Amerindian Allies of New France in the Seven Years' War." *Ethnohistory* 39, no. 1 (Winter 1992): 42-64.

———. "Treason at Quebec: British Espionage in Canada during the Winter of 1759–1760." *Canadian Military History* 2: no. 1 (1993), 49–62.

McCulloch, Ian. "Highland Chaplaincy in the French & Indian War, 1756–1763." www.electricscotland.com/history/scotreg/mcculloch/story3.htm (accessed September 15, 2009).

———. "'From April Battles & Murray Generals, Good Lord Deliver Me':
The Battle of Sillery, 1760." In *More Fighting for Canada; Five Battles*,
edited by Donald Graves, 15–72. Toronto: Robin Brass, 2004.

———. *Sons of the Mountains, The Highland Regiments in the French
& Indian War, 1756–1767*. 2 volumes. Fleischmanns, N.Y.: Purple
Mountain Press, 2006.

McCulloch, Ian, and Tim J. Todish. *British Light Infantrymen of the Seven
Years' War, North America, 1757–1763*. Oxford: Osprey Press, 2004.

McGuffie, H. "A Deputy Paymaster's Fortune: The Case of George Durant,
Deputy Paymaster to the Havana Expedition, 1762" *Journal of the
Society for Army Historical Research* 32, no. 132 (Winter, 1954).

McIlwraith, Jean N. *Sir Frederick Haldimand*. Toronto: Morang, 1905.

Malcomson, Robert. "Not Very Much Celebrated: The Evolution and
Nature of the Provincial Marine, 1755–1813." *Northern Mariner* 11,
no. 1 (January 2001): 25–37.

———. *Warships of the Great Lakes, 1754–1834*. Rochester, Kent, U.K.:
Chatham, 2001.

Marshal, Douglas W. "The British Engineers in America, 1755–1783."
Journal of the Society for Army Historical Research 51, no. 207
(Autumn 1973): 155–63.

Mason, R. H. *Life of General the Hon. James Murray, a Builder of Canada*.
London: J. Murray, 1921.

Mayo, Lawrence Shaw. *Jeffery Amherst: A Biography*. New York:
Longmans, Green, 1916.

Micheloud, Francois. "Canada's Playing Card Money." www.micheloud
.com/FXM/MH/canada.htm (accessed January 5, 2004).

Museum Records on Mortars and Shells recovered from the Coteau-du-Lac,
provided by Musée régional de Vaudreuil-Soulanges, Montreal, to
author.

Neatby, Hilda. *Quebec: The Revolutionary Age, 1760–1791*. Toronto:
McClelland and Stewart, 1966.

MacLeod, D. Peter. "Microbes and Muskets: Smallpox and the
Participation of the Amerindian Allies of New France in the Seven
Years' War." *Ethnohistory* 39, no. 1 (Winter 1992): 42–64.

———. "Treason at Quebec: British Espionage in Canada During the
Winter of 1759–1760." *Canadian Military History* 2, no. 1 (1993):
49–62.

Manders, Eric I., Brian Leigh Dunnigan, and John R. Elting. "80th
Regiment of Foot, 1757–1764." *Military Collector & Historian* 39,
no. 4 (winter 1987): 172–73.

Miksch, Heidi. "The Fort Ticonderoga King's Shipyard Excavation: The
Conservation Program" *Bulletin of the Fort Ticonderoga Museum* 14,
no. 6 (Fall 1985): 371–74.

Miller, Charles E., Donald V. Lockey and Joseph Visconti, Jr., *Highland
Fortress: The Fortification of West Point During the American
Revolution, 1775–1783*. West Point, N.Y.: Department of History, U.S.
Military Academy, 1979.

"Municipality of Sainte-Paul-de-l'Île-aux-Noix," www.ile-aux-noix.qc.ca/eng/tourisme/histoire.html (accessed 9 February 2010).

The Nautical Seaway Trail: Chartbook and Waterfront Guide to New York State's Great Lakes–St. Lawrence Region. Hammond, N.Y.: Blue Heron Enterprises, 1991.

Nicolai, Marin L. "A Different Kind of Courage: The French Military and the Canadian Irregular Solder during the Seven Years' War." *Canadian Historical Review* 70, no. 1 (1989): 53–75.

Paine, Gary. "Ord's Arks: Angles, Artillery and Ambush on Lakes George and Champlain." *American Neptune* 58, no. 2 (Spring 1998): 105–122.

Palmer, Dave R. *George Washington's Military Genius*. Washington, D.C.: Regnery, 2012.

Parkman, Francis. *The Conspiracy of Pontiac and the Indian War after the Conquest of Canada*. Intr. Michael M. McConnell. 1851. rev. ed. Lincoln, Neb.: University of Nebraska Press, 1994.

Peckham, Howard H. *Pontiac and the Indian Uprising*. 1947; reprint edition Phoenix Books, University of Chicago Press, 1961.

Phillips, Ruth B., and Dale Idiens. "A Casket of Savage Curiosities: Eighteenth Century Objects from Northeastern North America in the Farquharson Collection." *Journal of the History of Collections* 6, no. 1 (1994): 21–33.

Pound, Arthur. *Johnson of the Mohawks*. New York: Macmillan Company, 1930.

Quick, Estelle. *James Thompson: A Highlander in Quebec*. Tain, Rosshire, UK: Tain & District Museum Trust, 2009.

Ross, John F. *War on the Run, The Epic Story of Robert Rogers and the Conquest of America's First Frontier*. New York: Bantam Books, 2009.

Russell, Francis. "Oh Amherst, Brave Amherst." *American Heritage Magazine* 12, no. 1 (December 1960).

Sargent, Winthrop. *The History of An Expedition Against Fort DuQuesne in 1755*. 1855; repr., Lewisburg, Pa.: Wennawoods Publishing, 2005.

Sarkar, Shondeep L. "Microstructural Investigation of Renaissance Mortar from Montreal, Quebec, Canada." *Cement and Concrete Research* 22, no. 6 (November 1992): 1011–18.

Shy, John. *Toward Lexington: The Role of the British Army in the Coming of the American Revolution*. Princeton, N.J.: Princeton University Press, 1965.

"Sir Frederic Haldimand" in *Dictionary of Canadian Biography*, www.biographi.ca/009004-119.01-e.php?&id_nbr=2445 (accessed March 5, 2010).

Society of Gentlemen in Scotland. *Encyclopedia Britannica, or a Dictionary of Arts and Sciences*. 3 vols. Edinburgh: A. Bell and C. Macfarquhar, 1768–1771.

Stacey, C. P. "The Conquest of Canada, 1758–1760." *Canadian Army Journal* 6 (January 1953): 1–8.

Steele, Ian K. *Betrayals: Fort William Henry and The "Massacre."* New York: Oxford University Press, 1990.

Sullivan, Catherine. *Legacy of the Machault: A Collection of 18-century Artifacts.* Ottawa: Parks Canada: 1986.

Sutherland, Lucy S., and J. Binney. "Henry Fox as Paymaster General." In *Essays in Eighteenth-Century History, from the English Historical Review,* edited by Rosalind Mitchison. New York: Barnes & Noble, 1966.

Sweeney, Kevin. "The Very Model of a Modern Major General." *Amherst Magazine* (Fall 2008), www.amherst.edu/aboutamherst/magazine/issues/2008fall/lordjeff (accessed 12 February 2010).

Thomas, W. "Stations of Troops in North America, 1757–1760." *Journal of the Society for Army Historical Research* 14 (1935): 235–36.

"Treaty of Oswegatchie, 1760." *The Canadian Encyclopaedia,* http://www.thecanadianencyclopedia.com/index.cfm?PgNm=TCE&Params=A1ARTA0010705 (accessed on 28 March 2010).

Truxes, Thomas M. *Defying Empire: Trading with the Enemy in Colonial New York.* New Haven, Conn.: Yale University Press, 2008.

Vaugeois, Denis. *The Last French and Indian War.* Montreal: McGill-Queen's University Press, 1995.

Wayman, Matthew J. "Fortifications at Quebec, 1759–1760: Their Condition and Impact on the Sieges and Battles." *Journal of America's Military Past* 30, no. 1 (Winter 2004): 5–25.

Whitworth, Rex. *Field Marshal Lord Ligonier, A Story of the British Army, 1702–1770.* London: Oxford University Press, 1958.

———. "Field Marshal Lord Amherst, A Military Enigma." *History Today* 9 (February 1959): 132–37.

———. *William Augustus, Duke of Cumberland.* London: Leo Cooper, 1992.

Williams, Edward G. "Treasure Hunt in the Forest." *Western Pennsylvania History,* 44, no. 4 (December 1961), 383–396.

Wood, Robert F. *Captain Jesse Platt and the New York Provincial Troops in the French and Indian War, 1759, 1760, 1761.* New York: New York Genealogical Society, 1940.

Wrong, George M. *The Fall of Canada: A Chapter in the History of the Seven Years' War.* Oxford: Clarendon Press, 1914.

Index